WITHDRAWN

THE WAR AND GERMAN SOCIETY

ECONOMIC AND SOCIAL HISTORY
OF THE WORLD WAR

James T. Shotwell, LL.D., *General Editor.*

GERMAN SERIES

THE WAR AND GERMAN SOCIETY

THE TESTAMENT OF A LIBERAL

BY

PROFESSOR ALBRECHT MENDELSSOHN BARTHOLDY

FORMERLY, DIRECTOR OF THE
INSTITUT FÜR AUSWÄRTIGE POLITIK
HAMBURG

LATER, LECTURER AT
BALLIOL COLLEGE
OXFORD

NEW HAVEN : YALE UNIVERSITY PRESS
LONDON : HUMPHREY MILFORD : OXFORD UNIVERSITY PRESS
FOR THE CARNEGIE ENDOWMENT FOR INTERNATIONAL
PEACE : DIVISION OF ECONOMICS AND HISTORY
1937

Copyright 1937 by the
Carnegie Endowment for International Peace

Printed in the United States of America

TO THE MEMORY OF

CASPAR RENÉ GREGORY

WHO GAVE HIS LIFE TO THE SERVICE OF HIS FELLOW MEN
THIS BOOK WHICH OWES SO MUCH TO HIM
IS GRATEFULLY DEDICATED

EDITOR'S PREFACE

OF all the volumes of the Economic and Social History of the World War there is none that bears the scars of war more deeply than this last volume of the German Series. This may not be evident at first to the reader, who cannot fail but be impressed by the brave effort at detachment with which the book is written and who catches its high note of philosophic objectivity. It treats the story of Germany through the War years with a due sense of tragedy and of achievement; but its reticence and its silences bear truer witness to the impact of the War upon the German people than all the strident rhetoric of those who today speak officially for the Third Reich. For here the thoughtful, highly sensitive and thoroughly disciplined mind of the old Germany, of art, science, and philosophy, speaking with measured accent, presents the War and its consequences in terms of a Greek tragedy, blaming no one, seeking no special favors from fate —nor from those who capitalized misfortune to persecute the tolerant and the generous spirited, that company of exiles of whom Mendelssohn Bartholdy was an outstanding member.

I have spoken of reticence and silences. It is thus that one comes upon the incompleteness of the present volume. Planned originally to sum up the total effects of the World War upon the German people, it remains but a fragment of the intended narrative. This is not so much due to the author's sudden death, leaving an unfinished text, as to the fact that the subject matter itself—that which had a bearing upon some of the major economic problems in such a survey— was in part withheld from examination, and that the political interests of post-War Germany—and for that matter of every other country that had been in the War—were concentrated upon those elements of War history that could be molded to advantage in a better future and so drew a veil over the wasteful destruction of the War itself. Thus history shifted its ground as much of the past lost its meaning. Only a persistent human nature remained, to which the student of this tragic episode might turn as a clue to what had happened. And then it, too, seemed to change, at least in Germany. What was left? This question, still largely unanswered, is the elusive theme of the pages which follow.

It might be thought that with the passing of time not only the events but also their causes and consequences would stand out more clearly in the lengthening perspectives. It would be natural to suppose that the studies made of the War after the warping passions of the heat of conflict had subsided would tell a truer story than those made in the years immediately after the War, a story less biased by prejudice, more readily accepting evidence that might have been unwelcome to the participants in the events, one more informed by a spirit of genuine scientific investigation. This was the opinion of many of those to whom I turned for counsel in the early planning of the Economic and Social History of the World War. But as one looks over the literature of the post-War years down to the present and turns to it for guidance as to the meaning of the history of both the War and the peace that followed upon it, one is led to the disquieting conclusion that the impact of the War upon the intellectual and moral life of Western Europe and of the nations based on European culture did not die out when the actual fighting ceased, but rather developed new forms of controversy and misunderstanding. Like the theological warfare that continued after the Wars of Religion had been settled by political compromise, the claims and counterclaims of the nations of Europe not only kept alive their nationalist antagonisms but, by putting the emphasis upon grievances which were capable of being redressed, tended to lose sight of the underlying cause of the whole vast disturbance, namely the World War itself.

This was especially the case with Germany, and for a very good reason. The historian cannot blame the leaders of post-War Germany for attributing most if not all of the evils which that unhappy country suffered from in the decade following the War to the Treaty of Versailles, which sought to register the losses which it was to make good to an impoverished world and which, without a fair trial, ascribed to it and to its allies the aggression from which all these evils sprang. The accusation in the Peace Treaty and the penalties following therefrom became in this way the outward and visible sign of the devastation of the War as seen through German eyes throughout those sad years when every nation, victor as well as vanquished, was fumbling uncertainly with problems of economic readjustment and attempted recovery. In the confusion of those years the War itself was largely lost sight of by German publicists, economists and the public generally; the Treaty took its place.

EDITOR'S PREFACE

This development had not yet got fully under way when the German Editorial Board of the Economic and Social History of the World War was established in Berlin. By a strange coincidence its first meeting was held on Armistice Day, November 11, 1922. Stimulated by a conference with the Chairman of the Austrian Editorial Board, Professor Wieser, whose plan for the Austrian and Hungarian Series had been completed during the preceding months, the distinguished group of leaders in German academic, business, and political life which came together on that occasion faced their task with a high sense of its importance and of the opportunity which it offered to apply to the analysis of the facts of war that type of painstaking investigation and critical thought which had raised German science to its high place in the modern world. The only criterion which this committee placed before itself was that of the search for truth and the need for setting it forth not only for students in Germany itself but for those in every other country of the civilized world.

The Chairman of this Editorial Board, Dr. Carl Melchior, combined long experience in international finance with an intuitive perception of political realities, a rare combination and one that can never be associated with the rigid thinking of the doctrinaire. Among his associates were the great figures in German industry, such as Dr. Carl Duisberg, the statesman of the chemical industry; Dr. Hermann Bücher, at that time Secretary of the Reichsverband der Deutschen Industrie; Professor Max Sering, the economic specialist on agriculture; and the former Chancellor of the Reich, Dr. Gustav Bauer, representing the interests of labor. But it was the Executive Secretary of this group, Professor Mendelssohn Bartholdy, who furnished the driving force that made it a reality.

The plans for the German Series were far-reaching. It was proposed to cover practically every aspect of the impact of the War upon Germany as well as of its war-time economic organization. The Foreign Office was just beginning the publication of that great series, "Die grosse Politik der europäischen Kabinette," which opened to the world the documentary evidence for the diplomatic history of Germany from the war which created the Empire to that which brought its downfall. Professor Mendelssohn Bartholdy was one of the three editors of this great series. In his mind and that of the Editorial Board, the Economic and Social History of the World War was a parallel undertaking. While the full implication of this conception could not be evident in the early days, namely, that the War History was to furnish a test of the validity of Clausewitz' theory of war as an instrument of policy, yet it was a great conception which fired the imagination of my German colleagues, one worthy of the traditions of German scholarship and science. Unfortunately, it could only be partly realized. The War was not yet over in the economic sphere. It was still creating havoc in every country that had mortgaged its future and exhausted its supplies in the years of actual fighting. The full pressure of this exhaustion naturally found expression in the effort to collect reparations from the defeated Powers, and as this in turn was seen to rest upon the moral charge of their responsibility for having caused the War, it was inevitable that the war-guilt controversy should assume such proportions as to dwarf all other interests in the history of the War. Under these conditions the practical question began to be raised as to whether it was to Germany's interests to let the world know the full facts of the effect of the War upon her industries and her economic life generally. The French occupation of the Ruhr forced this tendency into one of almost religious belief that the Treaty rather than the War was the dominating cause of Germany's post-War sufferings. The starvation of the blockade was a bitter memory but it was fading. The hardships of war-time were accepted as logical and inevitable necessities. Moreover the War was apparently over and done with, whereas the Treaty still lasted on as a program of enslavement for a nation that did not feel itself conquered. Thus it came about that much of the central data for the German Series of the Economic and Social History of the World War became inaccessible, and even texts that were completed were not available for publication. Some twelve volumes were published and the richness of their offering will furnish some indication of what the German Series would have been if the original plan, consisting of almost double the number of monographs, had been carried through.

The situation which has just been outlined has a much wider bearing than the editorial problems of this History. It shows, on the one hand, that those in authority in the Republic were by no means careless of their country's interests in the long controversy over reparations, but, on the other hand, it shows how in the years immediately following the War there was still available in Germany an appreciation of the mission of intelligence in laying the basis for a civilized world. Many books have been written about the tragedy of modern Germany, but most of them, concentrating upon Germany's material and moral sufferings, have presented the Nazi régime as an escape and a deliverance. To the student of the history of the World War this is the opposite of the truth. Germany's tragedy was not ended but only intensified when it turned away from the question of what war itself is like when waged by nations of high industrial development to the controversial issue involved in the dispute over the Peace Treaty. It is true that the great debate over the causes of the World War is beginning now to produce more measured judgments and that history will profit largely from even the propaganda literature, just as real tolerance finally emerged from the theological battles of the sixteenth and seventeenth centuries. But the causes of the War are mainly political and diplomatic facts. The data of the War itself lie in another field. A survey of them would enable one to examine in detail the validity of the German theories of the nineteenth century that war was a continuation of policy and, therefore, a valid instrument of sovereignty. This theory cannot be overthrown by mere theoretic arguments. It must be met by inductive study, for which the laboratory of the World War offered an unparalleled opportunity. No other country was so well equipped as Germany to undertake this study and to follow it through to its conclusions; for nowhere else had the science of war been developed as it was in Germany and in no other country was the necessity for economic mobilization seen so quickly or carried through so thoroughly. Moreover, the War was lost through the blockade more than through defeat on the battlefield. Had the full political significance of these facts been seen, the study of war would not have been left to militarists, and the effort to find alternatives for it would have had a support in public opinion which, as it was, turned in confusion of thought to the emotional and reactionary leadership of nationalism.

This much has been said on the significance of the effort made to secure a well-rounded German Series in the Economic and Social History of the World War because it reflects the spirit in which Professor Mendelssohn Bartholdy approached the task of writing this final volume. A descendant of Moses Mendelssohn, the philosopher of enlightenment and the friend of Lessing, grandson of Felix Mendelssohn Bartholdy the composer, and a son of Karl Mendelssohn Bartholdy the historian, he brought to the study of jurisprudence, of which he was a distinguished leader, the many-sided gifts which made him an outstanding exponent of the best traditions of German culture. It was a tribute to his impartial and judicial outlook that he was chosen to represent Germany on the Arbitral Tribunal at The Hague, set up in connection with the administration of the Young Plan of reparations. He was honored by other countries as well as his own and held the honorary degree of Doctor of Laws of Harvard University; but in the autumn of 1933 he was obliged to seek asylum from persecution in Germany, and Balliol College, Oxford, created a lectureship for him. His sudden death in November, 1936, prevented a revision of this volume which would have brought it up to date and filled some of the lacunae, especially in the sections dealing with the economic effects of the War. Happily, however, the volume combined with fundamental objectivity the clear personal note of one who could rise above the warping prejudices of his time because of his fundamental interest in life itself. It is thus given to the public under the dual caption of a historical survey and "the testament of a liberal."

In a note attached to the manuscript, Professor Mendelssohn Bartholdy recorded his sense of obligation to the many friends with whom he discussed the subject-matter of the book while it was being written, and to the institutions which gave him generous assistance in collecting the material, especially the Institut für Auswärtige Politik and the Commerzbibliothek of Hamburg. The English text stands in large part as it came from his pen; but it owes much as well to two of those who worked upon it, Miss Lillian Gurry of the Royal Institute of International Affairs in London, who was at the time in the Library of American Law in Hamburg, and Mr. Arthur E. McFarlane who, as literary editor, contributed by both criticism and suggestion to more than turn of phrase or choice of expression.

J. T. S.

CONTENTS

EDITOR'S PREFACE vii

INTRODUCTION 3

PART I

GENERAL OBSERVATIONS ON PRE-WAR PLANNING AND PROPHESYING, ON THE FAILURE OF PLANS AND THE FUTILITY OF PROPHECIES, AND ON PERTINACITY IN THE OLD MODES OF THINKING

CHAPTER I.	Dispensing with Causality . . .	19
CHAPTER II.	Business versus Bureaucracy . . .	31
CHAPTER III.	Disregard of Economic Laws . . .	44
CHAPTER IV.	Financing War	53
CHAPTER V.	Financial Mobilization Plans . . .	59
CHAPTER VI.	The Hindenburg Program and the Devaluation of Money	75

PART II

THE EFFECT OF WAR ON THE CONSTITUTION OF GERMANY

CHAPTER VII.	Government: Political and Geographical Conditions before the War	91
CHAPTER VIII.	Government: The Change in Method, 1914–1918	106
CHAPTER IX.	Centralizing Forces of War . . .	115
CHAPTER X.	Municipal Imperialism	129
CHAPTER XI.	The Strain of War and the Revolution .	153

PART III

EFFECTS OF THE WAR ON INDUSTRY

CHAPTER XII.	Politics and Business in War-time . .	195

CHAPTER XIII. *Industry and Industrial Leaders* . . 220
CHAPTER XIV. *Some Post-War Effects* 249

PART IV
CONCLUSIONS

CHAPTER XV. *Material Effects* 265
CHAPTER XVI. *Moral Effects* 280

INDEX 297

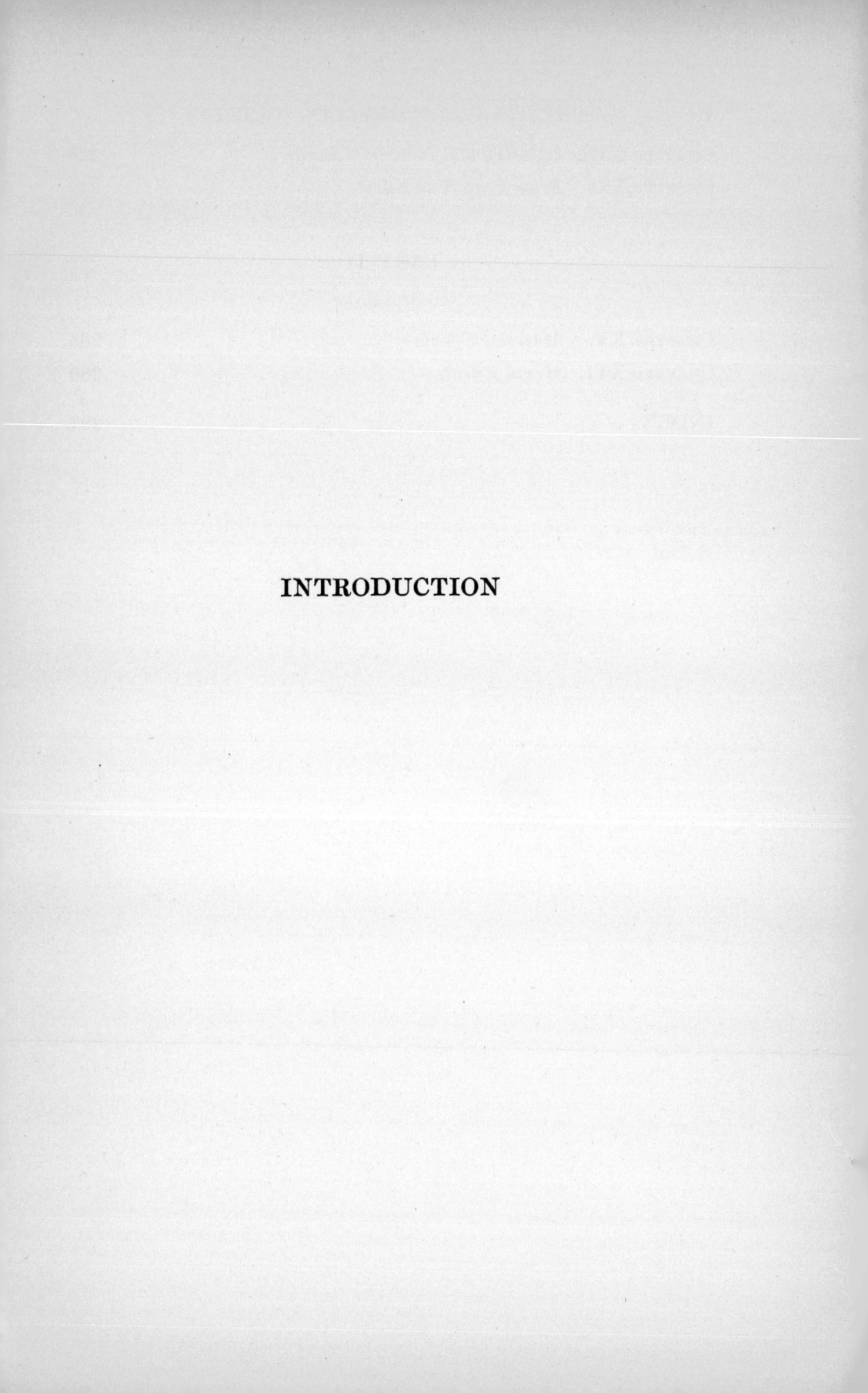

INTRODUCTION

INTRODUCTION

To estimate the general effects of the War on a country which was shaken to its depths by it and which, to have done with the immediate consequences of the War, had to undergo a political revolution and a complete change in its economic structure, would seem to be a bold undertaking on the part of a citizen of that country, when only fifteen years separate us from the War. Silence, some people might say, must be enforced in the sickroom while the patient still hovers between death and recovery; silence, most of all, on the part of those who could and should have spoken the salutary word of warning before disaster and disease were virtually invited.

There is truth in such a contention, but only a half truth. For a sick man, whose illness resulted from his living in a dark, stuffy room, a bilious misanthrope, will never get well if, with both windows and shutters closed, he is allowed to continue to be the plaything of his own moods, and enjoy the morbid illusions of a patient who must not be disturbed.

The attempt made in the following pages to discuss the effects of the War on Germany does not pretend to be more than an opening of the windows, the giving of free access to the open air, to the noise of the street, and to the vision of rain and sunshine alike in the case at least of the author's own sickroom. Premature though it would probably be today to form definite conclusions as to the social and economic effects on the world of the Great War, or even to generalize upon the situation of Germany or Russia as the losers or of Great Britain, France, or Italy as the winners of the War, it should certainly be possible for each individual country and for the social units within each country to condense their own consciousness of what they were fifteen years before the War and of what they are fifteen years after it into some formula which would sum up what war has meant to that community or group. Each country, whether it fought as a principal or an accessory, whether singlehanded, or as a member of an allied group, or as an independent associate, had to wage the war against war, which is the real task in every big armed conflict between full-grown nations, and wage it in its own way. Each country had to learn for itself and, incidentally, to show the world how far war could be made to fit in with its social order and its economic routine, and could in certain ways even be made to serve them, or, on the other hand, show how war came as an enemy to its social order and a destroyer of the wealth of a nation. And so with individual nations, with tribe and clan, with classes and groups, with ranks and professions within a nation, and finally with the single individual in his citizenship and his human life. There were currents of public and private life between 1902 and 1932 of such inherent strength that they ran their course throughout the entire period of the War without any deviation or slowing down; there were others to which the War simply gave an additional rapidity and forcefulness; and there were doubtless cases, too, where the flow of life seemed to have been changed or halted by the command of war. *Silent leges:* is not a law which cannot make itself heard a mere mockery of its own self? Can Life go on while the order of battle is Death?

The Economic and Social History of the World War wisely leaves it to every country to describe its own experience. The case of Germany, from 1914 to 1918, was as different from that of Austria, Russia, France, or Great Britain, as it was from its own case in 1900 or in 1913, or in 1919, or today. This volume, however, goes farther than that. It professes to state simply my own personal point of view. For the impersonal survey of political history it substitutes, deliberately, repeatedly, and it may be in partisan fashion, the personal diary, private correspondence, experiences within the narrow circle of friends and relatives; in preference to statistics it uses a housekeeping-book, a bank account, a series of income-tax returns in the author's own files. It relies on a talk with village neighbors, or with housemaid and cook, quite as much as a government or trade-union memorandum on fixed prices for agricultural produce, or on unemployment or a shortage of labor.

This may be one of the reasons why its main conclusions differ widely both from what may be called the official interpretation of the War in its effects on Germany, and from conclusions which might be popular with either militarist or pacifist.

No man who has lived through this war will lay claim to be able to see it objectively. We cannot simply accept the War as a fact having an existence independent of the human beings who were thrown into it. We sometimes hear those who were among the bravest in the field tell their audiences after the War that for the sake of the memory of their dead comrades, if for no other reason, war should be banished forever. Addressing members of the French ex-service-men's association and the British Legion who had come to take part in the unveiling of the memorial to the 73,000 British officers and men killed in the battles of the Somme and finding no known graves at Thiepval, the Prince of Wales declared that the names of the fallen must form no mere Book of the Dead; they must be the opening chapter in a new Book of Life, the foundation and guide to a better civilization from which war, with all the horrors which our generation has added to it, should be banished: "These names," he said, "and the names of the even greater host of the dead of France, the names of the dead of other nations who fought with us and of those who fought against us —all those, so long as we remember them, shall testify against the past, and shall call us to a better civilization. . . ." Nothing could be more honorable, in the old sense of the term, than these words coming from the future monarch of a great Empire and a soldier who fought in the War. The aim of this book, however, is not to indict war, nor to express the hope for an age in which men will have made up their minds not to tolerate the use of force in public affairs. But if I have confessed to my own lack of objectivity in the case of the last war I shall not try to make my readers accept my judgment upon it. The facts will be presented, so far as possible, without favor or passion; and if among the younger generation that may study them they are held to warrant new aspirations for the warlike attitude in public life, it is not within the province of this work to dissuade them from such a creed. We older people have only one thing to ask of them if they wish to requite our pains in telling them the tale of our own heartbreaking failure, and that is that they shall make at least a deliberate choice of war, if war it has to be, fully realizing how it will affect not only themselves but also their children's opinion of them, and that they shall not tumble into war again as the generation of 1914 must plead guilty to having done. The peculiar conditions under which Germany had to live during the War made easy the infection of her people by every poisonous germ that war can generate. We may see this in the two main differences between the two nations which had to bear the heaviest burden throughout the conflict, France and Germany.

Germany's armed forces, in the main, fought in enemy territory. There were only scant possibilities of home leave for non-commissioned officers and soldiers; and there was the strictest military censorship on letters and other means of communication between the fighting forces and the people at home. War in a nation's own territory creates a clear issue, common to all. It is defensive war in the narrower sense of the word, and carries with it, in favor of the people defending its soil, all the moral and material advantage which the Heraclean myth of Antaeus ascribes to the wrestler thrown down, but rising and renewing the struggle with the doubled strength drawn from Mother Earth.

Carrying the war into the enemy's country by a swift move of invasion means a certain measure of material safety for the home country. But we may well doubt whether that is not more than outweighed by the moral dangers besetting an army fighting in a foreign land. It will not conquer it, for that is not the point in modern warfare. But it will have to bring ruin and desolation to it, and set enmity between its inhabitants and the invading force for generations to come. And, all the time, it will be losing touch with the people at home and with the home country itself.

The greater moral danger, however, is, in such a case, reserved for those who have to remain at home. They feel the separation from their fighting men much more than the soldiers, active and with the compulsions of battle before them, can feel being separated from them. During the first months of the War those at home found their solace in Red Cross work, in sending gifts of love to those who had gone, in trying to help wounded prisoners, and in rallying the forces which they knew would be needed in the hour of peace. Martial law and the nervous dread of pacifist propaganda which had taken hold of the Ministry of War and of the Information Department of the G.H.Q. disposed of all this within a short time. People in Germany had to realize, from 1915 onward, that they must live the lives of women, children, and old men in a besieged town. Worse than that, they were cut off from their own defenders as well as from the enemy, and could do their giving only by reducing their daily ration of food and wearing their clothes to shreds.

The isolation of the fighting forces from their home country and the isolation of the home country from the rest of the world were the main reasons for the sudden collapse at the end of the War, and for the dissensions in both the army and the civilian population which have made it impossible for Germans to return to anything like normal conditions since 1919. A considerable part of the army, more especially many of those attached to the general and divisional staff, the commissariat, and the administration of occupied enemy territory still believed, up to the last days of the war that Germany's military strength was unshaken, and that the people at home had deserted the cause of the Fatherland. The bulk of its soldiers were honestly intent on being led home to take part in the reconstruction of the German state. On the other hand, the great majority of the people at home wished to see the War ended and, but for the memory of the fallen, forgotten. But others, especially youths just under military age, thought themselves cheated of their share in the glory of war; and, even before the Treaty of Versailles gave them a new battle cry, they tried to retain the outward symbols, and, through them, the spirit of warfare, and apply it to domestic politics.

These circumstances go a long way to explain the absolute power of war. Even so, however, we must note a remarkable tenacity of resistance to the changes which war is bound to make in a people, both in its social and its economic order of life. Habits in small things prove stronger than the combined forces of military rule within the country and military pressure from without. In some respects the easygoing, matter-of-course disregard of the War shown by some groups within the nation, and the corresponding difficulty of making them realize afterward what happened five or ten years before seem almost grotesquely out of keeping with the overwhelmingly vast and terrible facts of the War. One of the popular illustrated magazines of post-war Germany, the *Uhu*, had, in its issue of June, 1931, an article on "How We Looked in 1911," with a dozen or more reprints of photographs from the newspapers and magazines of that time. The whole article, a clever contribution to recent history, had one object: to tell the people of 1931 that all the things they had been priding themselves on as novelties of their own period had likewise been novelties for the long-forgotten, dead and buried generation of 1911. Infatuation for cinema stars and tennis cracks, speed records and jazz music, extravagant toilets on race course and Lido were as much in vogue in pre-war days as they are in those of our juniors. If this be life, the War dwindles to an interlude, passing quickly into oblivion, even though it lasted fully four and a half years of the twenty between 1911 and 1931. On the more serious side of the human pathway similar things are to be noticed. Among the big industrial concerns of present-day Germany we find only one or two in a hundred which were not of considerable importance before the War, either in their present form or as individual firms in some branch of industry which, since the War, has been reorganized as a vertical trust. It is the same with banks, private banks as well as companies. And not only that. If one regards the failures as a better indication of economic balance of power than the successes in prosperity, it is the same phenomenon again. The fissure which has widened to a breach, and made the building collapse, can be distinguished more or less clearly in the activities of the pre-war period.

Is it only in offices and institutions that this inherent conservatism is to be found? Is it the *milieu, juste ou injuste*—the average, exact or not—which reasserts its importance through the daily routine of peace work, leveling down the heroism and ridiculing the heroics of war-time? Cartoonists have often made fun of the Germans for playing schoolmasters to a world which felt it had outgrown them years ago. They would have enjoyed hearing of a new word which German pedagogues were using among themselves, ten years after the War, in their discussions of the psychology of teaching, the *Paedagogik der Aufrüttelung*, a phrase which has no English parallel. One might think that war had done enough to stir up the minds of people and shake (*Aufrütteln*) them out of all inclination for a complacent lethargy, to make the invention of a new category superfluous; but such is not the view of competent educationalists in Germany. They observed in their pupils of the 1920's a tendency to encrust their minds with a hard surface of technical ability, a cover of special knowledge and professional routine, so that neither human feeling, the warnings of conscience within, nor the most violent disturbances without, could penetrate the shell. The teacher, we were told, should take special care to agitate the liquid mass of his pupil's mind and prevent its becoming moldy, dull, almost dead matter within a hard, polished, glittering rind. Ten years after the World War, and with a generation of young Germans who were born into the War, many of them being old enough to remember at least the last years of blindfold killing, it was one of the chief problems of German pedagogues to look for new methods of rousing the nation from lethargy.

But it was by no means a problem for Germans only. The same phenomenon, an almost complete failure of the War to penetrate the inner sanctuary of men's and women's minds, has been observed in other countries, and in the case of people of an entirely different temperament and outlook. For this we have the word of Marcel Proust, who is nothing if not a realist in describing French society in Paris and the provinces depending on Paris. In the terrible volume, *The Past Recaptured* (*Le temps retrouvé*), in which he adds the final legend to his epic of the twentieth century, he writes of the attitude assumed by the salon of the Verdurins as soon as it begins to realize the War as a social fact. The circle which the Verdurins have formed remains true to its purpose, that of serving the social ambitions and the abject snobbery of its patrons. It proves its value as a social "cell" for its members by strengthening its hold on public life, for their benefit, even while the enemy is only an hour's drive in a fast car from their homes. They are loudest in their claim to genuine patriotism, in their denunciation, as pro-Boches, profiteers, and sneaks, of all those who abandoned them in the first confusion of 1914, and they always know how to find safe positions for their own flock in a government post. It is this group, with its eagerness for war and war to a finish (*jusqu'au boutisme*) that Proust tells us has never really been touched by a sense of what war means.

It might be said that the Verdurins thought of it because they had a political salon where every evening the situation of the armies and the navies was discussed. They did, indeed, give thought to the hecatombs of regiments annihilated and of passengers drowned; but some inverted mental process multiplies everything that touches our own well-being to such a degree, and divides by such enormous figures everything that does not concern ourselves, that the death of millions of unknown men touches us almost less unpleasantly than does a draught of air.

Madame Verdurin needs her wonted *croissant* every morning to dip into her cup of *café au lait* while she reads the news from the theater of war, and if she cannot get it the day is spoiled for her. The famous physician who is a trusted member of her circle writes a prescription for her which allows her caterer to have a special supply of pastry ready for Madame, in spite of war restrictions prohibiting such luxuries, an effort which takes almost as much time and pains as to get an obnoxious General dismissed by the Government and one of the "faithful" put in his place. In the end, however, things work out satisfactorily; and on the morning of the news of the sinking of the *Lusitania*, Madame Verdurin finds her favorite bit of crisp, brown-baked pastry on her breakfast table again.

Dipping the *croissant* in her coffee and creasing the newspaper so that it would remain wide open without her having to drop the morsel she held in her hand, "How dreadful!" she said. "Really it is more horrible than the most frightful of tragedies." But the death of all those drowned men must have seemed infinitely trifling, for as she was making these sad reflections she continued to munch her breakfast, and her face took on a look of quiet satisfaction, probably due to the taste of the *croissant*, so precious a specific against her headaches.

She is not "*aufgerüttelt*"; she offers the same made-up face to the terrible news of the latest outrage of war as to social arrangements in peace-time. The small things of her daily life, though in themselves rather unimportant in comparison with the sinking of the *Lusitania* or a sanguinary attempt to break the enemy line on the Chemin des Dames or on Mount Kemmel, are more familiar and closer to her than anything which happens on the Atlantic or in the devastated area. The *croissant* came from the neighboring baker's, and is on her breakfast table in her boudoir. The news from Jutland or the Masurian lakes came from far away, and its importance is reduced proportionately by the inexorable laws of distance. One of her servants reading the dispatch that tells the story of defeat or senseless destruction would perhaps experience a more direct contact with the event; for the newspaper in his hand or the concierge reading it to him are live things to him; and he might fling the paper into a corner or come to blows with his confreres about it. To Madame the news comes like the messenger from the battlefield in a Greek drama, who drops on the threshold, fainting from exhaustion, and with his last breath tells the tale of misfortune, only to be carried away into oblivion.

This impermeability in the face of the War was, of course, not peculiar to a political salon in the French capital; it was a common experience in every country, varying according to its own social structure and the habits of its daily life, but withal of the same kind. In Germany, instead of an intrigante like Madame Verdurin queening it over a circle of friends which pretends to have squared its circle and, because of this, to be superior to every other circle or group in the whole universe, it would have been a clubroom of respectabilities, made up of officers of militia and presidents of patriotic associations. They would have been continuing their wonted teamwork as commandants of prison camps, railway depots, or hospitals, or in some new service, that of the National Red Cross or the Bureau for Patriotic Information (*Vaterländische Aufklärungsdienst*). They would have been attempting to maintain the rules of social and political caste, to be exclusive, with their pockets always full of black balls in case an obnoxious intruder should have to be barred out of their local club or society. And, above all, they would have been trying to keep from being stirred and shaken by the common human appeal of the tragedy of the War. Or, on the other hand, the case might have been that of some staff of a trade-union secretariat, going right on with the business of classifying the working people as members or non-members of the Union; or of the elders of some Protestant church censoring a clergyman who preached Christ instead of the High Command's latest order against charitable feelings toward wounded prisoners; or of worthy bureaucrats who have kept to their old, self-sufficient sense of duty and integrity, who have looked upon the War as a kind of corruption which could be kept out of the house of Government by a strict enforcement of office hours and the rules of red tape.

Some of them against better knowledge, but the great majority in sheer ignorance, they refused to acknowledge the fact that in war they had come face to face with a gruesomely naked truth, in the sight of which men wearing their regulation, respectable clothes had become a ridiculous incongruity. They remained immune to the War to the last; and their candid belief that they would be able to maintain their own small citadel of traditional activity against the world conflict, however long it lasted, certainly helped to prolong it beyond measure and to make the end, when it came at last, more terrible to victors and vanquished alike than any treaty-made peace after a long war has ever been. It was only one of the by-products of the struggle between the armed forces.

But still it can be said that among the more important truths in the sphere of the social effects of the War is the fact that, as a consequence of this attitude of a large section of the "upper middle classes," the War over-reached itself financially. The crisis of 1922–1923, and partly at least, the German crisis of 1930–1931 hit those classes hardest, and not without good reason. They had tried, during the War, to eat their cake and to have it, too. They wanted to maintain a social status which was closely bound up with an orderly, we might even say a pedantic, kind of domestic peace, while they preached and glorified war, finding excuses even for its worst excesses. Against the brute forces of the War itself, the people belonging to this group maintained their position remarkably well. It was the economic breakdown which forced them to surrender. They had come victoriously out of the French Revolution and the Wars of Napoleon; the continental struggles for liberty and national unity during the nineteenth century had done them all the good in the world; and from 1871 to 1920 the party to which, I think, most of them belong in Germany as in England and France, the National Liberals, had been the strongest organization of mere bourgeois character. Inflation killed them, and inflation, in its turn, was, as communist doctrine did not fail to point out, a direct result of the policy which their group advocated during the War. Their downfall, however, belongs to the story of the aftereffects; it was one of the outstanding facts in the story of the new era in which people were trying to begin a new life free from war. In a story of the War we have to see them as they were at the time of the preparation for war and at the time of its fulfilment. And they were then an influential element in the social and political life of the nation and a powerful support, at the same time, of everything which could make for a wider development of national energies and national wealth, through a program which was essentially liberal, and everything which would maintain the old order against the "subversive forces"—in fact, of conservatism in its strongest form.

To give to this group and its attitude toward the War its due place in the survey of the effects of war is certainly not to minimize those effects, either during the War or afterward. The strength of active and passive resistance to the changes wrought in Europe by the events of 1914 and the four years which followed can be realized to the full without any undue deduction being made from all the acts of voluntary sacrifice and all the enforced suffering due to the War. There may be readers prone to call our description of the remarkable force of resistance offered to the influences of the War, as shown in many walks of life, an attempt to belittle the magnitude of the experience which the nation had to undergo, an attempt, too, that comes near to lack of reverence for the grandeur of death in battle. If so, we would simply answer that in this book there is no pretense of teaching reverence for the dead—a feeling which is so much bound up with everything that is best and noblest in human nature that we may hope it needs no teaching—but an honest attempt to tell of things seen and heard during the War and the years which followed the War. If it were not too much to claim to encompass in the span of a human life a world revolution like this present one, which we have lived through, I would say that this contribution to the Economic and Social History of the World War is not meant to be anything else than the story of the life of a man who at thirty had begun to take an active part in the political life of Germany, who was between forty and fifty years old when the War came and went, and who is now, when almost sixty, looking back and trying to find out what links him to his own first manhood in politics, to test himself and discover the break which the War may have made in his convictions and in his abilities, or, maybe, learn what deeper knowledge and stronger will he developed as a result of his experiences of those years. If a sincere lover of peace should object to a statement which seems to imply that the destructive power of war and its threat to civilization has been overrated, I would, again, ask him to regard the contents of this book not as a judgment but as the deposition of a witness.

And I would add, in concluding these prefatory remarks, that even making every allowance for the forces that resisted the War, for those of recoupment and perhaps of reactionary tendencies— that is, reaction toward a formal restoration of pre-war conditions— what was experienced from 1914 to 1918 is enough to awaken compassion in those who had to live through it, and to bring the responsibility for the War home to those whose duty it is to prevent a recurrence of it. It may be a matter of dispute how deep was the incision into the body politic and into the power of wealth in the belligerent countries. And it may be doubted whether the damage done, the destruction of towns and villages, the disabling of millions of men and women, and the disruption of industry and commerce is only a temporary infliction on those who actually suffer from it, or a permanent curse on the future of mankind. We may find some parts of the German body where the gash seems to have gone very near the place which would have meant bleeding to death. That would seem to be true of the fleet, or of the old form of military service and the loyalties it implied, or of the traditional conception of ownership of one's house and the privacies of life. While an almost complete recovery can be seen in some ways, in others, even at this time, the wound is hardly healed or may bleed again. Yet we may also find spheres of national life in which, from 1905 or 1910 to 1930 there has been hardly a break in a slow onward movement, a continuity which is the more striking for being quite unostentatious and, for the most part, unpremeditated.

One thing, however, cannot be questioned. The War has broken to pieces and trampled upon what confidence and reliance mankind had in a just and rational relation between work, in the broadest sense of the term, including our general conduct and mode of action, and the wages of labor, also in the broadest sense, including honors and rewards of every kind as well as punishment and loss of position. Security of tenure, moral and material, has been struck off the board. Nothing of necessity follows upon human action whether good or bad. The law, whether its origin be divine reason, or human will and the order of society, is in abeyance. Heretofore war seemed to imply a promise of recompense, at least to the commander-in-chief —a triumph and *otium cum dignitate,* dignified ease, if not exaltation to the everlasting stars. After this war one of the commanders curses his people for having robbed him of victory by their treason, and eats his heart out in mad dreams of revenge on political enemies within his own country. Another who seemed to hold victory in the hollow of his hand seeks to derive his real happiness from the humiliation of the vanquished foe. But he only finds the hated civilians lording it over him as soon as the Armistice has been concluded. He goes home embittered, looking for a new occasion for strife while all the world around him chants the hymn of peace; and, at last, a man who believes that he has wronged his country shoots him down in the street. These are the symbolic figures of modern war.

The moral destruction wrought by this war is a destruction which, as distinguished from the material damage, can be clearly recognized as the result not of the loss of the War, or of the treaties of peace, or international indebtedness and the depreciation of currency, but of war itself. And it is so tremendous in its scope and so far-reaching in its consequences that in comparison with it even the cruel devastation of the battle area does not count.

A battle has its heroism; death has its glory. The raging fire which laid a village waste becomes a pyre for those who conquered. But it is the terrible curse of war that the bravest take the glory they have won down with them to an unknown grave in a foreign land or at the bottom of the sea. There is no time so fitting for deepest mourning over those who died in a war as are the days which come fifteen or twenty years after its close. It is then that those who died to save their country should be alive in the full strength of their proven courage and of their love, to save it a second time. We look for men to take the helm—men in the prime of life who are able to shoulder the responsibility they owe both to their old and to their young. We look to them, we, the young who must be guided—we the old ones who must be relieved of our duties, now become too heavy. And we look in vain. For of those hale and powerful men who now, in age from thirty-five to fifty, should give guidance to the destiny of their nation, if the divine law of service and reward had not ceased to function, only a few have been left, and those few chosen by hazard, not by a test of value. Of those strong and healthy women, too, who should have borne them children and reforged the links of true motherhood between the generation of yesterday and that of tomorrow, few have been spared the cruelest fate that can befall a human being innocent of any guilt. For they were married to become widows; their lovers took the promise of undying loyalty down to their graves. With the women rests the hope of a nation. For them a war like this war means a long life of barren hopelessness. After 1918, a few men who had outlived their time, among them carried on the government, almost against their own will, till they became an abomination to those who had grown up during the War. Hundreds of thousands of immature boys and girls married to fill the gap caused by the War. While those older and better than they had lost not only their own lives or their own health, but the lives or the health of their unborn children, a generation without any ties of loyalty grew up, prepared for almost anything but hard work and a good laugh at bad luck. Perhaps the worst of all the evil effects of the War is this, that, while the men and women who have had to bear the loss show incredible courage, and, many of them, learn to defy even fate, those who have come after them are most of them prone to complain of their hard lot and to blame fate, or some enemy, for the unhappiness that is in themselves. That is the terrible mark that war puts upon those begotten during its reign.

PART I

GENERAL OBSERVATIONS ON PRE-WAR PLANNING AND PROPHESYING, ON THE FAILURE OF PLANS AND THE FUTILITY OF PROPHECIES, AND ON PERTINACITY IN THE OLD MODES OF THINKING

CHAPTER I

DISPENSING WITH CAUSALITY

THE first thing which strikes an observer of the effects of the War in Germany is the loss of all confidence in justice as one of the principles which regulate the course of human life. In peace-time the conception of a measurably just relation between effort of will and result, labor and the product of labor, crime or carelessness, and punishment or retribution, seems as natural to the mind of the good citizen as it is indispensable to the maintenance of the State. Of all the traditional beliefs in a measurable causality of events in human life, this one went down first. An irritating sense of everything depending on incalculable chance took its place. Chance was working the wrong way not merely from the point of view of law, a change which might be easily explained through the temporary silencing of the "still, small voice" of the law by the din of warfare. But things went wrong from the point of view of reasonable causality. Not so much the formal, outward laws of behavior as the intrinsic, logical relation between cause and effect seemed to have been suspended by the outbreak of the War.

Everything seemed to have been subjected to a law of absolute irrationality, to be left to mere chance. All things seemed made up of inexplicable and unpredictable *vis major* instead of human actions born of a will which uses the accumulated experience and knowledge of many billions of human lives to attain its end, and which has trained every nerve and every muscle of the body to serve it faithfully. Relations between cause and consequence which had been fixed as an element of thinking and planning in every sane human being's mind became uncertain and fallacious. Even in the War's own work of devastation, mechanical as it seemed to those who had made a study of, or had lived through, former wars, there was in this war an almost fantastic element of the incalculable and the unreal.

Death struck down the young and able-bodied instead of carrying off the old and the infirm. Success was a piece of luck, failure an error of Providence which entitled those suffering from it to curse Providence to their last breath. Every new day demonstrated the futility of the most careful preparations—the longer they went on the farther away moved all prospect of realizing them. Fortunes were made and lost, wealth was multiplied or dwindled to nothing without even a shadow of those reasons which normally make capital expand or contract under the manipulations of the Stock Exchange. War canceled causality. It seemed to do so, at least, to the German people.

A good many reasons may be given for the intensity with which this change was felt, this change from apparent sanity to apparent insanity alike in public and in private life. The immensity and the length of the War, the force with which it penetrated the whole nation and reached even the remotest corners, the universality of its influence, which lessened the old disparity between the immediate area of warfare and the home country—all certainly contributed to make the people as a whole, regardless of their interest in politics, their state of education, or their profession and walk in life, realize the change quite clearly, long before it could be measured by historians or sociologists. The main reason, however, why the iron of that disillusion entered so deeply and woefully into the German soul is to be found in a certain peculiar moral and religious predisposition on the part of precisely that element of the people which received the imprint of such an event as the War most directly and almost at once tried to react against it, or, as the case may be, conform itself to it consciously, and—in Germany—systematically. Under the surface of a rather superficial imperialism, beneath the verbose ideology of the *Grossmacht* complex, public life in Germany had remained much the same as it was in the later eighteenth and early nineteenth centuries. The upper middle class had gained considerable importance long before the humanitarian ideas of the French Revolution and the emancipation of the Jews destroyed the social barriers between, on the one hand, the Court, the nobility, and the highest grades in the civil service, and, on the other, the commoners and tradespeople. It had the strength as it had the weaknesses and defects of a social group that is more or less in flux, neither kept down in gloomy subjection as were the working classes at that time, nor elevated into immobility as had been the fate of the ruling gentry. The wealthier and more distinguished families of the bourgeoisie were constantly reinforced and given new life by new people who rose from the lower levels to the upper through higher education or commercial integrity and efficiency. Tradition certainly had its influence in this state of things, for the honorable part which loyal citizens took in the shaping of public life in Imperial Germany is one of the earliest memories of her childhood, eight hundred years ago. But the deciding factor, as it seems to us, was a break with that tradition. The constant tributes which had to be paid to different war chests from the beginning of the Thirty Years' to the end of the Seven Years' War had exhausted the towns. Their corporative organization had lost all reality; their community life had to be built up anew. That is why they felt comparatively young and full of enterprise; not only in newish places like Berlin, Weimar, or Mannheim, but in the old cathedral towns, or the free cities of the Hansa, or Frankfurt am Main and Augsburg. The conviction that a united German Empire, a center of world trade and a model in higher learning, arts, and crafts, was an indispensable element in the concert of nations, the *Weltregiment*—a conviction deeply embedded in the mentality of modern Germany—was not so much a heritage of the past to be maintained under changed circumstances as a vow to future generations; and the way to its fulfilment was to be prepared and kept open by constant efforts. Liberalism and delight in each step on this road of so-called progress were convenient forms of expression for that conviction. Liberalism combined easily with nationalism, and progress was, following the same line of thought, a justifying synonym for expansion. Among Germans of the Protestant faith nothing stood in the way of out-and-out adherence to these hopes and beliefs. Pacifism, which might have proved a disturber of their consciences, was found, if at all, in only a few. It was not to be mentioned, even in a town meeting, and much less in public speeches, sermons, or newspaper articles. Faithful Catholics to whom the arguments of national Liberalism did not appeal, stood aside. They were out of sympathy with the class consciousness of the townspeople. They had no use for a nationalism that sought to heap ridicule and abuse on their "ultramontane" allegiance to Rome. They nursed an instinctive distrust of measures that tended to increase Prussian influence in German affairs generally. And the rock-like immutability of their church certainly gave them more comfort in their hours of need than any satisfaction which some slight progress in the accumulation of wealth or resources could have done. If they had had a share in the government of the Empire, or even a mere prospect of ever being accorded such a share, they could have formed a valuable brake in the German body politic. They had no such share. Their influence was confined to parliamentary opposition. They were never allowed to play any responsible rôle in public affairs. In fact, the difficulty of reaching a leading position in the councils of the nation was much greater for a Roman Catholic of strong convictions than for a German of Jewish descent who had professed Protestantism. Energetic, progressive, challenging, and expansive, the middle classes in the Germany of the Second Empire were as zealously Protestant as they were liberal and nationalist.

The bourgeois element in the so-called civilized countries which constituted themselves the chief warring Powers from 1914 to 1918 had to bear the heaviest burden of the change from the rational to the irrational, from the calculable to the incalculable. Among the rulers of every kind, barons or junkers, bankers or industrialists, soldiers or professionals in the game of politics, faith is seldom to be found unless tempered by a strong admixture of cynicism. Contempt for human nature comes natural to them, even before they have met disaster and their people have failed them. The stronger their passion for righteousness and their sense of justice, the bitterer their comment on the inevitable result of their labors. *"Delexi justitiam et odivi iniquitatem—propterea morior in exilio."* Bismarck or Salisbury, Clemenceau or Curzon, Nansen or Hoover, whether they are patriots or humanitarians, have to drink the full cup of misanthropy. It is a poison, but it is medicine too, as poisons often are. The members of a ruling caste survive the shock of a war, whether it is a war of their own making or not, much more easily than the bourgeoisie, just because their caste believes unreservedly in its own national worth and merit, and in Divine approval of and rewards for them.

So long as such a belief is held, it can plausibly be used to explain what takes place in wars, and to allay the doubts as to the reasonableness of Creation with which a stricken people is sometimes plagued. A religion—and we may, for our argument, include in that term even the palest deism of the eighteenth and nineteenth centuries—always takes doubt into account together with faith and credulity. Its scheme of a predestined order of things includes war, earthquake, or pestilence, as measures for keeping the world going quite as truly as it includes the more peaceful of God's blessings upon those who keep his commandments and feel themselves entitled to have all that happens turn to their advantage. That may be, and is, in fact, explained in different ways, but the tenor remains the same. The explanation given may be that the Lord has to put human beings to the test of misery and misfortune; and this test, if harder to bear at the moment, is certainly not as cruel to those who fail to meet it as is the subtler temptation of easy good fortune. Such a conception of war as a period of probation, like Job's, is perhaps the only one among the traditional Christian exhortations to be patient and faithful in unmerited suffering that found many thousands of willing listeners even during the World War. Or the explanation may be that the ways of Heaven are strange, and have to be so, in order to make human beings realize that there are things they cannot explain with all their achievements of science and learning. Life is like a great carpet. God alone sees the beautifully ordered design on its face; human beings see only the reverse side, with its tangled web of threads and knots. It is only a very small fraction of eternal time and universal space that even a whole nation or group of nations in the moment of a clash of arms is able to discern: causality, unfettered by time and space may be in perfect function, while seeming broken or distorted to those who try to understand causality as a local matter going on from day to day. It is pointed out in the teachings of theologians that it is for hidden sins and shortcomings that humanity has wars visited upon it, and that, if war seems to strike the innocent, this only shows they are not as innocent, before the All-seeing, as they seemed to be in the judgment of the world. Finally, it may be that in war, in epidemics, in disaster, and calamity this lower world reveals its true character of imperfection and of undisciplined dualism of body and soul. These are faults which prevent its development on rational lines, let alone those of justice or sanctity—a conception which is often found to imply the belief that a state of misery and destitution in this world indicates that the true believer is on the straight road to the next and better world. The narrow lane of virtue is again contrasted with the broad road of sin; and misery promises heavenly balm to the believer's wounds after he has left the quarrelsome body behind him.

Faith such as this has helped human beings to outlive wars of an almost mythical frightfulness. The Thirty Years' War, the Wars of the Spanish Succession, and the Napoleonic Wars brought to the regions where they raged destruction far more cruel and insensate than the devastation of the World War, and some of them lasted even longer than the trench war in northern France and Belgium. They were wars in which towns were burned with their civilian populations in them, wars of torture and rape, of certain pestilence and foul corruption following in the wake of the armed conflict. Still, the nations which were ravaged by them, French, German, Dutch, Austrian, and Russian, did not break down under the ordeal. They never talked of the downfall of their world nor of the decline of their civilization.

How much faith can Protestant Germany, said to be the mainstay of the nation, be said to have retained in the years before the War? The loud complaint of the German nationalists of that period, that Germany when most powerful had become addicted to materialistic unbelief, may not have been true of the followers of the Catholic Center Party or of the Socialists, who at that time had all the privileges of a minority party that is excluded from the prizes of parliamentary life. But at least it was true of the great mass of the thriving, industrious, and rather commonplace commercial population which gave solid support to the Imperial Government, especially during the chancellorship of Prince Bülow. Another part of the governing classes, however, had kept its faith in a Divine Government of the World, as represented by the Sovereign; and, by them, those who served him in the army or as officials were regarded as secular officers of that Divine Government as truly as any ordained priest was a spiritual servant of the Divine Cause. This faith was bound up in an inextricable knot with the strongest national prejudice and with a fanatical zeal for the purification of the national character. People prayed for war, not as an evil to be inflicted on their enemies, but as a benefit for themselves, as a test for their bodies, a probation of their moral courage, as a showing up of their hidden weaknesses and sins, as a cauterizing of the sores in their body politic, as a castigation with the *fascio* of the *lictor*, as a promise of healthy, frugal poverty after the period of enervating prosperity which their country had enjoyed for too many years. This part of the German people clung firmly to that strange superstition—which in the cult of primitive people manifests itself in a way abhorrent to official Christianity—the belief that in a war which puts His followers to the test, the Deity puts himself to the test as well. In demanding the great sacrifice of life, liberty, and wealth, the Deity would be binding himself with a promise to his worshipers that if the people were ready to give their all for the War and to keep nothing back for themselves—which, it seemed to Germans during the first years of the War, they were ready to do— he would bless their arms and give them victory. Moreover, by so doing, the Deity would make manifest that after all he governed the world with justice. The individual may nurse the belief in a recompense in the next world for trouble and suffering during his "earthly pilgrimage." A congregation or a sect cherishing the same faith may, in times of persecution, save its soul by doing penance and mortifying the flesh. But this kind of stoicism is unattainable for any large body of men, whether in a great church or in a great nation. A nation wants confirmation of its belief in supernatural justice by a materialization of that justice in the form of worldly power and well-being.

Such faith in that kind of divine justice was the last remnant of that evangelical Christianity which had been a moral and spiritual force from the time of the Huguenots to the time of Zinzendorf. But it was this faith that went down during the first winter of the War, when the confirmation through a visible, manifest sign of God's being with the German Army failed to appear. It died out, in most people, one is almost tempted to say, at the same moment with the birth, and, later on, with the immense growth, of their faith in the man who more than anybody else represented for them leadership in war and politics—General Quartermaster Ludendorff. Indeed, the majority of these people at last came to the conclusion, at least subconsciously, that their belief in God had deceived them. Possibly this was because there was no God—the God of the French or the Russians being obviously a mere idol. Or, still worse, possibly it was because God was a Jewish or a Roman, but certainly not a Teutonic God. God having failed them, they transferred their allegiance to this German man, a son of that part of Germany which in its heart had remained true to its heathen strength, ever since Charlemagne had baptized the inhabitants by force and introduced Roman imperialism and Catholicism into this part of the world. Lower Saxony, the Hanse towns, Mecklenburg, with its old Wendish tradition, and Pomerania seemed to have become the true homelands of national manhood. The leader had to be a man who appealed to half-forgotten, heathen instincts, and the *signum* of victory an inverted swastika instead of the cross of Christ. Justification of the war, through religion, had failed by the end of 1915.

The inevitable reaction in people's minds became only stronger and more bitterly felt because of the fact that during the first months of the War they had experienced a unity of state and nation such as is rarely felt in times of peace. Both the glory and the suffering belonged to all, men and women, young and old, rich and poor. Even the strict division into soldiers and civilians enforced by the authorities during the period of mobilization could not weaken the passionate feeling of supreme pride in unity among people who only a few weeks before had been kept asunder by a thousand differences of religion, of regional pride, of social status, and political opinion. They knew that now at last they had been melted into one great mass of ardent power, moving in one direction, working in a common rhythm of labor, even breathing as one. It would be imperfect description to say that they were willing to share. They realized that life, from now on, consisted in sharing a common fate, unreservedly; and that for those who tried to preserve a hoard of their own, whether of material wealth or of skill and knowledge, the death of Ananias and Sapphira would be the appropriate reward. The first deeds of bravery gave a new pride to the infirm and bedridden in hospital or almshouse even as if they had themselves performed miracles of valor in the midst of battle; and the first losses were mourned and the memory of the dead revered by village and town as if they had been a single family. Such was the confidence inspired by the response given to the call for national unity that the day of supreme justice through perfect equality seemed to have come.

By the end of the first year and during the second year the reaction had set in. It had many causes; different observers in different parts of the country would probably disagree as to the chief cause. I came, at that time, into close contact with groups of soldiers traveling, on home leave, between Frankfurt am Main and Würzburg; and according to my experience the seed of discontent was sown when the men came back from the trenches or the artillery quarters in France to a changed homeland. Comparing notes with their people they began to feel the schism between the army in active service and the *Heimat* much more acutely than they had felt it when military censorship had stepped in between the soldier who must face the enemy without a thought of what lay behind him, and his people at home. They thought only of the soldier, of the time when his next leave would begin; and they had only the faintest notion of the real existence of the enemy, except through official propaganda. They began to realize the unreliability of the news published by the Government for home consumption. They began to share and nurse the grievance of the "man in the trenches" against the organization behind the front (*Etappe*) as being something repulsive, something almost ghoulish that had placed itself, monster-like, in the path between those who did the work of the battle and those who did the work of the field and the factory at home. The cleavage had begun in the censorship on correspondence between the soldier and his people; but it was immensely widened when he had his first, second, or third actual contact with the changed land of his father and mother, his sisters and brothers, his friends and comrades, and in some cases his old antagonists and rivals at home.

Changed in what? In my opinion mainly in the belief in a certain standard weight or measure used to ascertain the relation between— to use the simplest formula—what a man does and what he gets for it. I may seem to stress the point too much, and the feeling which I try to describe was certainly in most cases entirely subconscious, and might in many cases be said also to be unreasonable. I think it is most easily realized if one pictures the community embodying itself in a residential street in one of the many medium-sized towns in Germany that mean so much to the life of the nation. As a rule such a street is a very stable, conservative unit. The houses often remain in the same family, not only for a lifetime, but for two or more generations. Everybody knows his neighbors or, at least, knows everything about them. And in such a street, in 1916, a soldier on home leave might have heard the news of the neighborhood in some such way as this:

"The poor Schmidts in Number 1—of course they were the happiest, solidest people in the street. The father a famous headmaster; his five sons all healthy boys between seventeen and twenty-three, and his daughter one of the best girls in our *Wandervogel* Club. Two of the sons have been killed, one is missing, one has been blinded. The girl has become a radical pacifist. The father's school is going to pieces. The mother has not left her room for weeks and weeks.

"True, but, on the other hand, look at the Schneiders next door. The father, who was good for nothing except to worry his wife, is in charge of a large depot and gives himself airs like a field marshal. His five boys are only from six to thirteen years old, and the War will long be over before the eldest of them could carry a gun. Schneider is not two years younger than Schmidt, but he married ten years later because nobody would have him.

"And the widow Vogel in Number 3 and Fräulein Hase in Number 4? Why, one of them is getting wealthier daily and the other is starving. The widow has a son living in the Dutch West Indies. He has taken care of the money and sends her all the good things, and old Fräulein Hase, who was the kindest of souls and always gave you such nice presents has lost every penny because her income came from England, and there it is treated like enemy property. When the War began she gave every last thing to the Red Cross. But she has not had a fire in her kitchen all this winter."

Farther down the street there were the two bookshops, one of them with the shutters up. Its owner, who had established his business through his own ability and literary taste, with no help other than that of his younger sister, had enlisted. He had been a man of delicate health, a bookworm, as his enemies said, and had not even had to serve his military year. But, an enthusiast in everything, he had not been able to stay at home when the War broke out. As for the other shop, it had gone on as before. Its chief trade was in political pamphlets and in comic illustrated papers of the trashy kind. More than that, it was a famous gathering place for hangers-on of the *Gazzetta Nera* type. Its clientele had always been a sore point for the pride which the better class of his neighbors took in their street. His customers were outsiders, and nobody knew them. Yet, in some mysterious way, while the good citizens seemed to fade away and disappear, these outsiders, though most of them were well within the age of military service, had remained, nobody knew on what excuse, and had found ever new topics for scandal. The owner of the shop was said to be a Jew, but nobody knew it for certain; and his customers evidently were of the Jew-baiting type.

Three other shops had disappeared—a millinery shop, a salesroom for handicrafts, and a tearoom; they had all three been kept by single women who had given them up and returned to their families and to unpaid household work. Two delicatessen shops had grown up in their places. Food had begun to be scarce; people were commencing to fear rationing. The new shops promised substitutes, and perhaps, to a good customer, something of the real kind in addition.

Thus, between low comedy and tragic pathos, the life of the street had changed from its quiet, logical, matter-of-fact working day to a carnival in which nothing seemed to remain true to itself.

Was it because justice is an artificial creation of civilized society that belief in it was the first thing to disappear in the War? If so, it was followed by other standards of life before another year had gone.

Confidence in a measurable or "just" relation between action and reward or punishment, like the "just" relation between cause and effect, expresses itself significantly in the national development of the institutions serving both private and public insurance. When the War had exhausted itself and the period of reconstruction should have begun, one of the prime difficulties encountered consisted precisely in the loss of that confidence in a rational relation between action and effect which forms the base for any system of insurance. War makes people lose what we might call the habit of insurance. That may seem a strange argument to use in the history of a people under the stress of war; and a historian who is intent on reading the next generation lessons drawn from the failures of the past will probably object to it. Insurance would seem to be a commercial venture of doubtful merit if one looked at it only from the point of view of the higher ethics, for it offers security by making people pay only for some average share in the calculated probabilities of death, of damage, and even of every kind of crime, instead of having to pay the full price of it when it befalls them. But, on the other hand, it is closely bound up with the human instinct to save, and it had certainly permeated the life of the community to such a degree as to have become one of the main regulators of peace and industry. Post-war Germany had to do without it. The people despaired of being able either to take out an insurance policy on their own lives or of being able to make themselves beneficiaries by insuring the lives of others. Nothing could be foreseen or calculated in advance. It was only a gambler who could win, not a man of principle. Why then educate the next generation to a knowledge which in another war would again prove futile? Why work if the reward could be taken away by a force which prided itself on its freedom from that law which guarantees the wage a man's labor is entitled to earn? Why save if the capital which could be built up by saving proved, in fact, to be nothing more than a creditor's claim in a bad bankruptcy?

CHAPTER II

BUSINESS VERSUS BUREAUCRACY

DESPAIRING of justice as an effective criterion, men may still turn to other standards of life; and their next thought after their belief in the possibility of a reign of *suum cuique* has been discredited is usually a hearty striving for at least a full portion of *meum*. It is a change from idealism, whether sincere or pretended, to a materialism, which, besides being readily at hand, seems to have the definite advantage of being at least candid. People during the War had discarded, one after another, the paragraphs of their catechism of law-and-order as so many pieces of silly sentiment, and had told themselves and others how desirable it was for a patriot to get hardened.

They had forgotten, if it was Siegfried they took for a model, that the one soft spot between his shoulder blades proved more fatal to him than blows taken in front to an ordinary mortal. But they adopted the maxim that material gain was, after all, the only evidence of right action. Nothing succeeds like success, they told one another, when they discussed the outcome of the War and the different ways of getting over the difficulties of the hour. By the time of the first real efforts on the part of Germany to regain a foothold in world affairs, the bitterness of what had been experienced from 1915 to 1918 was, if not entirely forgotten, at least superseded by a strange belief in a new law which would regulate the conditions of national life and, in the end, secure a return to normality, the law of economics.

Much as the fathers of the German Constitution and the professors who had to expound its principles would have wished to direct the energies of political life to the exalted questions of Constitutional Law, the relations between Reich and component States, the fundamental rights solemnly guaranteed by the Constitution, or compulsory education as provided by it, the new start and rush of public opinion after the first months of the Republican régime took the people to fields of political discussion other than those prepared for them by the constitutionalists. The German people have often been said to lack the sense of politics; and the truth of this observation seems to need no further proof if we look at the turn of events after 1921. For instead of attacking the problems which, with a bit of luck, could have been solved by sober reasoning and hard work, they threw themselves on the two sets of questions which, under modern circumstances—or perhaps at any time—seem to defy popular understanding and popular effort most completely: foreign affairs, and the economic system—a system which, moreover, was struggling for the coördination of capitalism and socialism. A history of the social and economic effects of the War would miss the point if it did not know how to appreciate the influence of what we call *Politisierung* upon a nation which by tradition and character does not lend itself to the science or game—whichever one likes to call it—of politics. This "politicization" was a direct outcome of the War. Great havoc was wrought both by the amateurish and partisan criticism of everything the Foreign Office did or did not do, and by the stupendous amount of public lying which occurs whenever the finances of the State or of a big industrial concern resembling a state have to be explained (*sit venia verbo*) to a great mass of newspaper readers and other students of public affairs who are entirely innocent of any inside knowledge of the ways of business, and such havoc must be put down on the debit side of the account of the War, though this was only made plain to the world thirteen years after the last shot was fired.

Since the passing away of the first state of contentedness in Germany following the stabilization of the currency in 1925 and the phantom of prosperity which the British coal strike conjured up before the eyes of Germany, no other topic has been a greater favorite with the German who talks politics than the wasteful extravagance of the *Öffentliche Hand*, the Treasury and the pay offices of the municipalities. Sometimes the interest has centered on a specific case in which public finance was said to have neglected all the precepts of sound economy, the case, for example, of a subsidy given to shipping, or to agriculture in certain parts of Prussia, or to institutions which could not be said to be unequivocally devoted to science or the social services but somehow seemed to serve the interests of the Government of the day, or to the case of a municipal building which by its new style, by the grandeur of its plans, and by its ingenious devices was little in keeping with the general distress among all classes of the nation. An abundant opportunity for caustic comment was given by the action of many town councils in laying out garden grounds or perhaps a stadium with a magnificence unknown to the period of the Second Empire. To be resplendent, pre-war Germany had added stucco ornaments to post office or railway station, or a cupola of sham copper or gold to a government building. Post-war Germany embarked on public enterprises of a greater scale and on more realistic plans. But even the gratitude which should have been felt by the younger generation in Germany for the consideration shown its predilection for swimming and sun-bathing in the many artificial lakes or public baths established by most of the greater towns has not kept them from remarking on the expense connected with this their favored cult. According to most people, however, the worst of sinners were: first, the administrations of the different branches of social insurance, whose stately office buildings provoked the daily ire of all the good people who passed them in the street and believed them to have been built with the money which every employer of domestic or industrial labor paid into the insurance funds; and, second, the town councils, providing new elementary schools with swimming pools, cinema halls, stadiums, stages for amateur theatricals, and, in short, all the paraphernalia of an ocean liner for American millionaires—if one might believe what the Nationalist newspapers and stump orators of the opposition parties told their audiences about the schools in a district under socialist or radical administration.

Single cases of grievance, however, were not in themselves very important, most of them originating and ending in the local scramble for municipal patronage. But over and above them there was a widespread belief, and in the inner circle of the business community an uncompromising conviction, that during the last ten years the German capitalist and employer had been overburdened with taxes and insurance payments, including a high percentage of the costs of production for unemployment insurance. As it seemed to them, the employer had to maintain, from his private fortune or from the earnings of his business, an excessive number of officials with excessively high wages and plenty of holidays, an army of lazybones and do-nothings, meaning people who worked but evidently did not "create" money by working. For, quite the contrary, part of their work consisted necessarily in keeping businessmen from "creating" as much money as they could.

The great centers of industry and commerce like Essen or Magdeburg, Hamburg or Nürnberg, Augsburg or Frankfurt am Main, were prominent exponents of this theory. Industrial Saxony and Thuringia were the German States where it led to legislative steps which were meant to protect the economic life from officialdom, a curious reversion of the traditional rôle of the merchant and the official, who should be able to protect honest commerce instead of commerce asking for protection against them.

The new attitude of industrialists and capitalists generally was, partly at least, due to the change in the form of government rather than directly to the War itself. While Germany was a union of monarchies, with a few republican city-states in between, social distinction was, apart from the army and the higher grades of nobility, shared by the heads of administrative departments and a few select leaders of business, judges, prominent university professors, and, here and there, a luminary of one of the liberal professions. This was a state of things remarkably well expressed by the titles which were coveted by successful businessmen, and which were meant to resemble the titles given to high officials, a *Herr Geheimer Commerzienrat* (Privy Councilor of Commerce), or, as he was prone to be called *Herr Geheimrat*, becoming indistinguishable in this way from a Privy Councilor himself. Some of the older people in Germany may still remember the flutter which went through the upper strata of society when an Imperial title of *Wirklicher Geheimer Rat* (Privy Councilor in Ordinary), carrying the privilege of a "His Excellency" with it, was conferred on the head of a banking firm, or the sensation created by a leading industrialist who declined the same honor, which Emperor William the Second had intended for him. The Republic and the professed suppression of titles and decorations has wrought a remarkable change in this respect. Big business, and most of all the so-called "heavy" kind of industry, either looks down on the bureaucracy and buys the ablest members of the Civil Service to do secretariat work in its organizations or to become its lawyers and notaries, or it looks askance at officials. It distrusts them and complains of their high salaries and their long holidays, which have to be outbidden in the auction market of human ability and usefulness by the employer who wishes to lure the best kind of lawyer, administrator, or superintendent of labor away from the public services and enlist him in his private service. The economic crisis which came to shake Germany to her depths in 1931 was certainly to a great extent due to the general trade depression throughout the world, which in its turn was nothing but the necessary liquidation of the regular after-the-war boom in every kind of non-necessity of life. For the rest, however, we must not forget that the German crisis formed the climax of the vicious conflict between the old idea of a *Beamtenstaat*—government by a trained, permanent civil service— and the new conception of a *Wirtschaftsstaat* or *Industriestaat*, which insisted on being able to govern a country on essentially the same lines as a great business. The latter won its first, and perhaps decisive victory during the summer of 1931. At that time a government, closely allied to the leading heads of at least one branch of German industry and banking, determined by a series of emergency decrees to deprive state and municipal officials of their security of tenure, and especially of their security of title to pensions of computable amount after a certain number of years of service. Expectancy of pension and security of tenure were, apart from a certain social standing in connection with public office, the two allurements civil or municipal service had to offer in compensation for lower salaries and, more than that, for the manifold restrictions upon conduct and *Nebenerwerb*—extra earnings—which are corollaries to the dignity of office. The respect for social standing had, due to the War, made way for an exclusive, matter-of-fact recognition of wealth or patronage as the regulator of men's lives. Office, even that of a cabinet minister or a *president* (governor) of a state, could not give its bearer any distinction beyond that which he owed to private fortune, to personal influence with wealthy people, or in the administration of public funds or endowments. The shattering of confidence in the State as contractor of works or labor[1] was (or at least seemed for the

1. It is to be noted that the emergency decrees of 1931 did not reduce the salaries or pensions of those whom the State wished to enlist in its service in the future; but it took from old officials the right to fixed salaries and pensions—a right guaranteed to them under the seal of State, and regarded as *droit acquis* by the officials and their dependents—without even an excuse or the promise of any compensation. The sole promise on the occasion of the first reduction of salary was a solemn declaration that it was one of those things that happen once only, and then under extraordinary duress, and that it would last for merely some months, a declaration which had hardly been made when it became apparent that it was only so much dust thrown into the eyes of the service.

time being to be) clear gain to those who claimed that in their capacity as taxpayers they were the real mainstay of the nation and that, therefore, public service should not be what the theoreticians of utopian proclivities would make it, an instrument of good and just government, but a subordinate accessory to the organization of capital and labor which could very well take care of itself, at least in so far as general lines of policy and, above all, measures of taxation itself were in question.

Officialdom was the common enemy that made the representatives of differing and contrasting economic interests stand together—agriculture and the raw-material and refining industries, transport on land and sea, import and export trade, retail trade, certain of the "free professions," especially that of medicine, and finally the great organizations of commercial employees and shop assistants. The state of things that they objected to was not a mere situation, far less a mere system; it was a real enemy force they were out to dispel. Social insurance, to them, did not consist primarily of payments to the sick or infirm or the unemployed or the disabled, but of payments the employer had to make in addition to the salary or wages of young, able-bodied, and healthy men and women working for him; and, still more, it consisted of the office buildings of the insurance administration and of the officials who sat in leather chairs dictating unnecessary letters to girl typists, and week-ending or holidaying through all four seasons of the year, or of those officers who went from door to door to see that housewife and shopkeeper were punctual in pasting insurance stamps on the cards of their servants. Again, railway and postal service, state or municipal hospitals, public schools of every kind, *Finanzämter* (tax collectors' offices), factory inspection, statistics, and many another public service, meant not transport and communication, prevention or treatment of diseases, education, assessment of taxes, or state control to prevent abuses in the employment of women and children, but offices with inconvenient office hours, waiting queues at the counters, architectural extravagances of decoration and space, and the large staffs of officials belonging to these offices. The "natural course of economic life" which, from this point of view, was most obviously disturbed by State Socialism, consisted mainly in the employer of labor, the man who orders work to be done for him, appointing and dismissing those whom he employs, according to a businesslike calculation of exactly how much labor he needs from time to time, and, above all, how much he can spend on that labor in wages or salaries without reducing his profits and his income from investments. Instead of being able so to do he saw the State or some other public body stepping in and not only appointing the necessary officials but deciding for itself how many of them were needed, how many hours of work they would have to do and how they would be paid. But, to the business mind, the final insult was the fact that most of those officials got an old-age pension at a time of life when they were perfectly fit (and not a few of them quite willing) to continue working; and some categories of officials even acquired the right of a pension for their widows or children.[2]

The conflict between bureaucracy and business reduced itself to two main questions, the number of public officials and their scale of wages, and the necessity of such and such a single item of expense, or, to be more explicit, the question of who should decide on that necessity. The demand for a *Spar-Diktator*, a State commissary to

2. We are dwelling upon a region of the social map of the world which to the eye of a German looks different from what it does to that of a foreigner, most of all an Englishman or American. A German may think that free competition and an unrestricted use of private property and of the faculties of the individual is the system which leads to the greatest prosperity for the country at large and for the great majority of its inhabitants. He may think that the ever present poor themselves are better off in a society headed by a considerable number of very wealthy people than under a system which distributes wealth more evenly. But this same German will still hold to the conviction that as a matter of course the State should provide for at least two kinds of education, elementary and university, and for public hospitals. The latter, in the twenty-seven university towns, form part of the educational institutions of Faculties of Medicine, while other towns have their own hospitals for poor patients and for paying inmates who wish to get the best treatment for a relatively small sum. Endowments for scientific or educational purposes or for hospitals were a rare exception in Germany, even in periods of great prosperity and national expansion; and the leaders of the business world, in speaking of public waste and of the retrenchments they would carry through if they took over the Government from the "Marxists," by no means thought of making a change in that respect. In their view, as in that of their political antagonists, it seemed a proper function of the State to provide for the highest and lowest form of education, to maintain scientific institutions at its own cost, and to bear the expense of public hospitals. The only difference of opinion in that respect is as to including education in high school and college in the domain of State control, and of extending the cases in which education and hospital treatment should be gratuitous.

whom this decision should be entrusted independently of both Government and Parliament—in the sense that he could veto any expense even if proposed by the Department of State and voted for by Parliament—is easily understood if one considers why Parliament could not be responsible for permitting this kind of retrenchment. Representatives elected from small constituencies were put under heavy obligation to satisfy the special needs of their electors. Such needs might take the form of local railways, road making, stadiums, public baths and vast swimming pools, bonuses for local industries, cheap buildings for suburban flats, trams, the regulation of rivers, sanitary measures for unhealthy places, the clearing of slums, the support of a theater, and so on. Accordingly, such members of Parliament must be driven to make bargains of a more or less immoral character in order to please their constituencies. On the other hand, if Parliament is elected by proportional representation along party lines, each party has its own clientele of aspirants for office and its special kind of unproductive expenses to consider, whether military barracks and fortifications, or convents, settlement buildings, and the costly equipping of elementary schools with chemical laboratories, astronomical observatories, and museums of natural history and applied arts, or model prisons, State farms, or statistical registration for every walk of life. And finally, if Parliament, according to modern ideas, was to be an assembly of the estates of the realm, the relative importance and indispensableness of each of the estates —agriculture or industry, producers or consumers, the liberal professions or officialdom, town or country, the army or civilian life— would be decided and made a matter of the constitution itself; and Parliament would become a mere replica of the incessant guerrilla warfare between the departments of state in their rival claims on the Exchequer. Under modern circumstances, Parliament, in whatever form, was unable to be thrifty. That was a common complaint even before the War, but it was aggravated by the War, first because in general the War accustomed people to spend recklessly, and second, because discontent with the existing form of government, especially with the members of the commercial and industrial community, had learned to express itself much more strongly than it did before the War. That is why a journalist of changeable opinions, a hero of trench warfare, a man without professional ties or the education of an expert became, fittingly, the dictator of a people troubled by the undecided conflict of interests and values, and gained stability for his régime, after the first enthusiastic assault has put him in power, by taking upon himself all the more important departments of state and killing, by that real stroke of genius, the terrible hydra of departmental jealousies and rivalries, *Ressortpartikularismus.*

The weighing of expenditures is one of the most important tasks of government. In a collectivist state the question is not so much whether certain expenditures should be reduced in order that others could be more easily justified and more readily accepted by Parliament and public opinion. It is rather whether the Government should not take it upon itself to classify every expenditure made within its jurisdiction, even though it be private capital used in the course of regular trade and commerce as *necessaria* or *dubia* or *caetera*—necessary, doubtful, or merely gratuitous—to use the old terminology of the moralists. State planning would, in a period of economic stress, suppress all *caetera* expenses, suspend the *dubia,* and ask for documentary evidence before it conceded the *necessaria.* But during the period of transition from individualism to the position in which Germany found herself in the years after the War, the weighing of expenditures had been applied to the relative value of those outlays that were held properly to be provided for by the Exchequer. To take our case from the budget of the Reich, how would the following values compare? First, the gain to be had by going on with the building of a new cruiser of the pocket-battleship type, the value here being represented by national defense, by employment for shipbuilding yards, the encouragement of engineering, and considerations of domestic policy. Second, the advantage that would arise from raising legations in South America to the rank of embassies, the value here being in international relations, the furthering of trade with South America, and reciprocity. Third, what might be won by the granting of subventions to exporting industries with these objects: the building up of an active balance of trade in order to strengthen the gold basis of the currency, the increasing of employment at high wages through these industries, the creation of a weapon for the international negotiation of commercial treaties, and the attaching of such industries to the present form of government. Fourth, the advisability of the allotting—as a matter of domestic policy—of an emergency bonus to agricultural provinces suffering from an acute depression in prices. Fifth, the benefit that might come from a contribution to the fund for the support of scientific research and the publication of the result of such research, the so-called *Notgemeinschaft der Deutschen Wissenschaft* and Institutes of the *Kaiser Wilhelm Gesellschaft*. There the value would be partly ideal, partly in furthering new inventions to be used by national industries, especially those of chemistry, engineering, and aircraft. Sixth, we had the return that might come from devoting such money—by way of policy and patronage—to some organization for political propaganda. And so on. All this expenditure had to be kept in sound proportion to the standard of wages and salaries, and in sanctioning any of those expenditures the Government had to remember the need of State contributions toward covering the deficit in the funds of social and unemployment insurance administration, and similar deficits in the public welfare funds of municipalities and rural districts.

It was in the matter of this political function of government, the weighing of expenditures, inclusive of decisions as to their necessity or urgency, that the War had been the great perverter of morals and of sane judgment. War familiarized Government and people with the habit of taking things for granted which in normal times would not have stood the slightest test or scrutiny. War proved to be much worse, in that respect, than revolution. Revolution, it is true, makes a point of changing values, of "breaking old tables," and generally trying to make two times two equal five, or a chord from $C + E$ sharp $+ G$ sharp. But a revolution brings all this about through an irrational act of revolutionary will; it does not propose it as a rule of sound policy or a natural law. War commands people to submit to the necessity of its demands on human life, labor, and economic conditions as a matter of political morals, of logic, and of law. War itself is the supreme necessity which justifies every expenditure. Those who might doubt this and criticize the waste in war expenditures were told with great forcefulness they should be ashamed of even mentioning money or private property, that they should remember that their fellow countrymen were asked to give their lives, and were giving them without demur. Such considerations should forbid *them* to criticize mere money expenditures—money, too, spent for their benefit. And we have to remember that the abandonment of old rules of calculation was common to both producer and buyer, seller and consumer. For if, half the time, the Government paid extravagant prices for goods which could not even be tested before acceptance, in the other half it confiscated the goods and fixed compensation according to its own estimate. Its estimates, moreover, were not of what the goods were worth, but of what it could afford to pay for them. Or it regulated prices by a war emergency decree, and fixed them at a level which made production unprofitable and drove the article out of the open market. But always it was the firm conviction of everybody concerned that this had to be so, and that money calculations were something for *Händler* (shopkeepers), not for *Helden* (heroes). If a war be of brief duration this attitude of mind may end with it, and peace may restore ordinary ways of reasoning. The World War, however, made a lasting impression on the habits of thought, at least of the continental nations. The heroism which forbade any bureaucratic or commercializing doubts of the justification for the acts it was about to commit, transformed itself, during the post-war period, and with redoubled force during the two economic crises of 1923 and 1931, into a new philosophy of public morals called decisionism. It denounced caution as unmanly. It upheld the virtue of courage in taking the responsibility for the rights or wrongs of an ill-considered decision, on the ground that actually *taking* it, either this way or that, even if it proved wrong or unnecessarily expensive, is always better than shrinking from responsibilities and losing Fortune's fleeting moment while subtly reasoning on the chances of getting her cheap. The emergency decrees of 1931 were officially justified by the President and his Cabinet almost in the same words as those used by the Imperial Government in 1914 and 1918. In his radio message to the German people on August 4, 1931, Chancellor Brüning confessed that some of the measures taken by the Government during the three preceding weeks—the closing of commercial and savings banks, the partial moratorium, the State's guaranteeing big banks which had had to suspend payment, the closing of the frontier to tourist traffic, compulsory declaration by all taxpayers of their resources in foreign currency and the forced sale of such currency to the Reichsbank at a rate of exchange fixed by decree—might have proved ineffective and other measures might have proved very obnoxious; but, the point was, the Government had had to *act* at any cost.

Party politics have obscured the issue in question just as they succeeded in obscuring the story of the events at the close of the War and at the time of the Armistice. Socialist members of the Cabinet and Socialist influence on the coalition governments of the Republic generally have been held responsible for reckless extravagance—especially in raising wages and, consequently, salaries, by office inflation in the domain of social insurance and public welfare in particular, and by encouraging the luxurious equipment of elementary schools and apartment houses for workingmen. The Economic and Social History of the World War has another story to tell of post-war developments. Lavish spending of public money was, irrespective of the political allegiance of the post-war government, a relic of the War. The practice of the Ministry for National Defense was continued by the ministers in charge of national reconstruction and the labor ministers. The necessity of making provision for life claimed to be on the same level with the necessity of making provision for the destruction of life; and the habit of wholesale dealing between government departments or offices and industrial or financial groups and combines was by no means discontinued when it was demobilization instead of mobilization, turning swords into plowshares instead of the reverse, or reparation payments instead of war loans that were concerned. The root of this habit of using public money in a way which would not be tolerated in private business by any honest merchant was the same in post-war peace as it was in the War. Expenses could not be thoroughly sifted before the money was actually spent because the War had inoculated both the staffs of government and the servants of publicity with the belief that the end justified not only the deliberate choice of bad means, but—which is immeasurably worse—the seizing of any available means without first considering whether they were, in themselves, good or bad, and what kind of harvest the next generation would therefore reap as a result of such seed having been sown throughout the country. Patriotic purpose was enough to quiet the conscience. During the War the aim was, first to win. Then, after the hope of a decisive victory had disappeared, it was to prolong the War outside German territory and with sufficient vigor to obtain a negotiated peace. And, finally, it was to put off the inevitable end as long as possible. Criticism of that aim was tantamount to high treason, and criticism of the means used to attain it seemed utterly futile while the aim itself could not even be discussed. After the War the public aim was reconstruction, mainly of outward order, of transport facilities and overseas trade, of the equipment of industry for the manufacturing of export goods. And, again, it was the general conviction of the infallible righteousness of this aim which destroyed all attempts at a careful, cautious calculation of the necessary expense. Even those who were always loudest in the demand for a dictatorship which would formally consecrate this habit of dispensing with budgetary criticism are ready to acknowledge one thing. During both the first years of the War and the fifteen years since the War, that part of the public expenditure which *they* thought was most unwarranted and unnecessary was due to the same view on the part of the leaders of affairs, and it was this. Their program, they felt, could not be carried out—the War could not be won nor could a powerful peace industry, one able to compete with Belgian, British, American, or Polish industry, be built up on the ruins of the War—without the good will of organized labor, of trade-unions, and the German Social Democrat Party machine. That good will, propaganda of the Nationalist and Monarchist press contended, had to be bought by high wages and by pleasing the working class in various ways—by equal opportunity for education, by good and sanitary housing, by public recreation grounds and baths and stadiums—both during and after the War.

If this holds good of the immediate causes of reckless spending and the inability to weigh expenditure soundly we have to acknowledge, nevertheless, that the remote causes of these defects go much farther back into history than 1914. They are to be found wherever in German history policy in the narrower sense of the term—the *ratio status* of fifteenth- and sixteenth-century statecraft—formed the canon of government.

CHAPTER III

DISREGARD OF ECONOMIC LAWS

THE German terms for statecraft when it is opposed to justice and public morality, *Machiavellismus* and *Staatsraison*, are both borrowed words. In the clumsy fashion of such foreign words they indicate that the maxims which came without any special malice or insidiousness from the lips of the Florentine secretary or the courtiers of *le Roi Soleil* were alien to German thought. But their practice is not foreign to German history.

The turn which the financial policy of the Reich took at the beginning of the War under the direct influence of the *ratio status* conception forms a striking instance of the influence such doctrines may obtain, under the favor of war, in making for economic disorder, inflation, and virtual bankruptcy. That there was a direct connection between the way in which the authorities tried to finance the War and inflation, with its consequences, up to the crisis of 1931, has often been denied, though most economists seem to recognize that at least a general causation may be found.

The gold basis of German currency at the beginning of the War was solid. The gold fund of the Bank, 1,253 millions of marks in July, 1914 (with a note circulation of approximately 2,000 millions), had been more than doubled by the summer of 1917. On June 17 the Reichsbank showed a gold reserve of 2,533 millions. That was, obviously, not a result of normal monetary circumstances. The rise in the fund was mainly due to a series of measures of compulsion. They began with the withdrawal of gold coin from circulation and the enacting of special laws against agio-speculation in gold sovereigns, with heavy penalties for those who violated them (the decree of November 23, 1914). And they went on to the prohibition of the export of gold and the confiscation of bullion for coining into specie. There is a conflict of opinion as to the exact point, within that development, at which the first germs of inflation are to be seen. Dr. Schacht, in his book on the stabilization of German currency, emphasizes the fact that in the early stages of the War both the people and the Government had shown a remarkable power to resist the perils with which a war always threatens sound economics. He points to the fact that immediately after the declaration of war there were those—and they were both economists and politicians—who asked for a general moratorium. Indeed, they would not be satisfied with any but the most drastic measures of change from the normal and peaceful condition of affairs. For such measures were to secure a complete "silencing of chatter about laws in a nation under arms" and to bring all departments of civil government into line with the strict centralization and the obedience to command which prevails in the field of military operations, especially during mobilization. The Government did not, at the time, yield to this demand. It confined itself to a few special emergency decrees; and, in doing so, it followed the advice of the directors of the Reichsbank and of the most experienced leaders in the commercial and industrial community. They hoped to prove the sound condition of German currency by showing its ability to stand the assault of war and the consequent loss of confidence, unaided by measures of coercion and without any serious interference by Government with private ownership and normal trade conditions. They relied on the interdependence of capital in all the belligerent and the neutral countries. One has to remember, in this connection, that both the drastic application of the rules against trading and intercourse with the enemy (including, as the world was to learn, sequestration and eventual confiscation of enemy private property) and the imposition of a blockade on neutrals by a strict control over their intercourse with the blockaded country, came quite unexpectedly to German businessmen, even those in closest touch with banking and industrial life in the City of London and in Lancashire. They—or, for that matter, German experts in international law—are not entitled to blame the Government for lack of information or foresight in that respect. Not to have reckoned with the complete severance of every tie connecting the capitalists of the belligerent countries, even indirectly through common neutral business friends and correspondents, was the chief and the most fatal miscalculation on the part of German leaders in public affairs and of German financiers and industrialists.

On the other hand, even the first comparatively timid emergency decrees issued during the first two months of the War are evidence of the truth of the old saying that it is the first step that counts. We may even ask whether the emergency decrees of July and August, 1914, were not much more than a mere first step. Some of them were issued according to plan, in order that an essentially civilian Department of State might fit itself in with the mobilization of the last reserves, the *Landsturm,* on the very day of mobilization; others were clearly improvised, and the ill-omened decree which denied foreign creditors access to the courts, irrespective of their nationality and without regard to the British rule against "alien enemies," evidently belonged to the latter category. Taken together, however, they may be said to resemble a halfway house on the road to a general suspension of payments rather than a first step on the way toward State socialism, though in the end they proved to be nearer the latter than the former. Dr. Schacht himself points to the early date of the decree on *Geschäftsaufsicht,* that is, on the friendly control of businesses threatened with bankruptcy (Ministry of Justice, August 8, 1914). At the time it seemed innocuous enough. A debtor in normal times and according to pre-war legislation would have had to petition for an order of bankruptcy, go through the ordinary proceedings, turn over the control of his estate for the benefit of his creditors, and become liable to severe punishment in case of fraudulent or even grossly negligent failure to satisfy his obligations. But he was now allowed, by the decree of August, 1914, to put his affairs under the extra-judicial supervision of a kind of custodian, the *Aufsichtsperson,* which had the general effect of a moratorium against his creditors as long as the custodian himself did not recommend the opening of formal bankruptcy proceedings.[1] During the War this did not

1. The advisability of such a measure, from the point of view of preventing bankruptcy as long as there was any reasonable hope of tiding over the difficulties of the debtor, had been discussed by jurists and economists long before the War. A Belgian law of similar purpose had been praised as a model for German legislation; and in the Ministry of Justice itself the proposal had found influential friends who may have been willing to use the opportunity quietly to slip through a debatable bill as an emergency decree, without the cumbrous procedure of a parliamentary committee. It was not so much the contents of the measure in themselves which were objectionable, for it is a well-recognized principle of modern legislation to relieve the courts and their ordinary procedure as far as possible from everything which can be dealt with by arbitration, in a summary way, or by preventive measures. But this "friendly control" became one of the contributory causes of the general ruin of national economy, mainly through loosening one of the screws by which business morals had been held firm in peace-time. Debtors were no longer afraid of distraint levied upon their property, and far less of bankruptcy proceedings, with the odium they bring on the good name of the

amount to very much materially. The smaller cases of failure, which, in the main, give occasion for a *Geschäftsaufsicht*, would not have led to a bankruptcy, anyhow, in some cases because creditors would have been afraid to advance money to cover the cost of judicial proceedings and the remuneration of a trustee, and, in others, because the debtor was on military service and therefore exempt from answering a summons to appear in court. The effect of the emergency measure was moral, not material, and that is why it did not pass away with the material situation from which it had emanated, but lasted well on into the post-war period. It led to the habit of relying on a laxer practice of enforcement of commercial obligations, not only in a state of emergency, but as a matter of ordinary routine.

Still more serious were the consequences of another early war decree, that which denied foreign creditors recourse to the courts. The authorities tried to justify this measure by the supreme necessity of an undisturbed general mobilization both during the mobilization period proper and during the months that followed. According to the official explanations given by the Ministry of Justice, it was meant to release German debtors from the necessity of defending themselves in a court of justice against a claim by a foreigner at a time when all energies should be directed toward national defense. The first wording of the decree was so ill-considered as to exclude even the subjects of an allied country from suing in the German courts; but later on, strong objections on the part of neutral creditors—Swiss and Dutch —led to a loosening of the provisions. The break, however, could not be cemented by simply conceding something to those who complained the loudest.

It was at the very moment that neutral or allied participants in German national economy—that is to say, subjects of the United States, Italy, Austria-Hungary, Rumania, all the South American States, Sweden, Norway, Denmark, the Netherlands, Turkey, Persia, China—or of every country in the world but Serbia, Russia, Belgium, France, the British Empire, and Japan—should, from the German point of view, have been encouraged in the belief in the unshakable strength of the military, civil, and economic constitution

---

debtor or his firm. Putting themselves for protection in the hands of a trusted confidant, they felt they had done the honorable thing and had escaped the blame for having abused the credit given to them; it was war, an act of God, not their own mishandling of affairs which had brought this to pass.

of the German Empire. But, instead, their confidence in the reliability of what, in most parts of the world, is still considered as the *fundamentum imperii* was shaken by a denial of recourse to the courts which seemed unwarranted except as a measure of utter despair. Their feelings were akin to those of a German who in peace had enjoyed the hospitality of one of the enemy countries, had returned this hospitality by doing what he could for that country, either in the form of work which its nationals were unable or unwilling to do, or by spending his income in it, or by putting his savings into one of its banks, and then, as a return for his trust in the unwritten laws of hospitality, had had his property confiscated, and had, himself, been interned in a civilian prisoners' camp. The share a foreign creditor takes in the prosperity of the debtor country is not quite as distinctly obvious as that of the foreign worker, engineer, teacher, or other guest in a country which has tendered its hospitality to him in peace-time. It is enough, however, for him to feel that he has been deceived in the trust he has placed in some given or implied promise of equal recourse to its courts of justice, as a corollary to international intercourse. The damage caused by a measure which certainly was not meant to inflict but to prevent hardship was immeasurably greater than the value of the property or the amount of money involved. Together with war sequestration of private property, forced sale, and the consequent confiscation of at least part of it—whether resulting from a doubtful rule of common law, from an emergency decree of a belligerent country, or from a reprisals order of another—the denial of justice to foreign parties in civil cases was a terrible blow to private property, to the capitalist system, and to the idea of a *jus civile* protected by non-political courts of law. Law itself seemed to have given place to the brute force of national egotism as made manifest in war.

Could the currencies of belligerent countries remain intact when measures like these had to be taken to safeguard them for the time being?

The judicial moratorium against foreign claims is, in retrospect at least, closely bound up with the financial policy of the German Government and the Bank of Germany during the later stages of the War. If they had even considered the possibility of financing the War, if only in part, with the help of foreign loans, the moratorium decree of August, 1914, would have been unthinkable. Credit will only be given for securities—and that is hardly practicable in wartime, when every public and private resource of the belligerent country has to be kept at the disposal of the Government, to be realized upon at a moment's notice—or under the fullest guarantees of prompt and fair justice to the creditor, without discrimination against the foreigner as such. To make such discrimination, in favor of one's own nationals, a law of the land, especially in the case of pre-war debts which had been incurred under terms of complete legal equality for foreigners and nationals alike, was tantamount to saying that Germany was resolved to stand apart and to finance the War from German resources as they stood at the outbreak of the War, provided that such resources were protected against all claims from beyond the frontier, whether they were well-founded claims or not.

In itself, this resolution taken at that time shows how imperfectly those who directed German policy realized the actual nature of the struggle, or how much they overestimated the importance of a military success during the first stages of the War. The story of the indignant surprise with which the permanent officials met Walter Rathenau's first suggestion of a systematic provision for a sufficient store of raw materials is well known. The War had always been thought of as a war on at least two fronts, with overseas trade in a very precarious condition even if Great Britain did not take part, and with a possible blockade of German ports if she did. But the question of substituting other sources of raw-material supplies for those ordinarily to be had in Central and Eastern Europe, in the colonies, and America, does not seem to have presented itself. If it had, the problem of providing for this part of the war expenses would have had more serious consideration than was given it, so far as can be gathered from published data on the financial preparation for the War. Other war expenses may be met by government bills and the printing of paper money; but war material from neutral countries, except in cases of barter with a country which needs surplus raw materials from the belligerent, has to be paid for in gold. From the moment when it became clear that Germany did not count on foreign loans, but intended, on principle, to finance the War out of her own resources, neutrals lost interest in the maintenance of German currency as an integral part of the currency system of the world. For this system is tacitly based on the assumption that international high finance will calculate its profits on international loans made on the supposition of a certain interrelation of currencies, with just such a margin for mutual alterations of value as makes the business of quoting exchange a paying affair, but without allowing the currency of any single nation, even in war-time, to become entirely independent of this international system of loans and rates of exchange and to live on its own resources.

The experiment of providing for the cost of the War from the national capital would have had a better chance of success if it had not been accompanied by two misdirected attempts to protect the substance of this capital. The first has been discussed in the foregoing pages. The second was perhaps still more fateful in its consequences, as concerning the internal value of money and domestic economy. German capital was to be protected, according to this doctrine of war finances, not only against withdrawals of credit on the part of foreign capitalists, but against all taxation on the part of the Government itself so far as such taxation might represent a levy on capital. War loans were to be underwritten by German possessors of capital in return for a threefold security—the defense of German territory, the denial of justice to foreign creditors, and the decision of the Government not to tax capital nor to raise the discount rate, as England, for instance, had done in spite of the complaints of the commercial world.

It may be, though this is by no means certain, that the personal régime, concerning which critics within Germany and without have given so many details since its downfall, is partly to blame for these errors of judgment. In a monarch or other *de facto* head of the State it is often, and especially in a time of crisis, a supreme merit to be slow of intellect, simply because this will make it difficult for his advisers to explain things to him. A slow intellect combined with a painstaking, conscientious attitude toward high-sounding plans and bold schemes makes the best kings and presidents. The German Emperor had a remarkable faculty of grasping even difficult questions more quickly than most people of his *milieu;* and even severe criticism of his failure to be what he wished to be, or to show himself as he really was, will not deny him a strong sense of his responsibility toward God and a sincere striving to be worthy of his predecessors. But he was, almost constitutionally and from his youth, a prey to any man among his advisers who had a ready wit and was prompt in proposing solutions for difficulties. If the German War Cabinet of 1914 and 1915 had had to obtain the assent of either of the two subsequent Presidents of the German Republic instead of the Emperor for their scheme of financing the War, they themselves might have dropped it before even proposing it to the head of the State. As it was, they could count on a quick assent to a plan which had the merit of paying, simply by its enunciation, a high tribute to German patriotism, even though it was patriotism of the unheroic kind looked for from those whose contribution to the common cause is only money. We can hardly blame the Emperor for having failed to realize, at the time, truths which his advisers themselves either failed to see or did not dare to point out to him.

We paint in the blackest colors the miserable miser who parts from his hoarded treasure of dead silver and gold with greater reluctance than does his poor neighbor from health or life, and we are ready to condemn him to the innermost circle of Hell. But in the justice due even to the meanest of creatures we should reflect on the utter thanklessness of the sacrifice he is making to his country. A man who gives life and limb in the war can know that in this act his country takes pride, and honors him for it. He dies in order that others may live. Blinded, he may hear around him the shouts of joy at the glorious sunshine that again shines upon his land, and may rest content in the happiness of others whose lives would be a dark prison but for his deeds of courage. Crippled, he may find comfort in seeing the marvelous efforts of his fellows to replace the lost hands of their brothers by redoubling the work of their own. This sacrifice makes for recuperation and regeneration. The capitalist who parts from his money (or to take a more tangible case, the German housewife who has to give up the copper in her kitchen and the linen in her cupboards, where it has lain for many generations as evidence of thrift and patient skill) has no such comfort, nor can the capitalist look forward to any compensation for his loss. He must know that to sign one of his country's war-loan bonds may mean the loss of his money; and he will be unable to find his recompense in any hope that a good use will be made of his sacrifice. As a capitalist, he must know, furthermore, that this is the deadly flaw in the system he and his kind belong to, because it is the only case where he cannot see a corresponding gain to another capitalist result from his own loss. The Government, on a superficial view of the situation, may tell itself and the people that national wealth (*Volksvermögen*) is carefully preserved and perhaps even increased during the war. It may say that such national wealth is not changed in substance but only in form, if, instead of goods, coin, or claims in foreign currency, it consists of one huge claim of the national capitalists upon the Government. And it may argue that its credit would be able, by some mysterious power, to survive the loss of such goods, coin, or claims in foreign currency as had gone to pay the costs of war, had enriched foreign purveyors of war material and, so far as they had been changed into goods of another kind, had exploded in a literal sense, causing as much supplementary destruction of other substantial capital or basic securities for capital as was in any wise possible. The owner of the goods or the coin, however, cannot deceive himself, or be deceived into even a momentary belief of that kind. He sees that those things which, as he has been told again and again, were his property, the things proper to him for his own use and pleasure as well as for his share in public service, are gone; and if, while giving them up, he is told that this is not a loss or sacrifice at all, but has to be accepted in order to maintain his capital intact, he learns the bitter truth of the saying about adding insult to injury.

CHAPTER IV

FINANCING WAR

IT would benefit our knowledge of the economic effects of war immensely if we could determine, by exact methods of reasoning, what change it would have made in the post-war situation if a military *tour de force* had, against the odds, given a decisive victory to the Central Powers before the United States entered the War. We should like to think that it would not have made as great a difference as those who believe in the power of war would have us assume. Even a treaty of peace as much in favor of the Central Powers as the treaties of 1919 were against them would have left them burdened with a public debt of fantastic dimensions, with the urgent necessity of artificial measures to get rid of it—probably not without inflation—and with a precarious claim for a war indemnity against the enemy countries, which in that case would have clashed with the claim of the United States, and perhaps of other neutral countries, for the repayment of their war loans. By the figures for the Great War, Germany and her Allies would have had, in 1917, an internal public debt of about 150,000 millions of marks, or about 37,000 million dollars. They would certainly have forgiven Russia her eventual war indemnity in return for the separate peace they had been able to conclude with her. And they would, of course, have been unable to force conditions of peace on either Japan, the British Dominions, or the South American countries. But they would have demanded, in all probability, the payment of at least 30,000 million dollars from Great Britain, France, and Italy—that is to say, about the sum which at that time these countries owed to the United States.

After a prolonged struggle over the priority of commercial pre-war debts, pre-war public loans, war loans to allies, and reparation payments, during which time several of the debtor countries would have been reduced to a state of bankruptcy and German trade would accordingly have suffered with them, by their being forced to dump goods, the Government of the United States, supported by public opinion, would have made a proposal for an all-round rearrangement, first to prevent further dumping and disturbances of the currency system, second to secure disarmament, and third to reduce, or to suspend, or, finally, to forgive, *pari passu*, reparation debts and debts due to war loans—in fact virtually the same proposal as that made by President Hoover in June, 1931. This proposal would have been received with the utmost feeling of relief by the debtor countries, and with some reluctance by Germany, but we may perhaps assume that the recognition of an unwelcome truth and of the right of the United States Government to proclaim it to the world would have opened the way to a belated solution of the economic crisis.

If our guess is not too wide of the mark, the economic effects of a reversal of victory in the Great War, or, in other words, a reversal of the method of financing the War between the Allies and the Central Powers would have been almost nil. The situation has been somewhat complicated by the fact that the greatest neutral creditor country joined its debtors as their associate during the later period of the War. The "inter-allied" character of the financial relations between the United States and the European belligerents in 1917 and 1918 made it easier for the American creditors to conclude a series of accords in mitigation of the debts owing them by their individual debtors, while the difficulty of finding a convenient relation between the reparation debts and the inter-allied debts was not similarly overcome. One side of this difficulty must not be overlooked, though it is the side farthest away from the light of impartial history. The financial policy of the German Government is blamed most heavily by those who hold that it was a political blunder, besides being economically unsound. Their theory is that a foreign loan binds the creditor country in a subtle way to the fate of its debtor and that a belligerent should therefore try to get a loan from a neutral country to prevent its joining the enemy. It is an argument which cuts both ways, and certainly one which should not, in fairness, be used by the advocates of war as an arbiter between the belligerents, for the neutral creditor country which had helped both parties, crediting supplies of war materials and even permitting the issue of loans to both of them on its stock market, would certainly be entitled and, by its playing so essential a rôle financially, be enabled to step in as soon as the complete defeat and ruin of one of its debtors threatened, and ask for an "inconclusive" treaty of peace, a "rotten" peace. Still, it was a widespread belief in Germany, very useful to nationalist propaganda against international finance, represented by Wall Street, that the United States would not have entered the War had it not been influenced by its capitalists, who felt that their claims on French and English debtors would be endangered by a German victory.

The lesson we can draw from the real event must needs be one-sided. In the case of the War it reads that a country which tries to finance its war by internal loans loses doubly if, as was the case with Germany, it loses at all. It has nothing to hope for in the way of mediation on the part of a neutral creditor. Its debt toward its own subjects is completely disregarded in the fixing of its obligation to pay reparations or an indemnity. Relief can come only by inflation sweeping away the internal debt, by the threat of dumping, and by communist state monopolies bringing the foreign creditors to a reasonable reduction of their claims.

If we follow the event, we cannot distinguish the economic—or *in specie* the financial—consequences for German credit and German currency of Germany's having lost the War from the direct effects of the financial policy initiated in 1914 and followed up to 1918.

It is true that as early as July, 1914, the technical possibility of an increase in the circulation of notes was provided for. A bank-note holder's legal claim to be paid its face value in gold was summarily abolished—a proceeding which, at the time, was divested of part of its funereal aspect by a solemn declaration by the authorities to the effect that "mark would always be equivalent to mark," a slogan which during the inflation, and still more during the period of under-revaluation of the "old" mark claims, won a notoriety that even endangered the lives of responsible officials at the pay offices of the State. In addition to the Reichsbank and the privileged note-issuing banks of several states, new vehicles for the issue of paper money were created. The *Darlehnskasse*, a central credits fund, was established as an independent institution under the control of the Reichsbank, and was given the privilege of issuing notes called *Darlehnskassenscheine*—the word *Schein* meaning in German, ominously enough, not merely a certificate or voucher, but also a mere semblance or pretense—and security for the new bank notes was vested in deposits of stocks and shares, stored-up supplies, and the like, valued at a more or less conservative estimate. The *Darlehnskassenscheine* were given the character of legal tender for bank notes. Treasury bills and notes were accepted as sufficient cover for paper money.

It is equally true, however, that all this was meant not as a step toward inflation, or even a preparation for such a contingency as inflation of the kind which resulted from it, but simply as a means of easing a situation of transient difficulty. Single measures and, so far as there was any kind of plan, this plan itself, can only be understood as part of the general attitude of the pre-war governments toward war, a strange mixture of overconfidence and a skepticism akin to absolute despair of success. Every German, we might almost say, overestimated the efficiency of institutions, and believed in an unparalleled state of thorough organization and preparedness, which would make war itself a kind of prolonged mobilization, according to plan, and with almost an obligation on the part of the enemy to behave in the way German foresight had made him behave on the green cloth of the General Staff *Kriegspiel,* or, on paper, in the mobilization plan. Such was the confidence placed by all those concerned with Government in the so-called Schlieffen Plan—a confidence which, with civilian ministers and other advisers of the Crown, went so far as to make them feel entirely free of responsibility for anything which might happen after war had been declared—that it seemed to be assumed that the thing would function by itself. Everybody believed in the Plan. It said that after so-and-so many weeks France would be practically put out of the fight and the German forces could then be thrown against Russia. And in so-and-so many months they would secure a good basis for the conclusion of a continental peace. But at the same time, practically nobody believed in the ability of any of the men in responsible positions to carry the Plan through by his own individual strength and energy. Such belief was lacking in General von Moltke, the Chancellor, or his Secretary of State for Foreign Affairs, or in any of the party leaders, or in the Emperor, or even in Admiral von Tirpitz. Everyone felt convinced that if the Plan did not go through as it promised to do on paper nothing could save Germany. It was this despair of human powers, of the ability and resourcefulness of the generation of 1914, which was so much in evidence in the speeches and acts of Chancellor von Bethmann-Hollweg, and was displayed so pitiably in the way the leaders blamed each other for the miscarriage of the campaign both on land and on sea. Even the war enthusiasm of many young people, students and college boys mainly, was utterly distrusted by the authorities as being outside the domain of strict command and the machine-like functioning of orders. The watchword of the Chancellor—"no more parties, Germans all of us"—was meant to be an exhortation to all those active in politics to stand aside and let those commanding in the War do their duty in the service of the Plan. Above all, people must not come forth with any independent contributions of their own. How could a people which had told itself for centuries that it was the people of *"Denker und Dichter,"* of thinkers and dreamers, of slow-working peasants, painstaking artisans, and pedantic professors, be trusted to act in a sensible way except on orders which had been carefully prepared years and years before?[1] Such a policy could not be maintained for any length of time, and it was patently and outrageously untrue to say, at any period of the War whatever, that time worked in favor of the German cause. It worked against it from the beginning. For the longer the War lasted, the more would success depend on renewed effort independent of the stale organizations of 1914, on individual feats of courage and resourcefulness, on radically sincere thinking, and on telling superiors the truth. Above all, it depended on the whole people knowing that every single individual had to strain all the nerves of his being to take his share in the conduct of the War and make it his own personal affair, not as a suffering victim, but as an agent of the will of the German democracy. That, however, was just the thing which the rulers and the officials in charge of the conduct of the War thought would lead to certain disaster. None of them would have believed in the possibility of either the army or the people at home holding out to 1917 and 1918, if anybody had predicted such a thing in the August days of 1914; and with many Germans the obsession of lack of trust in their own people was so strong that it led them to believe everything which the enemies of that people told them

1. The German people's hero worship of Hindenburg and Ludendorff, which extended far into the camp of the Socialists, offers only one more argument for this thesis. They were both of them entirely unforeseen forces, hailed by the people, but really supported by a relatively small band of personal followers, while the official mind either doubted or openly opposed them. General Hoffmann's book of war memories, *Lost Opportunities,* and the Valentini Memoirs are the best guides to the truth about these matters. Another instance of German inability to cope with an unforeseen event was the way in which the negotiations for the Eastern Peace—that with Russia and Rumania—were conducted, and the possibilities of a real peace, on these occasions, neglected.

about its having committed felony and high treason during the last months of the War, and even to pander to the atrocious "dagger stroke" lie—which put the blame for final "betrayal" upon the Socialists.

The financial policy of the Government of 1914—and we may quote the authority of Dr. Schacht again for saying that it was "in the first instance the financial administration of the Reich and not the Reichsbank which was responsible" for that policy—was in perfect accord with the idea of a war which would be won, through the Schlieffen Plan, in a few months or could not be won at all.

To apply for foreign loans would have called for the courage to depart from the designated road, for force of initiative, and pride in personal responsibility. To ask the people for subscriptions toward an internal loan in the first two years of the War meant simply nothing to the Government. It was a mere formality, except in so far as it demonstrated the readiness of the people to support the War in any way which seemed appropriate to the Government.

The change came when subscriptions to new loans began to lag behind the amount of the floating debt. Up to the year 1916 the proceeds of a loan were always sufficient to cover Treasury bills in circulation. In 1916 the amount subscribed was still 6 billion marks greater than the current credits in the Treasury. The fifth War Loan, however, left 2 billion marks of floating debt without cover, and this margin increased with every new loan till at last it amounted to nearly 40 billions, or almost half the nominal value of all the War Loans taken together. The amount payable on bank notes in circulation rose from less than 3 billion marks in July, 1914, to about 13 billions at the end of 1916. In 1917 the effect of the "Hindenburg Program," through which the rational relation between labor and wages had been finally discarded, disclosed the failure of the financial policy of the Reich. The close of 1917 shows a circulation of 19½ billions which was to increase, by November, 1918, to more than 28 billion marks (with 48½ billion marks of floating debt resulting from Treasury bills, the Bank of Germany alone being in possession of more than 69 billions of such bills). Per capita, the notes and coin in circulation had risen from about 110 marks in 1914 to about 430 marks in 1918, that is to say, had nearly quadrupled. Virtually, inflation had set in.

CHAPTER V

FINANCIAL MOBILIZATION PLANS

Two instances of the inherent weakness in planning war merit further consideration: the so-called financial mobilization plans of 1891 and 1910 and the Hindenburg program of 1916. Criticism of the Hindenburg program need not imply any reproach to those who drafted it or had to carry it through. It had to be improvised under great stress and pressure, and its authors did not pretend to be doing more than keeping the War going and postponing a collapse which some of them saw was near even in 1916. In the case of such an emergency measure its ultimate success rather than its immediate failure would shatter belief in the Pythagorean table of economics, or in the righteousness of the commandments of the social catechism.

It is otherwise with a plan thought out in peace for the financing of a future war. A calculation of that kind should leave no unanswered questions. If it fails to lead to a clear solution, either the system of notation or the intellect of the man who uses it must be at fault.

It is the custom to speak of the measures which were taken by the Finance Department of the Government immediately after the outbreak of the War and during the early fall of 1914, as the financial mobilization of the country. Thus Professor Lotz in his contribution to the Economic and Social History of the World War,[1] or, more recently, the official publication of the German Record Office on preparations for war in the two chapters which are devoted to preparatory measures of financial or economic character.[2] By using this term historians of the War seem to indicate the deliberate character of financial war policy. It is fixed long before the event and has to move in a prescribed direction whatever may happen; it implies the renunciation of that voluntary effort on the part of the people which should accompany the moral *furor* of a popular war, that is to say, a war of defense against a blatant, unprovoked aggression.

The plans for this "financial mobilization" (*finanzielle Mobilma-*

1. *Die Deutsche Staatsfinanzwirtschaft im Kriege*, pp. 16 ff.
2. *Reichsarchiv, Kriegsrüstung und Kriegswirtschaft* (1930), I, 336 ff., 433 ff.; cf. Volume of Annexes, Nos. 68 to 101.

chung) have been discussed in connection with the question of the responsibility for the War. No wonder, for, assuredly, to plan a future war in all the details of the course it should take is exactly the thing which a German proverb calls *"den Teufel an die Wand malen,"* that is, "Paint a picture of the devil on the wall of your room and he will soon be there himself." It is much easier, however, in 1934 than during the years immediately following the War to deal with that side of the question.

We have come to distinguish preparedness from preparations in a much clearer fashion than before. Germany undoubtedly did her best to make every possible preparation for the War, which had been said to be inevitable by statesman after statesman in all of the armed countries in Europe and also by many American observers of European affairs. Undoubtedly, too, Germany lacked preparedness, which certainly is more important than the other thing.

Today we are able to recognize that, whatever the intention of those who prepare for war, the essential feature of every mobilization plan, financial, industrial, or military, is not the wish for a war which it might seem to imply, and far less an intention to demonstrate by a war that the preparations were adequate and carried the certainty of success with them—a childish delusion for the simple reason that preparations are almost always competitive. On the contrary, such mobilization plans are bureaucratic overestimation of the value of plans and systems, of organization and preparation, to the detriment of all the potentials which make for victory in a war, quickness of resolution, adaptability, power of improvisation, resourcefulness, and, more than anything else, directness of action.

The character of the plan for financial mobilization in case of a Continental war which was formed in the Nineties of the last century expresses itself appropriately in the individuals who drafted and approved it. In many respects the reign of the young Emperor had been a conscious change from, and even a brusque contradiction of, the Bismarckian principle of government. It was a change from the old order, in fact, which, to the men and women in the entourage of the Emperor, seemed fully as mid-Victorian as the England of Macaulay and Tennyson seemed to the "Edwardians." In one respect, however, the year 1890 did not mark a change. The new régime had its two camps just like the old; the policy of the military cabinet and the General Staff was quite as distinct from the official policy of the

Chancellor and his secretaries of state as it had been in Bismarck's time. The plans for financial mobilization were due to the initiative of the competent civil authorities, not to the military spirit of military men. And the man who more than anybody else is responsible for the maturing of the plan and for winning the Emperor's sympathetic interest in it, was a commoner who was not even remotely connected with anything smelling of militarism. He was not a courtier like the Eulenburgs, nor a *junker* like von Podbielski, nor a conservative bureaucrat like Dr. Delbrück or von Bethmann-Hollweg; nor a Christian Socialist like Count Posadowsky-Wehner, but a man who had made his reputation as mayor of a distinctively liberal commercial town—the Prussian Minister of Finance, Dr. Miquel.

It is difficult now to realize how modern the régime of 1890 not only looked, but really was, at the time. The Emperor found very little to change in the army, except perhaps those few changes called for by personal dislikes and predilections. He was honestly intent on continuing the traditional foreign policy which, as he saw it, had suffered from Prince Bismarck's growing fretfulness, especially in his dealings with Russia and Austria.[3] The field of the Emperor's modernist activities was domestic policy. Its general trend expressed itself in a resolute plan for government regulation in matters of social welfare and social insurance; a marked preference for the development of science and engineering through the technical schools of higher learning (*Technische Hochschulen*), combined with a hearty dislike for the humanistic learning of the *gymnasium* and the universities; a most liberal promise of support for the expansion of municipal enterprise—manifesting itself in the special royal favor shown to the Lord Mayors of rising industrial and commercial centers, even outside his own Kingdom of Prussia—and an evident conviction that the foundation of a great Empire such as Germany had become was to be found neither in law nor good administration of the old, thrifty, and perhaps a little narrow-minded type, but in industry and engineering (*Technik und Industrie*), supported by,

3. Cf. the passage in Lady Gwendolen Cecil's *Life of Robert, Marquis of Salisbury*, III, 222, about Bismarck's relations with England at the time of the Gladstone administration. In 1885, "the domineering fretfulness which had become characteristic of his old age had been exasperated to madness by the divided rule and policy which obtained in the Gladstonian cabinet."

and in its turn supporting, trade and commerce, shipping and transportation, in short, in the material achievements of an industrial age. It fitted with this policy that the young Emperor liked to choose his ministers of State from every walk of life, thus breaking the hard-and-fast rule of advancement within the ranks of the Civil Service. Prominent among the men chosen by William II to carry out his modern ideas was the above-mentioned Johannes Miquel, Mayor of Frankfurt am Main, that city which, more than any other in Germany, stood for civic pride in independence and of liberal-minded democracy, the city, too, which under the mayoralty of Miquel (and of his successor in office, Adickes) had begun to praise the value of stronger local self-government as opposed to the prevailing order—that of a state policed and administered from the top down, an *Obrigkeitsstaat*, directed by the central authority toward a a goal which, to the provincial centers of national life, might seem distant even to invisibility.

For such a man the contingency of war evidently must have meant the consideration of what a town like Frankfurt am Main and municipal administration in general would be able to contribute to its conduct, as well as what the central Government could do. His estimate of the efficiency of the central Government in a case of extreme need was probably a very moderate one; he would think that the *Obrigkeitsstaat*, which was past its prime in any case, could not be equal to such a situation, and that civil service, diplomacy, and government bodies would have to be supplemented, and perhaps in the long run superseded, by a council of men who were wont to master fortune as well as to superintend the routine work of others, captains of industry, bankers, and prominent city officials like himself, a kind of General Staff of Economics.

The younger generation in the army and the rising men in the Admiralty had for many years learned to put their hope in the General Staff. They saw in it an institution which, in the face of conservative military tradition, had "made itself," a school of modern intellectualism. It was opposed, almost to the point of open hostility, to the old privileges of aristocracy within the army, to crack regiments and historic names. It took its pride in the solid, civic ability of the individuals composing it rather than in the splendid tradition of the Prussian army as a whole. To the General Staff the War meant not a brilliant attack, with the probability of certain death for the officers galloping before their men, nor even the silent grandeur of a sacrifice common to all, but railway transport on such and such a day of the mobilization period, special safety measures for the industrial districts with the greatest productive capacity for war material, secret service, and propaganda, getting control of the whole machinery of economic and political life, and, above all, the making certain of the undisturbed execution of the Plan. They certainly had no use, in their scheme of war, for Thersites, and would have made short shrift of him had his criticism reached their ears; but they had still less use either for Achillean "moods" or for superhuman bravery, which defied the statistics and calculations of the daily average turn-out of men and material for the War.

It was Miquel who as Prussian Minister of Finance first urged the necessity of having increased financial reserves available in case of a war.[4] It was strictly within his province to do so, and not to wait for

---

4. A glance at the list of books and pamphlets dealing with financial and economic preparedness during the last decade before the War confirms the impression that the men who tried to draw attention to this problem were almost without exception members of the commercial community, financiers or economists, most of them liberals. Thus K. Helfferich, *Das Geld im russisch-japanischen Kriege* (1906); M. Warburg, *Finanzielle Kriegsbereitschaft und Börsengesetz, Verhandlungen des 3 Allgemeinen Deutschen Bankiertages zu Hamburg* (1907); J. Ludwig, *Kriegführung und Geld, Vierteljahrshefte für Truppenführung und Heereskunde*, Bd. 4 (1907), S. 293 ff.; W. Behrend, "Die Kartoffel im Kriege," *Preussische Jahrbücher*, Bd. 134 (1908), S. 319 ff.; H. Voelcker, *Die Deutsche Volkswirtschaft im Kriegsfall* (1909); Jacob Riesser, *Finanzielle Kriegsbereitschaft und Kriegführung* (1909, 2d ed. 1913); G. Schramm, *Die Verhandlungen und Beschlüsse der Londoner Seekriegskonferenz* (1911); E. Bippard, *Das staatliche Getreidelagerhaus* (1912); H. Fröhlich, "Deutsche Volksernährung im Kriege," *Schmollers Jahrbuch*, Bd. 36 (1912), Heft 2; A. Dix, *Volkswirtschaftliche Kriegsfürsorge, Vierteljahrshefte für Truppenführung und Heereskunde*, Bd. 10 (1913), S. 441 ff.; C. Ballod, "Deutsche Volksernährung im Kriege," *Preussische Jahrbücher*, Bd. 157 (1914), S. 101 ff. The book published by Mr. Riesser, a well-known protagonist of free trade and a liberal of Jewish descent, created a stir in public opinion throughout the world. An article by the French Senator Charles Humbert, entitled "Le nerf de la guerre—comment l'Allemagne prépare la mobilization financière en même temps que l'autre," in *Le Journal* of December 2, 1909, moved the Emperor to have a special report on Riesser's book made by the Secretary of State for Finance. (Cf. *Kriegsrüstung und Kriegswirtschaft*, Volume of Annexes, No. 99, p. 343.)

a move on the part of the Ministry of Finance of the Reich. For the offices of all Imperial Secretaries of State, with the exception of the Chancellor's office, were, to quote Bismarck's well-known dictum in his Memoirs, mainly destined to assist the Chancellor in his negotiations and arrangements with the Prussian departments of State. They provided him with the necessary staff of experts on technical questions which might come up, and formed a purely ministerial bureaucracy practically without executive power. The Prussian Department of Finance was the more competent to deal with the question of financial mobilization, as it had to work in close departmental touch with the Prussian Ministry of War, which, of course, was so all-important that the Reich had no War Department at all. Still it remains a significant fact that, of all the Prussian Ministers of Finance since 1871, it was the one who came from the ranks of municipal government and was entirely innocent of militarism who took the matter up. It is due to him that from 1891 the Ministry of War made an annual computation of the amount of ready money which it estimated would be needed for mobilization and for the maintenance of the army, instead of having such a calculation made only at greater intervals of time, and that the amount was estimated for each of the thirty days of the mobilization period, while heretofore it had been given in a round sum. Even this action of the Minister of Finance led to nothing more than an attempt to ascertain how much cash would be needed at the moment of a declaration of war to bridge the period from mobilization to the first decisive battle. After that—it was only a successful battle which could be taken into consideration—German and foreign capital must regain such confidence in ultimate German success that it would place itself at the disposal of the German Treasury at a reasonable rate of interest.

The first move by which Dr. Miquel had initiated the new scheme for financial mobilization in 1891 was not to be the last. In the first place, it was followed almost automatically by the creation of separate departments of financial mobilization in the Treasury Office of the Reich, in the Prussian Ministry of Finance and in the Secretariat of the Bank of Germany. As Prussian Minister Miquel opposed, first of all, the proposal which had been favored by the directors of the Bank and which tended simply to replace gold coins, as they went out of circulation, by bank notes of small nominal value. He used, in this conflict of opinion as to whether the more radical measures or this mild and transient one should be adopted, the right of veto by which the Minister of Finance is allowed to suspend a decision of the Prussian Cabinet; and thereby he prevented an arrangement between Prussia and the two Federal institutions, the Treasury and the Bank. During the Nineties of the last century Miquel is said to have had important conferences with the Chief of the General Staff, Count Schlieffen, who at that time began to remodel the defense plans of the older Moltke and to base German mobilization, in case of a war against Russia, on an offensive movement through Belgian territory, while Moltke, in conformity with his estimate of the importance of Metz and Strassburg as the centers of a glacis for defense, had insisted that an eastern war should admit of a decision in the east. It is certainly more than a coincidence in dates that at the time when the Schlieffen Plan had been fixed, and a German offensive through neutral territory to the rear of the French line of fortifications had been decided on by the military authorities, Miquel, now an old man about to resign his office, sent a special memorandum to the Emperor (November 11, 1898) which contained a kind of last will. In this paper he insisted on the paramount importance of the *Zwangskurs* for paper money from the very beginning of the war, a measure which he says, "no theories of economists or considerations of trade should prevent us from taking." During its further course, he says, the war would have to be financed by loans.[5]

Opinion in military circles still tends to the belief that Count Schlieffen would have been able to obtain at least a temporary success for his plan if war had come in his time. Miquel might likewise have been able to win the support of international finance for his plan. If we had to agree with that opinion it would lead us to the conclusion that a new chief of the General Staff or a new Minister of Finance should never be allowed to rely on the plan his predecessor in office had adopted. The least we can ask of those who have to take upon themselves the responsibility for carrying out such a plan is to have thought the plan out for themselves and to be able, therefore, during the course of the actual event, to reënact in their minds the motives which led them to form it. Then, and then only, would they be able, with complete authority, to change it at a time

5. *Kriegsrüstung und Kriegswirtschaft,* Volume of Annexes, No. 90, p. 300.

when failure in detail could still be redressed by abandoning the weaker parts of the plan for other and sounder ones.

But apart from such conjectures, we can only recognize the fact that both plans, having evolved from the minds of the two men who were admittedly the most brilliant holders of their offices between 1890 and 1914, miscarried at the hands of those who tried faithfully to execute them in 1914.

When the World War had given the lie to all those who had theorized about the impossibility of a protracted war under modern technical conditions, many people were inclined to be wise after the event and to blame the economists who, they said, had misled the Government in its preparations for the War by eliminating all consideration of a longer war from their theories. It is to be doubted whether the Government paid much attention to academic discussions on such a theme. But apart from that it is hardly to the point to blame the theorists for their failure in foresight. Those who had to take the decision would not have listened to them in any case. Judging from the attitude of the councils which were held in 1891, and from many similar ministerial deliberations during the following years, the problem of the war's probable duration was kept strictly out of sight. The only question that mattered was how quickly the first important military event would follow mobilization, or, eventually, whether a resounding success of some kind could be obtained by a surprise attack executed almost simultaneously with the declaration of war by troops which were not on a war footing. It is a common experience with capitalists, who in their dealings at the Stock Exchange have to work on the most deceptive news, that it is not the skepticism or the diffidence of the "burnt child who dreads the fire," but the unshakable optimism of the gambler that must be first in their calculations. An inquirer into the origin of wars should not forget to learn to what extent speculation on what speculators will do during the first stages of war can influence, not only the way in which the first war news is made up, but the actual mobilization plans and the first attempts to engage the enemy; and one should also learn to what extent the plans of a General Staff are bound up with the belief that military successes in the first weeks of a war are all-important on account of their reaction on the foreign exchanges, much more important than a carefully thought-out plan for the longest possible resistance in case of an early mishap.

Another minister of finance, a self-made man like Miquel, playing his own hand in a cabinet of courtiers, gentry, and Tory bureaucrats, Secretary of State Wermuth, in 1910 laid before the Emperor a report on financial measures to be taken by the Government in case of war. He reminded the Emperor of the fact that, according to the estimates for 1909, the first day of mobilization alone meant an expenditure of about 120 million marks. That was more than the amount in the War Fund of the Reich. The Ministry of Finance, in order to meet financial demands in the case of a war, proposed a series of extraordinary measures which were mainly destined to increase the gold reserves of the Reichsbank and to protect its gold supply. The legal obligation of the bank to pay out gold for bank notes presented at its counters was to cease at the moment of the outbreak of the war. Treasury notes were to be increased by 100 per cent; treasury bills were to be used as bankable paper money securities; and special credit offices with the privilege of issuing notes equivalent to paper money were to relieve the Reichsbank of part of its task as a credit-giving institution. All this, however, was only a more or less mechanical device to get over the monetary difficulties during mobilization time. After that, as the report points out, the money to finance the war would have to be found mainly through loans.

The memorandum is, like so many official documents of that period, drawn up *ad usum Delphini*—"to conciliate the Dauphin," as the French used to say in the days of Louis XIII. For the Emperor had not ceased to be a Dauphin in this sense, that his entourage and most of his ministers were trying to make things look smooth to one who was often petulant, and whose sharp and rather gloomy wit liked to dwell on the weaknesses and flaws in other nations' and other men's politics. They often thought more of how to handle him by giving their reports a turn pleasing to his well-known views and prejudices than of basing them on the merits of the matter itself. The latter reproach cannot in justice be leveled against Secretary of State Wermuth. He was very much in earnest about the subject matter behind his report. He was one of the few men at the head of affairs in this period who put their conscientious opinion above pride of place and above the self-flattering conceit of their own indispensability, for the success of their good cause, one of the few who were ready to resign rather than give in. His opinion upon sound finance in a modern industrial state was that death duties must form a considerable part of the budget on the income side, and that the objection of conservative capitalism against this form of taxation—that it tended to destroy capital at its base, and what was worse, took away the strongest incentive for the formation of new and the steady increase of old capital—was entirely at fault; for death duties, by keeping capital in circulation among the people through the medium of a strong Exchequer and correspondingly easy money rates, encouraged each new generation to build up a new fortune of its own. The landed interests and the greater part of organized middle-class opinion were against the proposal, and so were the governments of the States, to whom that kind of reinforcement of the Federal Exchequer would have been a real danger signal for their sovereignty within the Reich. The man who braved opposition of such differing and almost equally terrifying character certainly did not lack courage. But even he could not look lightly upon the possibility of having to gain the Emperor's attention and sympathy for his plan by playing up to his fancy and making sound finances and an honest budget—things which, as he saw them, in themselves meant everything—look as if they were only a part of the "shining armor."

The situation in 1910 was not unlike that in 1931 and 1932. The Minister of Finance was hard pressed; in 1910 he had to meet unexpected and perhaps unforeseeable demands on the Exchequer, chiefly for armaments, while in the recent crisis he had to meet them in the main for social insurance payments and emergency loans to the eastern frontier provinces. But he met them under conditions which either forbade a further rise in taxation of any kind, or at least lent to the opposition to such taxation, on the part of those who would have to bear the brunt of it, an almost furious strength of resistance. Everybody agreed on the absolute necessity of balancing public income and public expenses, if not by increasing the income, then by curtailing expenses. And the difference between the arguments of 1932 and those of twenty years earlier consists mainly in the respective threats used on these two occasions. In 1910 the bogey was not yet bankruptcy; it was a continental or world war and its danger to a country which could not rely on an almost unlimited credit, based, in its turn, on reserves of marketable securities running into many billions of marks. Even so, as the reports of the Secretary of State and of the Prussian Minister of Finance both point out in almost the same words, the Government must in the end be obliged to resort to war loans in order to raise the necessary funds, and through war loans—about the precarious character of which the memorandum contains a memorable sentence—arrive at depreciation of currency and perhaps government insolvency.

However that may be, an argument based on the danger of possible inflation would not have served in 1910, while the argument of readiness for war would probably have had its effect upon the Emperor, won him over to the side of the death-duties program, and, by stabilizing the budget, might perhaps even have lessened the danger of war. We have thus to make ample allowance for the legitimate desire of a Minister of Finance—who at that time was Minister of Economics and Labor, too—to find a conclusive argument in favor of his plan. But even if we divest the contents of the memorandum of everything which was meant to influence its Imperial reader, we are left with the impression of an entirely inadequate financial provision for the contingency of war on the part of the responsible Department of State.

Two main arguments appear when we consider the inadequacy of plans for financial mobilization. The first proceeds from the fact that the plans were elaborated with all due care by the most competent officials of an administration which had the merited reputation of being one of the most conscientious and at the same time one of the most efficient in the world. In spite of that, it is not only the general idea of the plan which is entirely at fault—a thing which may occur in the work of the best of administrations if its task is set by some extraneous power of command—but the means which it designates are similarly at fault, partly through weakness and partly through a dangerous overreaching of the economic strength of the nation which they call for. It is as if the immoral character which a government has to take on during a war had imprinted itself upon these preparations. The plan, as the memorandum of 1910 explains it, does not shirk the most drastic measures; indeed, from the start it takes the line of silencing the law while war is in progress—meaning in this case, not the mere laws of contemptible scribes, advocates, and professors of jurisprudence, but the laws of capital and interest, and even the code of international loans and credit. All these measures, however, are clothed in the most innocuous sheepskin of bank acts, money-printing orders, and normal exchange practice. The gold coverage is practically done away with; but the utmost stress is repeatedly laid on the necessity of S. 17 of the Bank Act, the legal statute of the gold-basis system, remaining in force. The relation between gold reserves and circulating bank notes is mentioned as if it remained intact at 1 to 3; the Bank, it is expressly stated, would not lend or advance money to the Government except for full collateral. But the plan itself contains a whole series of measures calculated to create this collateral, which the Government is obliged to hand over to the Bank, a mere fiction. The War Fund of the Empire, on which the traditionalist conception of a war between Germany and France rested, is mentioned twice—besides being spoken of by the Emperor as ridiculously inadequate—but in a self-contradictory way. First the fund is to be carried in specie from the Julius Tower in the Spandau fortress to the vaults of the Reichsbank and is there to contribute to the gold reserves of the Bank and so to enable it to print more bank notes. But when the fund is mentioned for the second time it is in connection with the necessity of the Chancellor of the Exchequer's finding "available capital assets," *greifbare Aktivkapitalien*, capital on which he can lay his hands at once, the memorandum regretting to state that such capital is not at hand, and that, failing other tangible assets, the Government would see itself obliged to resort to the War Fund. To dot the *i*, the memorandum speaks of the sum, 120 million marks, as being available. And that, following this train of thought, can mean only one thing, that it is the 120 millions which would have to be seized and spent in the same way as the 200 millions of Treasury Bills, the 300 million marks of overdue customs and taxation payments, and, finally, the subscriptions to war loans which are mentioned as further means for providing the Government with money.

The most remarkable feature of the memorandum, however, is that though it bears the signature of the Secretary of State who tried to restore the finances of the Reich by the introduction of death duties, it does not even mention the possibility of paying the costs of the war (after mobilization had been carried out and been paid for from a special fund) out of the proceeds of special war taxation. Loans are expressly stated to be the only possible method for finding the money to finance the war. The question whether domestic or foreign loans are to be preferred for that end, is not asked. To answer that question it would, of course, be necessary to know against whom the war is to be fought, whether it will be fought out of dire necessity, in evident self-defense, with no freedom of choice, or as a means of maintaining or even enhancing the influence of the nation in the councils of the world, or to get rid of a rival, or, to use the phraseology of nationalists, as an iron tonic for a people suffering from weakness and debility due to a prolonged period of peace. War can be of this kind or that, but without knowing whether it belongs to one or another category the war cannot be financed even on paper.

Nor is there even the slightest mention of requisition and confiscation as a more direct and honest way of carrying through mobilization, though it had been the practice for many decades to minimize the cost of maneuvers by quartering troops on towns and villages, riding roughshod over fields and meadows, and offering the property owners only a meager compensation, or rather a kind of fee for usage if they were not military-minded enough to be satisfied with the service their property had rendered to the national defense. Costs of mobilization could be almost entirely dispensed with if the "act of God" which war represents, in so far as every belligerent government declines the responsibility for having committed this act of its own free will, entitled the Government to use the entire estate and property of the country for mobilization purposes. Railways and other transport facilities, postal service, including telegraph and telephone, every kind of supply for men and animals on military duty, aeroplanes and cars, broadcasting stations, timber, mechanics' tools, fire engines, and so on could be taken over without any payment whatever. Or, perhaps they would be paid for after the conclusion of the war upon the production of certificates of requisition by those who at such a time might still care to be recompensed for their special contribution toward the defense of their own country.

Such a right of the Crown—well known to English law—has two peculiar features in common with special war taxation, as opposed to paid-for mobilization and war loans. The first of these features is that both requisition and taxation reduce to a minimum the profits of the middleman, the profits of the contractor made from mobilization, and the profits of the financial agent and the banks made from loans. The second peculiarity is that the individual who works for, or otherwise contributes to, mobilization without being paid for that service, and, though in a minor degree, the taxpayer who contributes to a special war levy knows, or at least may imagine with good reason, where his services, his contributions, his sacrifices, and his payments go. In the other case, the case of paid-for mobilization and war loans, he is confronted with bureaucracy, which tells him that on patriotic grounds and as a good citizen he ought not even to try to understand what it is about, and would probably spoil the mechanism if he sought to do anything by himself above and beyond what he is commanded to do and is paid for, which is to sign a number of papers, state his age, family connections and religion, and be present in various bureaus at certain fixed hours. He further observes, perhaps dimly during the first weeks but with increasing clearness afterward, "the go-between trade." If he has any reason to be discontented with anything even remotely connected with the war and complains about it, he is sure to find a representative of Nationalist or Communist propaganda behind the counter of the tobacco shop, or at the barber's, or in his favorite drinking place, ready to tell him that it is Big Business, Wall Street, and all those damned Jews whom he and the country have to thank for the mess they are in. And this he promptly believes; for, in fact, he is entirely unable to understand, and has been kept purposely in the dark about the financial activities called for by either a domestic or an international loan.[6]

Plain common sense is enough to tell us, first, that half the success of a contest of any kind lies in letting as many people as possible feel that they have or will have helped to win it, and, second, that if the battle is lost it will save not only the government but the various elements of the nation much venomous and mutual recrimination as to the reasons for defeat if, during the struggle, they have all, as much as possible, been taken into the confidence of the government

---

6. A further illustration of the difficulty of following the transactions of war finance and of the no doubt unintentional ambiguity of official explanations may be found in the memorandum of the Directors of the Reichsbank of July 12, 1904, signed Koch and Glasenapp (*Kriegsrüstung und Kriegswirtschaft,* Volume of Annexes, No. 96, p. 334). In this memorandum the Directors agreed to the plan for an official forced quotation for paper money, to be declared on mobilization. The legal gold reserves were to be transformed into paper money so that this paper money could be trebled by the issue of other bank notes. International finance could hardly be deceived by such a device. But the deception could be practiced on the German people, who were induced to put their confidence in the continued validity of the Bank Act, because, to use the words of the memorandum, the letter of the law had been kept though the intent of the law had been frustrated.

and allowed to know, as far as possible, what was going on—plans and changes of plans, improvisations, and everything else.

An obvious impossibility? Certainly not in the case of a country which has been suddenly attacked and which has to improvise means of defense and counterattack, nor in the case of a power that intervenes in a war between two others. The impossibility is merely in carrying out abstract plans made for the contingency of a war that will fit in with these plans instead of following its own laws.

Inadequacy of planning becomes even more evident if we follow another line of argument. The memorandum of 1910 follows the example of the mobilization plan of the General Staff by envisaging not a concrete case of war between Germany and a specified enemy power (or as many concrete cases of war as there were potential enemies of the German Empire) but war as an abstract proposition, a war which of course would be waged by Germany, but without anything to indicate against what other country or countries, for what reason, whether in the enemy's country or with the danger of enemy invasion of German territory, whether on land or on sea, with or without support from the resources of the colonies, or whether alone or with allies. The only sentence of the memorandum which shows a consideration of the psychic or moral situation in which Germany would probably meet the outbreak of war, is, characteristically enough, entirely negative in its content. It says—with remarkable candor—that patriotism, even in the shape of a *furor teutonicus* at the outbreak of war, is in itself no sufficient guaranty of the success of a domestic war loan; the main thing to an investor is security of investment, vouchsafed, in the case of a war loan, by the credit that would be made secure by sound financial measures on the part of the government of the belligerent country.

The argument would lead to very dangerous conclusions if it were followed, for quite evidently it disposes of the difference between the potential attitude of a foreign and a domestic investor. The latter will hardly insist on the financial soundness of his own government's policy before the war and in the first stage of the war; he will rather agree with Emperor William the First's marginal note on one of the newspaper articles which, in 1875, had held over Europe the prospect of imminent war:

To be successful in war the army which takes the offensive must have the sympathy of all noble-minded people and countries on its side, and public opinion must cast its vote against him who unjustly provokes war. . . . Whoever goes to battle without justification will find public opinion arraigned against him; he will not be able to find allies to join him, nor will he find *neutres bienveillants* or any neutrals at all. He will be the enemy of the world.[7]

The World War showed us the soundness of the old Emperor's observation. Except perhaps in Austria-Hungary, popular opinion was at once in fever heat about the question of the just cause of the War, without troubling in the least, even in neutral capitalist centers, about the financial consequences of the possible outcome of it. This will remain the chief point in any critical argument on war plans, that they deal with war in the abstract, while an actual case of war either makes all planning look ridiculously inadequate and desultory in comparison with the effects of the psychic storm which drives the whole nation along at a pace no mechanical contrivances could ever develop, or demonstrates by the utter failure of its plans made beforehand that a planned war, happily, is a thing impossible even from the military point of view, but much more so in the field of finance and economics.

7. *Die Grosse Politik der Europäischen Kabinette 1871–1914*, I, 282 (No. 181). *Die Auswärtige Politik des Deutschen Reiches 1871–1914*, I, 19.

CHAPTER VI

THE HINDENBURG PROGRAM AND THE DEVALUATION OF MONEY

THE case of the so-called Hindenburg program—that is, of a group of governmental measures designed to raise the output of war materials by the forced labor of the adult population in 1917—differs widely from that of the memoranda on financial mobilization to which we directed our attention in the foregoing chapters. It grew up from the hotbed of emergency, in the critical period of "a war of lost opportunities," while the financial plans of 1891 and 1910 were seeds sown years before they could possibly reach the light and ripen. At the time when Dr. Miquel's plan was drafted the contingency of a world war was not seriously contemplated, and if the Emperor sometimes indulged in prophecies about a future Armageddon it was certainly not a war of continental origin, with Russia, Great Britain, and Italy aligned against Germany that he had in mind. Even in 1910, when the Triple Alliance had ceased to be a reality and the "Entente Cordiale" was, not merely in Germany but in many quarters, held to be tantamount to an alliance, the authors of the new German plan for financial mobilization did not—and perhaps could not—contemplate a war against one or more enemy powers by whom their country would be attacked or whom it would for its part attack. William II certainly had not given up the hope of uniting continental Europe under his leadership, and the diplomatic documents published since the War give abundant evidence of both Prince Bülow's and Von Bethmann-Hollweg's power to resist, in the main successfully, the would-be influence of a group of soldier-politicians whom they suspected of too marked a disposition for war. A combination of peaceful intentions and preparations for a defensive war as a rule makes futility of planning more apparent than does a deliberate project for the carrying through of a war which has been engineered in bad faith. One might say, thus far, that excuses or at least explanations of failure are not lacking in the case of the German financial plans.

One cannot say the same of the "National Service Law," which embodied the Hindenburg program. Peace with Russia and war against the United States were new and uncertain factors at the time this plan was conceived, but otherwise allies, enemies, and neutrals were well defined. The lessons of two years of the changing fortunes of war had taught the Government that facts had to be faced. By then, to plan measures in the abstract must surely have seemed the height of folly.

But in spite of all the reasons that made for a sober and realistic policy, the plan of 1917 proved as unreal as the designs and calculations of twenty years before had proved to be. The War had taught the value of propaganda if nothing else, but a law that professedly applied to every man and woman in the land, a law with the intrinsic force of direct appeal to the nation as such, was as little understood and remained, for the average man, as unintelligible in its real purpose and effects as had been the secret memoranda of Cabinet Ministers in pre-war times.

Even the name under which the plan of 1916 became known was calculated to mislead the man in the street as to its origin and aims. The plan for the adoption of a measure of forced labor (*Arbeitspflicht*) for the adult population, in order to comply with the demand of the military authorities for more soldiers and at the same time more supplies of war material, bore the name of Field Marshal von Hindenburg simply because his name was the only name left to conjure with in Germany. The plan had many different roots, some of them of militarist, some of socialist nature, while others grew from the individual manias for efficiency of war officials, theorizing industrialists, and inventive engineers. The chief responsibility for the law which formally created the facilities to carry such a plan through, the *Gesetz über den vaterländischen Hilfsdienst*, or National Service Law of December 5, 1916, lay with the Secretary of State and Vice-Chancellor Dr. Helfferich, the pioneer of German world policy (*Weltwirtschaftspolitik*) in the days before the War when Greater Germany meant the Bagdad Line and the Mannesmann Concessions in Morocco. Dr. Helfferich was the trusted supporter of the interests of German finance, industry and shipping in a cabinet of mere lawyers, bureaucrats, and military men. He was also the powerful organizer and leader of that "national opposition" to the German Republic and the Weimar coalition dominating its councils, which, upon his death in a railway accident (shortly after the murder of Walther Rathenau) became the field of Dr. Hugenberg's energies. In addition to Dr. Helfferich, the Prussian Minister for War, General von Stein, the first director of the War Office (*Kriegsamt*), and General Gröner, a specialist in technical warfare, and Colonel Koeth may be mentioned among those who conceived the Hindenburg program or took a hand in carrying it out.

The origins of the plan are manifold. Three of them must be mentioned because they are certainly in a kind of way the necessary motive power of any such undertaking as the 1916–1917 plan, or, for that matter, the similar plan proposed during the economic crisis of 1931. The crisis itself is of course the most important among them, both as a material crisis (whether, as in the War, a shortage of supplies, of munitions, and of most of the necessaries of life, or, as in peace, a shortage of credit, of money, of buying power) and as a moral crisis. The great new plan which was to save the situation had as its predecessors, many smaller, less pretentious schemes and efforts, the failure of which was most likely connected, in popular opinion, with the incompetence of the men who up to that time had been in charge of affairs. Even in a country where any warning doubt as to possible failure or shortcomings was termed a crime against national honor, and where the military censor was omnipresent, it had become evident by the fall of 1916 that the Supreme Command demanded more supplies of men and materials than the country could produce and still maintain its past standard of economic life and the prevailing conditions of labor. Raw materials had been *bewirtschaftet*—put under public control—it is true, since Walther Rathenau made his first successful onslaught on military bureaucracy in 1914. For well over a year everything which could possibly be done in the way of taking stock of existing supplies and creating reserves of supplies had been done by an organized effort of war offices and bureaus in regard to necessary raw materials. A list of these drawn up during the first months after the beginning of trench warfare included all the materials which might become scarce in Germany and the allied countries if the War were to continue for a year and a half or two years longer. Two kinds of raw materials which were not included in that list, and, in fact, had been treated as inexhaustible—coal and iron—had begun to lag behind demand and expectations. When the Supreme Command, driven by General Quartermaster Ludendorff, told the authorities in Berlin that all factories, offices, and even agriculture and the victualing trade must be combed out for men able to do military service behind the lines in the place of *Landsturm* men who would be sent to the trenches; that, further, the supply of munitions not only must be kept up at the present rate but would have to be considerably greater than heretofore; and, finally, that it was impossible to say how long, even when all this was done, the War would last, the central authorities began to realize that coal would give out, and that with a shortage of coal, iron, even though available as raw material, could not be put to use and transported. The War Office was, by that time, in full control of everything which could be controlled by official administration. It had the statistics, and its chief was exactly the man to gauge the difficulties of transport which, in addition to the difficulty of a sudden increase in production, would arise if the demands of G.H.Q. were to be satisfied. Coal and iron were both found to be *Kriegsrohstoffe* —war supplies. The allotment of exempt workers to all factories and mills, and the distribution of the product of the coal industry were entrusted first to a mixed commission of military and civil authorities and representatives of the industry itself, the Coal Adjustment Board (*Kohlenausgleich*), and later on to a Coal Commissioner (*Reichskohlenkommissar*), while iron fell under the control of a Steel Adjustment Bureau (*Rohstahlausgleichsstelle*). The case of coal was extremely difficult to handle because the commissariat had to apportion the quantities needed for industrial purposes, for transport, and for household consumption, after war needs were satisfied. War needs took precedence, household consumption being put last— with the proviso that discontent in the industrial areas had as far as possible to be avoided or mitigated by special favors. Transport consumption was comparatively easy to divide between military service in the wider sense of the word, and civilian needs which could be curtailed or even set aside. The real crux of the matter was with industry itself. Even the War Office was, in many cases, unable to control the use made of labor and coal supplies by factories or industrial combines, especially where an establishment or chain of establishments had, since the outbreak of the War, been partly transformed into a munition or other war-supply factory while it still continued its old business, perhaps doing so by using the by-products of one industry as material for the other. The need of primary materials like coal or metals was so urgent that the owners had to use warlike methods in order to keep their works going and were willing to make even out-of-the-way arrangements if only they could hope again to be put on the list of war industries (*Kriegswichtige Betriebe*).

We have the confessions of some of the men who were in charge of the War Office and its affiliated industrial departments in 1917 and 1918, acknowledging that distribution became more difficult from day to day, and that a long-term arrangement on a fixed ratio for every kind of consumer's group became quite impossible. Plans for distribution, Dr. Koeth tells us, had to be changed from month to month, for there was always a deficiency in the coal supply owing to shortage of labor, transport difficulties, climatic conditions, sudden alterations in orders from the Western or Eastern Front, or other reasons. The only way to deal fairly with all the different demands was to drop the attempt to apply any hard-and-fast rule; today they had to favor one kind of industry to the disadvantage of households generally, tomorrow they would have to prefer the household demand of a certain region to that of the industries of another province. And we know from the memoirs of military leaders how keen some of them were and what astonishing means they used to get a larger share of deliveries for their own sector than a neighboring commander could obtain; and how even the conduct of military operations by G.H.Q. sometimes suffered from rivalry between the Eastern and Western commands. None of these people really could be said to serve only their own personal and private interests, for with very few exceptions they believed their own share in the conduct of the War and the maintenance of economic life—also in support of the War—to be at least as important as that of their competitors. The universal sense of the general need, from which nobody could have detached himself even if callous enough to wish to make private profit from the common suffering, a feeling which by that time had taken a firm hold on the people at home, worked itself out in a curious loosening of private and business morality in all dealings with the central authorities. If they were guided more by a consideration of interests than by an impartial law in making their orders of distribution, as evidently they had to be, it seemed permissible for everybody to put his own judgment as to his needs, and the indispensability of certain raw materials or labor facilities to satisfy them, above the decision taken in a Berlin office where they could have no real knowledge of conditions in the provinces, and to state those needs in a manner to make them seem imperative as compared with others.

It is hardly possible that with such a state of things there should not be rumors and imaginary beliefs that undue preferences were given to one industry or industrial combine rather than another. The Hindenburg program, in popular opinion, saw the beginning of the preponderance of the Ruhr-Westphalian steel and coal industry in German public life which, in fact, had manifested itself long before the War, even in foreign policy, and which certainly had no stronger influence on the Government in 1917 and 1918 than in the first two years of the War.

A second, contributory reason for the 1916 plan was purely military in character. Rightly or wrongly, the Prussian Ministry of War in which war officialdom was centralized—Bavaria and Württemberg with their separate War Ministries remaining comparatively independent in matters of military and political importance, but without the possibility of independent action in questions touching industry and finance—had come to believe that disaffection was spreading, not only in the form of criticism, which, after the futile attempt to storm Verdun, had broken the bonds of censorship, but also in a more concrete form, thanks to propaganda which a few months later would have been called Bolshevist, though at that time it seemed to emanate from political socialism. It may have been a complaint on the part of trade-unionists, who were necessarily in close touch with the war bureaus, which confirmed the generals in their natural impatience with members of the masses who seemed ready to disobey orders, and thereby sowed the first seeds of the "dagger thrust" legend. For trade-unions began to suffer, during the late summer of 1916, from the opposition of the radical wing of the Socialist party, and some of their leaders who knew how hard they had worked and how much they had won in the way of material alleviations for the working class by coöperating with the military authorities were naturally inclined to become very angry at the charge of having forgotten their socialist creed and paid homage to Caesar. They had undoubtedly done more to prepare the way for the kind of nationalization which in Germany is called *"Sozialisierung"* and even for socialism itself than the individualists who opposed the obstinacy of their consciences to the general submission to war as a

HINDENBURG PROGRAM AND DEVALUATION 81

fact. Be that as it may, the War Ministry felt itself responsible to G.H.Q., especially to the political bureau at G.H.Q., which became more and more important as General Ludendorff's influence increased, for the general disposition or frame of mind of the country. They had been blamed at times when the military leaders paid short visits to the capital for letting the people get out of hand; and they welcomed a scheme which, outwardly—though less so, in actual fact—made labor a semimilitary organization. Outwardly it did so, in so far as the committees which were to decide on whether one had already done work in connection with the War and therefore could not be required to enlist under the new scheme were to be presided over by an officer of the *Generalkommando*, that is to say, the executive authority upon which civil administration of the smaller states and the Prussian provinces had devolved with the outbreak of the War. The two official assessors on the committees were to be nominated by the War Office. And labor had actually become half military in so far as industry and organized labor could, under the new plan, be made even more pliant than before to the wishes of the Supreme Command and the War Ministry.

It would be a grave error, however, to attribute the idea or the working out of the plan chiefly to the War Ministry or to "militarism." The plan corresponded to the wishes of some at least of the officials of the Ministry, but it could never have originated with them or materialized through them. Bureaucracy in the War Ministry has always been of the heaviest type, very difficult to move and filled with a stolid pride in good old methods and *règlements*. The propelling power of the new plan lay in the leading industrialists, with the Vice-Chancellor as their spokesman in the Cabinet, on the one hand, and trade-unions on the other. Trade-union leaders had been confidentially informed of the proposed "national service" (*Vaterländischer Hilfsdienst*). They had insisted, from the first, on the democratic character the measure must necessarily have in order to win the assent of the Social Democrats as a political party; they had found a sympathetic hearer in the Chief of the new War Office, General Gröner, when the main lines of the measure were discussed in November, 1916; and they had agreed formally to coöperate by delegating one of their foremost members, the leader of the Union of Metal Workers, Alexander Schlicke, to become an official member of the War Office, so that the new scheme might function to the satisfaction of all. It seemed to be a significant fact that both men, Gröner and Schlicke, came from Württemberg, the German home of national democracy or democratic patriotism, whichever one likes to call it. In Parliament things did not go nearly so well as when the trade-union leaders had conferred with the authorities at the Ministry of War. Dr. Helfferich, competent as he was in a meeting of shareholders or directors, never knew or cared for the good will of Parliament, least of all of a minority in Parliament, and waged an unnecessary battle over a few clauses of the new law in the Reichstag. On the other hand, the undersecretaries and other departmental officials in charge of the bill had to make a series of concessions which, from the point of view of military centralization, should have been fought to the last. The staffs of the social insurance bureaus (*Krankenkassen*) and similar institutions, the personnel of labor secretariats, the employees of banks and insurance companies and, last but not least, newspaper workers, were under the new law to be exempt from the duty of doing war work. Women were excluded—they would not have fitted in with the trade-unionist character of the plan. Workmen's councils were established in all the bigger industrial establishments, except State railways. Dr. Helfferich won a Pyrrhic victory in that respect by a vote of 139 against 138 in the Reichstag, a memorable occasion as showing the real strength of the movement toward State socialism as early as 1916. Compulsory arbitration for labor conflicts (*Schlichtungsstellen*) was, against violent resistance from the Conservatives, extended to agricultural employment.

The Reichstag adopted the law by 235 votes against 19 on December 2, 1916. The general committee of the trade-unions, on December 8, issued a manifesto, addressed to all workmen and employees that were members of trade-unions. The manifesto called on them to support the National Service Law wholeheartedly. Members of trade-unions, it said, would not need to be compelled to work. They were accustomed to it. They did it as a matter of duty. None of them would wish to stand aside when the territorial army of workers for national defense was formed. Moreover, workmen and employees would be able to take an ample part in the formation of that army and even to control to a certain extent the working of the new system through local works committees (*Betriebsausschüsse*) and district conciliation boards (*Schlichtungsausschüsse*). Trade-unions should direct special attention to the election for these committees and boards. If this was done and coöperation was freely given, organized labor would have its full share in the rebirth of Germany which would take place after the War.

A few days later the various trade-union groups held a conference at Berlin in which they confirmed their readiness to take a full share in making a success of the National Service Law. They published a resolution, unanimously adopted by their 500 delegates, which said:

> The representatives of some four million organized workmen and employees assembled in Germania Hall on December 12 declare their readiness to coöperate with all their forces in carrying out the National Service Law.
>
> The classes represented in the organization of workmen and employees are willing to put their whole strength, as a complete unit, at the service of the country, in order that the plans of our adversaries for the destruction of Germany may fail.
>
> The assembled representatives expect that the Imperial Government and the War Office will give far-reaching encouragement to the legitimate demands of workmen and employees in the matter of better conditions of labor, higher wages, and guaranties for the maintenance of free association (*Koalitionsrecht*). We also demand stronger measures against profiteering in food and other necessities of life and a fairer distribution of existing supplies, so that the working population can fulfil the demands made upon them.

Radical Socialists and Communists have condemned in no uncertain terms the action of the trade-unions in their eagerness to coöperate with the military authorities of the War Office, especially with General Gröner and his successor in office, General Schenck. They have declared the manifesto mere eyewash; according to them, the trade-union leaders and the whole staff of the trade-unions simply wished to be on good terms with the District and General *Kommandos* in order to escape active service at the front for themselves or their friends and clients. That is again one of the phenomena of war-time, that rumor can ripen in a few moments, whereas in normal times years are needed to enable it to pass for the truth. The blame which anti-militarists tried to fasten upon the promoters of National Service is not quite fair.[1] National Service could be and was honestly believed

---

[1] It served them well in fomenting industrial disorder during the winter of 1917–1918, after the Treaty of Brest-Litovsk, and the incomprehensible

by the trade-union leaders to be a preparation for the new order of things which would come, almost by itself, at the end of the War, whether the event was to be a German or Allied victory, or a peace of conciliation. With the end of the War the committees and boards established according to the National Service Law would have come to stay, while the military members would automatically disappear. They knew, in addition, that as long as the War lasted they could almost certainly count on being hand in glove with the War Office itself, the staff of which was anything but militarist in the cartoonist's sense of the term. They were a hard-working lot of men, whose politics were best described under the term National Democracy, fighting for practical results and not for the glory and excitement of fighting. They had a strong admixture of red-tapism, a thing by no means unknown to trade-unionism; and, all alike, they were addicted to the fetish of organized efficiency in administration, with a remedy at hand for all things demanding one, and an appeal against every decision, within certain limits; in fact, a rule of conduct for every conceivable situation and the proper etiquette for every step to be taken. Coöperation was, on both sides, honest. It is again only fair to both sides to say that during the two years from the promulgation of the National Service Law to the end of the War and the formal abrogation of the law by the Revolutionary Council of the People's Commissaries, in almost every case the representations of the Central Committee of trade-unions in the case of regulations for carrying out the law or the execution of its provisions found favor with the authorities. And the attempt of the more conservative employers' associations, especially the United Iron and Steel Industries (*Verein Deutscher Eisen- und Stahl-industriellen*) to modify the law in the sense of making it more difficult for a workman to leave his place for National Service work with a higher salary, were steadfastly resisted by the Government, on the recommendation of the War Office.

The Economic and Social History of the World War contains a volume on the effects of the War on labor in Germany, by one of the soundest leaders of German trade-unionism, Paul Umbreit.[2] His fi-

---

refusal of the Prussian Government and the Prussian Parliament to accept the inevitable adult franchise with equal voting strength for all, that is, the franchise which, since 1871, had applied to the Empire as a whole.

2. *Der Krieg und der Arbeitsverhältnisse.*

nal judgment on the National Service Law, which, on the whole, it is his aim to defend and even to praise, is a singularly clear exposition of the insanity of war economics. He says (p. 262):

The National Service Law certainly did much, during the period of nearly two years in which it remained in force, to heighten the volume of war production. Its immediate consequence, however, was the decline of German industry and, in the case of raw materials, a complete impoverishment of Germany's economic system. Anything and everything that seemed of any possible use for war purposes—factories, machinery, laboratories and every kind of institution—was forced into the compass of this, the last mobilization of all available forces, and was used up in it. The downfall of our fatherland, in the long run, was not halted by this procedure; it was made complete and universal. National Service completely exhausted the forces of resistance which lived in our people, and in the end led to Germany's unconditional surrender to the conditions of peace imposed by the enemy. As a measure of strategy or a political device the Hindenburg program failed, because it overstrained the forces of the nation. As a measure of social policy and of national economy the National Service Law, on the contrary, was a success; and the working-class, more than any other, had reason to be satisfied with it, thanks to the form it had taken in Parliament through the coöperation of the trade-unions with the political parties. The guaranties which had been introduced in the interest of the employed as a corollary to compulsory service were so satisfactory that there was never a labor revolt against the National Service Law. Neither were trade-unionist organizations in any way oppressed by it; on the contrary, their position was strengthened and they won great numbers of new adherents through the amplification of war industry. With the end of the War came the abrogation of the National Service Law, by decree of the Council of People's Commissaries, on November 11, 1918. The works committees, however, and the conciliation boards remained, and the provisions of the law in regard to them have been reënacted in the laws of the Republic.[3]

3. A similar judgment, from the point of view of German capital, was pronounced by the then Minister of Finance, Dr. Schiffer, during the debates of the Weimar Assembly in 1919: "I don't want to criticize the Hindenburg program from the military point of view. Economically it was a program of despair and did an enormous amount of damage. A reaction of the most disgusting character set in. Expense was no longer taken into consideration. It was as if a premium had been put on luring away the workmen from one industry to another offering higher wages, or to a position more secure from enlistment in the army. In the place of organization, disorder reigned, with-

Nothing was farther from the minds of those with whom the Hindenburg program originated than to strengthen the position of the Socialist party. But that was the only tangible effect it finally had. Through its disregard of every sound relation between work and wages it helped to create conditions which, even apart from the effects of inflation, would have made the return to a normal state of things in industry and labor almost impossible. The severity of the reaction against the power secured by trade-unionist organizations under the National Service Law was one of the most conspicuous features of the political revulsion in Germany. It is one of the personal tragedies of this time that the second President of the Republic, in order to undo some of the consequences of the war program connected with his name, felt compelled to sign the emergency decree by which the National Socialist Party was put into power, their program being to restore the German nation to the condition in which it fought the war from 1915 to 1917.

The monetary disturbances which came to their climax in the inflation of 1923–1924 cannot be traced to a single source nor can the Hindenburg program be said to have been one of their primary causes. We should be nearer the truth if we likened its influence on German currency to that of an abnormally narrow gorge through which the waters of public finance had to take their course, accelerating their pace as the gorge became deeper and deeper. The primary causes were doctrinarianism, as it manifested itself in the financial mobilization plans and the inherent weakness of the policy of the Government —if it can be called a policy—in trying to finance the War mainly through an anticipation of a speedy and decisive victory. Public

out any fixed relation to reality. In fact, the system from which we suffer today began to develop. The material and moral damage done was absolutely terrific." For a contrary view compare Lotz, *Die deutsche Staatsverwaltung im Weltkriege*, p. 108, who holds that at the end of the War—*a fortiori* during the last stages of the War—the causes of inflation and ruin had not yet arisen, or at least, that the later events would not necessarily have followed as a consequence of the financial policy of the Reich during the War and the practices under the National Service Law. Professor Lotz repeatedly states that the damage which, as he too concedes, was done to national economy by the financial and industrial policy of the Government and the trade-unions, was in his opinion curable (*heilbar*) as late as 1918–1919. He puts the blame for the irremediable damage upon the Peace Treaties and the post-war policy of the Allies.

credit lasted through the first two years of the War, digesting the internal loans which were to cover the bill of military and political expenses for the next six months or so. It did better, on the whole, than could have been expected. Its chief mainstay, during that period, was the profound belief of the people, and especially those with small savings and a moderate income, in the War as their common destiny. If they were taking refuge in war as a means of national policy somebody might certainly have had enough common sense and enough cynicism, too, to say: If we are planning wars let us train ourselves in preparedness for them. Let us distribute the task among all in the most rational way and conduct the war, once it has been launched, in a way which will mean a minimum of loss and a maximum of gain. To do that, our financial policy must be one of calculating the cost, spreading the risk over a long period, and involving as many other countries as possible in the system of war credits we shall need to carry the war through if a military success is not given to us by pitched battles.

But as this was not a planned or an intended war—though it had often been rehearsed on the green cloth of ministerial war offices—everybody believed in the necessity of carrying its burden as his ordained fate, and the heavier the better. To the common people who subscribed to loans to the best of their power great strength of endurance grew out of such a conviction. To the Government it was the reverse—a dispensing with solid, sober reasoning and with that sense of stern responsibility which should have rested on the heads of officialdom even during the reign of war. The amount of short-term treasury bonds, which meant the debt owed by the Reich to the Reichsbank (or in other words the amount which had to be raised through the next internal loan if the Reich was to be able to redeem the bonds when due) had risen from 897 million marks in October, 1914, to 3,412 millions in October, 1915, to 7,856 in October, 1916, and to 22,679 millions in October, 1917. It was doubled again during the next year, and almost doubled from 1918 to 1919. But 1916 to 1917 showed the maximum increase.

That is one side of the question. The other is that taxation during the War went quite as unmistakably wrong as did credit policy. It was not only that war profits were allowed to escape taxation during the War to a remarkable degree—especially if Germany in the War be compared to Great Britain. Taxation, where it really reached out and made a financial success of a special surtax, as it did in the cases of the additional taxes on coal and on cigarettes, defeated its own ends by fastening on just the kind of object which had to be purchased in enormous quantities by the administration itself. The tax was laid upon the buyer, and the principal buyer who paid anything that was asked for was the Government, which had tried to raise money through taxation.[4] That is where the Hindenburg program came in and, causing expenses to rise to a sum irretrievable, through internal loans, let it become a patent truth that at the end of the War —whenever it did come—there would exist a public debt that could not be repaid to the creditors, if it could be paid at all, without serious danger to the currency and to capitalism in general.

Inflation, arising from a plan for financial mobilization which proceeded on lines of strictly capitalistic reasoning, and Dictatorship, arising from a program for national service which seemed to stabilize the trade-unions in their dominant political position—that is what follows when war takes a hand in the game.

[4]. Compare R. Kuczynski, "Deutsche Kriegssteuerpolitik," in *Annalen für soziale Politik und Gesetzgebung,* Vol. 6. It is to be noted that Kuczynski criticizes the financial policy of the post-war governments even more severely than that of the War Cabinet.

PART II

THE EFFECT OF WAR ON THE CONSTITUTION OF GERMANY

CHAPTER VII

GOVERNMENT: POLITICAL AND GEOGRAPHICAL CONDITIONS BEFORE THE WAR

Our introductory remarks may be open to the objection that war as they view it, is seen as a merely negative force. Even the eulogists of the warlike spirit admit that as an agency of destruction war is unparalleled; indeed, they glory in that capacity of war to destroy anything that is not fireproof and to unburden, once and for all, the household of a nation of all those things which have been accumulated by generation after generation, till they have become useless and even meaningless to the present. But that is, according to those who hold war to be amply justified by the lessons of history, only a preliminary or accessory effect of war. They attribute much greater importance to the constructive forces born of an armed conflict between the nations. Unquestionably, civil war often helps to create a new national body, with a constitution in which the elements of blood and iron form the strongest constituents. International war might do the same thing for the world, or for that part of the world put to the test by it. With such an effect of the World War we are, for the moment, not concerned. But we have been told—a good many high-school textbooks in modern history may be quoted for it—that war is a physical and spiritual cure for every nation that dares to wage it. By war the body politic is cured of slackness; war is the remedy without which right stagnates. Leadership is acknowledged where, during a long period of dull peace, the nation had confided in debates and the resolutions of the Council of State. A new sense of responsibility, we are told, is awakened in those whose orders involve the life and death of hundreds of their fellow men, almost as a matter of routine. The technique of organization is put to a test, often with surprising results. Put all this together, and we might safely conclude that through a war a change for the better must come to the government of a nation, both in form and substance.

That is the contention, put forward by the partisans of war, to which we have to direct our inquiry in the following chapters. War, in the case of Germany—that is, a war believed by the people to be a defensive war, but fought mainly in the enemy's country, with, consequently, an acute separation of the fighting forces from the people at home, and, finally, a war lost not so much in open battle as through exhaustion—certainly undermined, if it did not finally destroy, the moral equilibrium of the nation. It gave the most formal *démenti* to the belief that an adequate adjustment of merit to reward is possible, to say nothing of such an adjustment being the regulative lever in the watch of human life. War, moreover, demonstrated the futility of planning, whether for peace or war. But did not war give more than it took away? Were not the losses on the moral side more than balanced by an enormous material gain on the side of political power and conscious national strength?

In order to estimate the change wrought by the War in the constitution of Germany we have to think of that constitution not as it was in force immediately before the outbreak of the War, and, indeed, not as a written law consisting of so many articles, but as the traditional attitude of the German subject toward the State and toward Government.

How that traditional attitude has changed is shown by a recent pamphlet by a German writer of fiction who, in the nationalist group of literary men in post-war Germany, stands out almost as Wilhelm Tell stands out in Schiller's drama, a man apart, difficult of access, devoted to the idea of his own powers, valiant in action but as powerless to explain it or to understand the action of other people as a child. The author of *Volk ohne Raum* forms one of the few signal cases where a man's life was reversed by the War—and this does not mean simply broken, as many men's and women's lives were by the deaths of sons and daughters, or by being struck down themselves—blinded or maimed or shocked out of their minds. It means that outwardly and inwardly his life was changed into the opposite of everything it had been. He came of old Frisian peasant stock, honest heathens from whom in the eighteenth and nineteenth centuries there had sprung Protestant clergy and teachers. His ancestors were people of the soil, homely, just, and righteous people, ideal "good men and true," in the genuine sense of the term used when an English jury is called.

A man to whom descent from a long line of landed squires means more than anything else today, Hans Grimm, in his youth went out into the wide world, lived for many years in South West Africa and South Africa and fought hard to be a poet, instead of simply living the life into which he had been born. He wrote and published four or five books, stories of African folk which read with the best Indian stories of Rudyard Kipling's halcyon days, and a book of travel which contains about the best comparative appreciation of German and English character in German literature. These volumes were hailed by a few intellectuals who in 1913 were looking for a young man who could write unadulterated German. But before the War or during the first years of the War people in general did not care much about them, and some were hardly noticed at all.

Then the War came to reverse all that. The *Uitlander* came back to Germany for good. He bought a farm where, as he found out much later, his forebears had lived in the fourteenth and fifteenth centuries. He wrote three new books, one at the command of the military authorities or their press bureau during the War, and two on his own account during the years of the bitterest internecine conflict. He was one of the extremist partisans. He renounced the poet's gifts with which the language of his country had comforted him during the *Wanderjahre*. He became a pamphleteer, deliberately and ruthlessly using his literary technique for propaganda of the bitterest kind. Almost at once, he was hailed as one of the leading novelists of the day. His books sold by the hundred thousand, and in spite of his protests his name was used in party warfare as one of the signs under which the National Socialists strove to gain the victory over Jews and Marxists, and to give Germany, as they said, her third incarnation as a sovereign empire, or her first, as Grimm himself seems to think.[1] It is from the pamphlet in which he confessed his political faith that the sentence which might be placed at the head of this section has been taken.

"In a new country," it says, "life is, in general, different from that of people in Europe, especially in Germany. For, contrary to nature and quite needlessly, all the subtle complexity of Germany's national life has been infected by the long-standing malady of princeling rule and the rank growth of bureaucracy."

That is the judgment one of the protagonists of the younger generation in post-war Germany passes upon German Government in

---

1. Terms like that of a "Third Empire" originate not so much with international as with civil war. It is interesting to compare the description of General Harrison's "Fifth-monarchy men" by Sir Walter Scott in his Cromwellian story, *Woodstock*, Chapter XI.

the past. In future, if we agree with the lessons he learned from the War, Germany will never again bear with a federal constitution. The old loyalties to the home country, whether of Guelph or Wittelsbach denomination, whether duchy or kingdom or free town, belong to the past. Government, so it has been decreed by the War, can only be a centralized rulership over the whole of Germany. If the term centralization is rejected as being un-German, or, to be more precise, French, we might call it a single government of German men over the whole of Germany. Its members are to be chosen less for their technical administrative abilities or because of official civil service careers that end almost as a matter of course with a seat in the Cabinet, than for the confidence which the people put in them—not, of course, indirectly, through parliamentary elections or on the advice of, and nomination by, the leaders of political parties, but by a process of almost mystical relationship between a true leader and his retainers.[2]

To a foreign observer this may, at first sight, seem a conception of government which has no relation whatever to reality, and he might feel confirmed in that view by noticing how many adherents of this war creed show a violent dislike of even the word *Realität* or *Wirklichkeiten*. They claim, indeed, that it is simply cowardice to talk of the obtainable instead of pledging oneself to a political *jusqu'au boutisme* which demands the fulfilment of a radical program to the last degree, and a readiness to die rather than become the slaves of compromise. Appearances, however, are deceptive; the

---

2. This belief in leadership as a living principle of government plays an important rôle in the minds of the younger generation of Germans, irrespective of their party or non-party allegiance. Such intellectual groups as the followers of Stefan George (many of them of Jewish descent, and belonging rather to the left than to the center or the right), for instance, must be understood to include in truly German fashion two contradictory elements, one of them democratic in the sense of the term in which the Western world uses it, insisting strongly on the freedom of a German who will not bow to prince or prime minister, far less to any lesser dignitary of State or Church, and the other aristocratic or even feudal in character. Usually the latter prevails. It leads the followers of this creed to abhor the idea of representative government. If the man, it says, who is to govern because he is the best and noblest of all, were to try to represent the crowd he would have to lower himself. A leader has to live above his retinue much as the captain of the ship has to live apart from officers and crew.

Nationalist creed is much more intimately bound up with many of the ancient intricacies of German constitutional history than its prophets or their followers seem to realize—or would like to acknowledge if they realized it.

For one thing, a critical observer of the German attitude toward government should not neglect the part which conscious pride in their national history and even a subconscious traditionalism plays in the case of the educated classes of a country which, up to the beginning of this century, based its system of government on a civil service manned by students of the humanistic faculties, theology, law, logic, and history. In political thought Germany may claim to be one of the oldest nations in the world. Her tradition of sovereign imperial government extends over more than a thousand years, with only a short break during the middle of the nineteenth century when the last vestige of Habsburg predominance over the greater part of Germany had disappeared, and southern Germany was still undecided whether to trudge along in the way set for her kingdoms and grand duchies by Napoleon, or to espouse one of the political causes which were seeking to enlist them.

Racially, the German people is composite. Slavonic ingredients prevail in its eastern part; the west and south, including the important southeastern bridge that reaches out toward Italy and the Near East, show many ties of consanguinity with Rhaetians, Italians, and Mediterranean French. In the north the transition from purely German Lower Saxons to Frisians and through them to Dutchmen and Flemings, or to Schleswigers and Danes is almost imperceptible; in nearly every town and in many provinces, especially in Franconia and Hessen, there is a sprinkling of Jewish blood, and among the aristocracy and the upper ten thousand, generally, Danish, Swedish, Russian, French, Italian, Hungarian, and Spanish ancestry makes itself felt, sometimes to the almost complete displacement of the German element of descent. On the other hand, however, the German has a strong conviction of being aboriginal, the country he lives in today having been his country from time immemorial, "from the Maas to the Memel, from the Adige to the Belt," in the words of the national hymn. Many of his greatest representatives in literature and poetry, in the fine arts and in statesmanship have been born and have lived in the frontier provinces, at the farthest outposts of this territory, standing on guard to keep it together in its integrity. They know they dwelt in this country long before Gaul was conquered first by Rome and then by the Franks, or the British Isles by Saxons, Danes, and Norman-French, or northern Italy, and even Rome, by the Goths, or southern Spain by the Moors. With the belief in the direct descent of a true German from the people who put the Romans to flight in the time of the Emperor Augustus and with a tradition of their farm or manor having been in the hands of the same family throughout the ages, maybe for nearly two thousand years, many of them combine a strong suspicion that Germany would still be a nation of free men with a clannish form of tribal government if, first, their forefathers had not succumbed to the brutal imposition upon them of the Christian faith by Charlemagne, the conqueror of the Saxons, who baptized them with blood and iron, and if, second, they had not been prepared, by this first infiltration of alien thought, to succumb, later on, to the subtler influences of Roman law and statecraft in the early Middle Ages. It is in northwestern and northern Germany, among a peasantry which preserves more customs and manners of clearly heathenish origin than any other community in Europe, that this tradition is strongest. But elsewhere, too, it has its adherents. In smaller numbers and without the same kind of attachment to the soil, but with a violent hatred of foreign-born people and foreign institutions, it has them, above all in the frontier districts of northeastern Bavaria and Bohemia, in the Tyrol and the adjoining German valleys and in Westphalia, the seat of the old Vehmic courts of summary justice.

Other people of a less romantic disposition and a worldlier outlook still cling to the cultural tradition and heritage of the Holy Roman Empire with its unparalleled wealth of civic life in Basle, Constance, Augsburg, Nürnberg, Frankfurt, Cologne, Bremen, Hamburg, Lübeck, and Danzig. From this tradition many liberal reformers took their conception of a natural alliance between the ideal of a great empire common to all and a homely citizenship rooted in the peculiar conditions of a commercial center, a great harbor, a university or seat of clerical studies, or a craftsmen's town—a conception on which most of the policy of German Imperial chancellors rested before Vienna had become the capital and the central seat of a cumbrous bureaucracy. An offspring of this fifteenth- and sixteenth-century *entente* between the monarch and his most loyal townspeople, an *entente* which had been tested in many foreign wars and finally sealed by a common effort to establish an enduring *Landfrieden*, a "land-peace," in the face of the turbulent and pretentious robber barons, is to be found in the predilection of the eighteenth and nineteenth centuries for duodecimo states, the *Kleinstaaterei* or the petty-state conglomerations of southern and central Germany. The bourgeoisie of the bigger towns in those small states, one of them the capital, another perhaps the seat of local industry, the seat of a bishopric or a former free city which had been incorporated in the State, formed the real bodyguard of the dynasty. The German version of *God Save the King*, which was sung in every state whenever the monarch's birthday or a tour through the provinces of his realm gave occasion for a celebration under the national flag, contained a very remarkable reference to the close relation between the crown and its loyal citizen subjects. The opening verses with their salutation to a victorious war lord, crowned with the laurels of battles fought and won, did not accord with most of the reigning sovereigns of the smaller German states, who took the duties of civil government much more seriously than the military rank which appertained to their station, and were, at least in their old age, respected much as a patriarch was respected in the golden age of bucolic lore. The hymn fitted the situation much better when it came to

> *Nicht Ross nicht Reisige*
> *Schirmen die steile Höh*
> *Wo Fürsten steh'n.*
> *Liebe des Vaterlands,*
> *Liebe des freien Manns,*
> *Gründet des Herrschers Thron*
> *Wie Fels im Meer.*

And when they sang of the finest thing a monarch could feel himself to be, and told him, serenading before the windows of his residence, that he could truly know no prouder feeling than that "neither cavalry nor infantry could give him that secure hold which he could find in the freely given love and loyalty of the good citizens of the country," they were only reiterating the sentiments which had made the free towns of the old German Empire stand by the emperor against pope or king or Grand Turk, against territorial lords, bishops, barons, and peasants' leagues.

A third historical association of more importance to the German conception of government is of more recent growth. It is the political creed of those who see in the rise of Prussia to the rank of a great military and civil power and in the War of Liberation against Napoleon, or finally in the Bismarckian structure of a smaller German Federation, the true foundation of German sovereignty and government. Their chief indebtedness is to the genius or the indomitable strength of will of a few leaders. These forced the people, and in many cases a weak monarch, into a rate of progress and aggrandizement to which they were violently opposed in the beginning; and only with much grumbling and protesting did they submit to it later, even as they gave it no praise until all was done and the gods had signified their pleasure at the extent of the sacrifice. Thus it was with Frederick the Second in his glorious feats of arms, and his international intrigues against all the world, both within his Prussian domain and without; and thus it was, in 1813 and 1814, with Scharnhorst and Yorck, and during the whole struggle against Napoleon in the case of the Freiherr von Stein. They had to force, all of them, their will and their views on the king, on the ministers, on public opinion. Thus it was with Bismarck, whose fiercest battles were not with Napoleon the Third, or Gortschakow, or even Count Beust, but with the court party, with members of the reigning house, with egotist Prussianism among the leaders and spokesmen of his own class, and with a few ambitious militarists trying to mar foreign relations on their own account. It is in a different fashion that history has told the story of their deeds. It has heaped abuse on them, or piled up praise; in turn it has blessed them as the great heroes of national resurrection, and cursed them as enemies of their own people and destroyers of their virtue. But on one thing all are agreed, that these men were greatest and most formidable when they stood alone, without other support than their own moral and intellectual qualities gave them. It was not a game of command and obey; these men, even the King, often had to persuade others rather than give orders to them or even simply to stand by their own convictions without a following, till time showed them to be in the right. Their best they always did singlehanded.

Thus history shows that among Germans there are, roughly, three different traditional attitudes toward government.

One, found mainly in the north and northwest, holds that government is local government and self-government, a ruling by trusted men chosen by their equals within a community of people of the same blood and the same religion, leaving the greatest possible measure of independence to each single member of the community, and extremely distrustful of professional public service and of paid officials. It is republican in substance, and if it admits an Emperor he is more a sublime idea than a tangible fact; their Emperor is the *"heimliche Kaiser"*—the secret emperor—of the German legend, who sleeps somewhere in a mountain cave till the day of national reckoning comes, or whose name is used when a court sits in secret to deal with an infamous crime.

The second, mainly in central, western, and southern Germany, is devoted to a form of state government, which should be largely modeled on city government. Essentially bourgeois, it has a fair appreciation of the importance an efficient civil service has in the maintenance of law and order, and also believes in moderate progress brought about by a careful system of education. During the last two centuries it was monarchist, but by no means imperialist, liberal in a conservative way, and comparatively easygoing in political matters.

The third, mainly in the old Prussian provinces east of the river Elbe, but with many followers in Saxony and northern Bavaria, is inclined to believe in the necessity of a governing power which rules independently of the consent or even the good will of those over whom it holds its sway. Success, with this form of government, results not from coöperation or from a general sense of duty and obedience to a superior—that would be a most misleading view of the essentially Prussian system of government—but from a constant struggle in which finally the will of a single strong man will emerge triumphant, thanks not least to the battle given him by the opposition, or, if he belongs to that opposition himself, by the existing order. Traditionally, Prussia is a monarchy, but as history has shown, the system is in no way legitimist. It has no place for an emperor, and during the forty-seven years from 1871 to 1918 the King of Prussia remained the real force, while "Emperor" was merely a title borne by him. The agency of government, under this system, was the army and a political administration of the agrarian provinces which stood in close personal relation to the army.

These attitudes, all of them emanating from practical experience rather than from speculation, all of them resting on proven merits, form the conservative side of German politics; those who adhere to them prefer to rely on pride in the past rather than on the ability to do new and better things in the future.

History, however, is never alone in forming the mind of a people. Time is not more powerful in that respect than space is; and, in the case of Germany, the geographical situation has a special meaning for the development of public institutions.

The main fact to be remembered is that Germany, with practically insuperable natural boundaries on the north and south, has had no fixed frontiers on the east or west for many centuries. International conflicts, wars, and an hereditary enemy complex resulted from this state of things. And, defying nature, the solution adopted has been one that has taken great rivers, which in their courses should unite the human effort of all those fortunate people through whose territories they flow, and has turned them into things to be cut into pieces and distributed like so many parcels of private property among as many different leaseholders. In the case of every big river in Central Europe—Rhine, Elbe, Danube, Oder, and Vistula—this policy has been adopted. But that is a question of international policy which does not concern this history. What matters is the importance which the undefined boundaries to the east and west of Germany have for German domestic policy. The conflict between "Westerners" and "Easterners," so well known to all students of the World War, has, in a different sense of the words, been an ever recurring problem to German politicians, who have had to steer their way between the two currents of constitutional practice.

A misplaced and misleading definition says that the line between the two parts of Germany—one of which is as much mixed up with its eastern neighbors as the other is with its western ones—is the course of the Elbe; just as a similarly mistaken term in the German politics of the last century spoke of a *"Mainlinie,"* a line marked by the river Main, as being the boundary between northern and southern Germany. Not the smallest bit of the valley of the Main ever belonged to northern Germany; the boundary runs along the heights which border the north side of the valley of the Main and its northern tributaries. Nor has a single bit of the Elbe Valley ever belonged to the western part of Germany. The Elbe Valley and all the land and the river systems to the east of it have a peculiar character, in that as much as 75 per cent of the land consists of great estates worked by a kind of serf labor, or seasonal labor from beyond the frontier; while of the western part as much as 85 per cent is in small farms cultivated by the owner and his family. The contrast in the popular attitude toward life is not less marked than the contrast between the peasant-owned and the State-farmed or serfs' country. In the east, human life is governed by a strange mixture of determinism and strong-willed obstinacy on the part of the individual. In the west, life is taken easily; a tolerant skepticism of the opinion of others—more tolerant if they are persuasive, and more skeptical if they are domineering—and a long-suffering patience, by no means irreconcilable with a shrewd instinct for a good bargain, count for as much in life as does—among the Germans of the east—a severe regard for duty and a profound conviction that life means either ruling others or being ruled by them. The Westerners like to talk; social intercourse shows them at their best. The Easterners like to act in silence; they listen better than they talk.

To add to all this, there is a difference which is neither racial nor merely geographical. The western frontier districts always had and still have the advantage of direct contact with neighbor civilizations—French, Franco-Swiss, Belgian, and Dutch—a contact which, even in periods of acute conflict like those of the War of the Spanish Succession, the Napoleonic Wars, and the French campaign with the Allies, or that of 1923–1924, has its special merit in helping to form national character and to build up an intelligent public opinion on government. Throughout history there is hardly another case, as far as I can see, of the directness and thoroughness of the influence of public opinion and the attitude toward public affairs of one country on another—except, of course, in cases of annexation and forceful imposition on the part of an invader—parallel to the case of French influence on Germany, first in the time of Louis XIV, and afterward, in much stronger measure, during the French Revolution and the Napoleonic Empire. Every walk of life shows traces of it, from public administration in the "separation of powers," to that of civil procedure. Then, during the nineteenth century, there was an almost complete supersession of German common-law procedure by the principles and practice of the *code de procédure civile*, down to the *juge de paix* and the *conseils de prud'hommes* from which the German labor courts have sprung. Even the office of the *huissier* has been embodied in German law. And this is also true of roadbuilding, of the language of military command, but above all of every sphere of government and parliamentary life. It was an influence which went on almost undiminished even during hostilities and in spite of the hereditary enemy complex, in spite, too, of its being an influence entirely one-sided, the first cases of any decided influence of German institutions and ideas on public life in France having been brought about only by the re-annexation of Alsace and Lorraine after the World War. If it ceased to work directly beyond the Vosges and the Moselle during a war or a post-war period of more or less closed frontiers, it merely took a detour through Switzerland, where the contact between the French- and the German-speaking sections only became the closer when France and Germany were estranged from one another, and through Walloon-Flemish Belgium and the Netherlands. Geneva and The Hague, since 1914, have become the centers of influence of the French language and French thought on the Continent.

It is otherwise with the eastern provinces of Germany. If we leave the Austrian question aside for the moment, and think only of the eastern frontier north of the Danube, contact with the eastern neighbor has, during the centuries, meant for Germany the opposite of what has been meant by contact with her neighbor of the west. Neither Czechs, Poles, nor Russians—nor, if we include Austria, Slovenes, and Hungarians—had impressive models of public institutions to show their German neighbors. Their contribution to the political mind of Europe was an intense nationalism, partly due to oppression, as in the case of Poles or that of the minorities in Hungary, and partly growing out of the Pan-Slavist movement. The political influence of the east on Germany, up to 1916, was confined to three distinct and conflicting contacts. The first was that of the monarchs, which meant a great deal to German foreign policy during the Sixties and Seventies, and even later on occasionally made a spectral appearance as the ghost of a Holy Alliance of the Emperors against western liberalism, without its being able to do more than make both the Tsar and the German Emperor look unreliable in the eyes of their allies, and sometimes in their own eyes too. The second contact was that between the landowners, pastors, teachers, and estate agents of German origin in the Baltic provinces of Russia and their relatives and friends of the same class and profession in Prussia. The influence of the Baltic barons went to reinforce that of the Prussian landowners in the old Prussian provinces, and to accentuate the difference between the political views of the Westerners and the Easterners in Germany, coinciding to some extent with the different outlook of Lutherans and Roman Catholics; for the Baltic barons were strongly Lutheran, while most of the owners of big estates in western and southern Germany belonged to the Roman Catholic faith and, politically, to the "ultramontane" Center party. The third contact, however, served to a certain degree to counteract the other two. It was established by the eastern Jews, not so much by those in the grain or fur trade—who passed from one country to another without taking much interest in politics apart from the bribes they had to pay to customs officials—as by those who fled from Russian persecution. For many of them who meant to proceed to the United States or to England were unable to do so and stayed in Germany.

Before the War the influence of the East on eastern Germany was by no means strong and of merely one character. The conflicting impressions brought home from their casual visits on the one hand by courtiers, diplomats, or military attachés, visitors to a big model farm in the Baltic countries or guests at a big-game hunt in Poland or Galicia, and on the other by liberal intellectuals or Socialists, were not calculated to help the political education of the German people as a whole.

During the War even this kind of confused contact with Russia was almost entirely lost. Official relations ceased, as a matter of course, and family feeling among the members of the reigning houses turned into real hatred, made worse by the disappointment of hopes built on the *Heimattreue*—the loyalty to the old country—of German princesses married to members of the House of Russia, or on the vaunted intellectual influence of the German Emperor over his cousin. Neither the Scandinavian countries nor Rumania, much less the Polish or Czech circles which aspired to national independence, had ever been willing to form connecting links between the German and the Russian people as political bodies, such as Switzerland and the Low Countries did in Western Europe. They became less and less willing to do so during the War. The influence of the Baltic landowners and their retainers became, for a time, exceedingly strong with the German High Command and with the Nationalist movement in Germany, which, since 1915, has received some of its strongest impulses from people of German origin in Austrian Bohemia and in the three Baltic provinces of the Tsarist Empire; but that was a specific war influence, and in the end served only to make the revolutionary reaction against German-Baltic landowners more terrible in its work of murderous destruction. An undue influence ruthlessly exerted brought about almost the same process of self-annihilation among the Jewish element in eastern European politics. Jews had proved useful servants to German administration in the occupied territories in the East, if only because of their language, an eastern Yiddish which was a mixture of Hebrew, German, and Polish understood even by many peasants in White Russia and the Ukraine. In some cases they became advisers to German authorities; almost everywhere they had acquired a freedom of movement between the border provinces of Germany and Austria-Hungary on one side and Russia and Rumania on the other, which, during the last stages of the War and the post-war troubles in these regions, led to an excessive influx of Russian, Polish, and Galician Jews into Germany; and much of the virulent anti-Semitic agitation in Germany resulted simply from a series of cases of corruption (of the old Russian and Austrian kind) in which eastern Jews figured, along with Germans of undoubtedly immaculate descent, and from the bitter envy and indignation of small traders in the eastern German towns. These believed they were being undersold by the Jewish newcomer, always suspect of sharp practice and without doubt willing to be content with a lower standard of living; or they felt they were deprived of the good will of their customers by big department stores, most of them owned by Jews.

After the War, contact between eastern Germany and Russia would probably have implied as impressive a lesson in communism as contact with France had meant a lesson in liberalism and the art of political oratory. That, however, was prevented, first by militant communism itself which, at the time of the Soldiers' Council's rule, before the Constituent Election, had made itself very unpopular with the great majority of Germans even of the working class; and then, later, contact was barred by the ever stricter enforcement of that part of the Peace Treaty which was apt to be construed as the erection of an insuperable barrier between Germany and Russia. In that respect the policy of the Little Entente, which in its international aspect is outside the sphere of this history, reacted forcefully on German domestic policy, on social conditions, the state of public opinion, and the balancing of political views generally, in Germany.

To the elements of preponderantly historical origin—the three political groupings, republican peasants, constitutional and parliamentary bourgeois, and dictatorial landowners and industrialists—two further elements have thus to be added. One is, again, the very definite, and, at many periods during the last one hundred and fifty years, the almost overwhelming, influence of French thought and French methods of administration on western and southern Germany. This, one might say, applies to the whole section of Germany lying westward and southward of the western and southern confines of the Elbe Valley, running roughly from the Böhmerwald to the Fichtelgebirge, the Thüringerwald, and the Harz Mountains down to the heath of Lüneburg between Hamburg and Bremen. The other is that rather indefinable and complex impression on the political character of eastern and northeastern Germany resulting from the contact with eastern neighbors and, still more, with emigrants and fugitives from Russia.

CHAPTER VIII

GOVERNMENT: THE CHANGE IN METHOD
1914–1918

THE constitution of 1871 was itself an almost ideal compromise between those conflicting claims of antagonistic systems of German politics, and as long as the founder of the second German Empire held the Government of both the Reich and Prussia in his hand, the danger of that Government overreaching itself remained very slight. The man who, in his personal bearing as well as by his descent was bound to satisfy the need of one part of the German mind—the need of giving unquestioning obedience to an iron (if flexible) will—and who had all the qualities required to make him the object of the most enthusiastic hero worship, took, on his own initiative, and one might almost say with his own hands, every possible precaution against a central dictatorship. The contingency of such a dictatorship, apart from his, Bismarck's, own, was certainly a very distant one in the Seventies of last century; but the German constitution provided as carefully—with every kind of brake and every possible counterweight lest a single will within the Empire should become too powerful and, in the end, too well able to impose itself on its partners in the German administration—as if that constitution had foreseen the tendencies toward dictatorship in post-war Europe. Constitutionalists had, to comfort them, the *Bundesrat* as the representative of the coalesced sovereign will of the states, and the *Reichstag* as the assembly elected by universal franchise, a well-balanced relationship between federal interests and the idea of a great, single nation of sixty million Germans. For them the members of the *Reichstag* were the spokesmen, and for them spoke the Chancellor himself, more than any single member of Parliament, when he addressed the *Reichstag*. Both the peasants of Oldenburg, Westphalia, northern Hannover, Holstein, and Schleswig, and the junker farmers of Mecklenburg, Pomerania, and Prussia could feel that they were allowed to administer their own affairs and be masters in their villages or their districts, the latter because of the fact that the *Landrat*—the District Government Commissioner—was a man of their own class, usually himself the owner of an estate in the district, and the former because of the general practice of leaving the peasant farmers to work out their own salvation, unmolested by most of the rules and regulations which prevailed in the towns or in interstate commerce. The Emperor and his Chancellor, to them, were legendary figures rather than agents of executive power. Berlin was far away from the country where, except for the Sunday sermon, real life went on without too much talk. The Chancellor himself enjoyed his independence of character as a country squire at Varzin or Friedrichsruh, and, above all, the supremacy of his power of office and his unparalleled prestige as the real ruler of Germany and, more or less, the pilot of European policy in his age. They all felt secure in their independence because they knew Bismarck's own personal conception of government. At the same time, people in southern Germany and in the Rhineland had every opportunity of having their say in German politics. Elections for their own Parliaments of Baden, Württemberg, Bavaria, and Hesse-Darmstadt were hotly contested, and while the Monarch would have been entitled, according to the constitutions of these states, to form a cabinet of men in his confidence—even as if he had been a president of the United States—it became a well-established practice for the cabinets in the southern German states to be formed in accordance with—if not in compliance with—party strength in the Diet. They were National Liberal in Baden, Liberal-Democrat in Württemberg, and either Liberal or Catholic Center in Bavaria, with the upper house in all three states playing much the same rôle as the House of Lords has done in Great Britain since the Parliament Act of 1911.

Complaints about cumbrous or even arrogant bureaucracy were, of course, heard in Germany as in every other continental country; and sometimes the antagonism between the different sections of public opinion showed unmistakably, long before the time when the socialist program came anywhere near to being practical policy, or to taking a real share in public opinion. But on the whole the administration remained as nearly invisible as is possible in a country like Germany, much more so, at any rate, than in Austria-Hungary or in France. This reticence was practiced as a matter of *Staatsklugheit*—of governmental prudence—in Bismarck's and Hohenlohe's time; and, later on, it was imposed on the bureaucrats by the young Emperor's predilection for engineers, technicians, and naval experts, all of them impatient of the law and its servants—people, it seemed to them, who were there only to invent difficulties and raise objections.

The War changed all that. In the War the Government overreached itself—anybody could see that—and it may also be said that the War brought out flaws and false pretensions in the Government which had long existed without causing much comment. It is difficult, if not impossible, to say whether that is primarily or mainly due to the peculiar German situation in 1914, or whether it is an innate corollary to war on the great scale in any case and everywhere. No doubt the constitutional arrangement by which, on the outbreak of war and almost automatically, the executive power is transferred from the civil to the military authorities, did much to raise reasonable doubts as to public administration in the minds of the public, and to make restive and critical those who had, before the War, been patient and long-suffering about public affairs, almost to the point of criminal indifference. Throughout Germany, including Bavaria, in spite of her special prerogatives of sovereignty, the military districts became the administrative districts, in some cases including the territories of several of the smaller central and northern states. The Emperor, as Supreme War Lord, was represented by the general-in-command (*Kommandierender General*) of the district, or, to be more precise, the lieutenant-general-in-command, for the general-in-command himself had to go on active service, and in his place it was usually a retired general who was called upon to reënter service and become the regent of the district. Nor was he a representative official only; he wielded an almost unlimited power in the case of civil administration and political rights generally, as well as in military matters. The conception of his office was essentially different from that of the Cabinet Minister or Secretary of State or Civil Governor (*Regierungspräsident*) whose functions were to be fulfilled by him. It was not service which was expected of him, but command. He was the military commander, *Militärbefehlshaber*, and as such had to exercise civil executive power in its entirety. Civil servants remained at their posts, at least those who had not been called to the colors, and except for the courts of law, the independence of which was strictly maintained, worked under military orders. In addition to this, the general-in-command had a whole staff of officers and officials of military rank. Most of them were retired on grounds of age or disability; and, in the later stage of the War, they were officers who had been wounded or contracted some illness which prevented them from doing active service. It was pure chance if any of these men who formed the government of a district and who, of course, were practically exempt from either ministerial or parliamentary censure or control, was either trained in administration of any kind, or was able to master the technique of civil government by sheer energy of will and quickness of intellect. Many of them were unable to do so, and some of them were unwilling, having their own ideas about the unnecessary fuss trained civil servants used to make about their work, thinking how easy it was for a businessman, or an officer, or any other man with ordinary common sense to administer, if not strict law, then at least a sound measure of equity to everybody concerned.

The people had thus more occasion and likewise perhaps a better opportunity of getting in touch with the authorities and of judging of their impartiality and efficiency. They had to ask all kind of permissions to do things which needed no special permit in times of peace. They volunteered information which they thought was essential; and during the first few months of the War the spy mania gave the information departments of the *Generalkommando* a lot of trouble. People were forced to go to the censor for *imprimaturs* for newspaper items or general literature, and to obtain leave to hold meetings, and so on. Favor or its opposite began to play a rôle it had never played before in administration; and where in peace-time businessmen (and idle men too) had often grumbled about there being too much *Gründlichkeit*—pedantic thoroughness —in the Civil Service or the courts of administration when dealing with petty cases, it became quickly the reverse under the new régime. Decisions were speedy, and, as must be the case with summary decisions, arbitrary; and suspicions of favoritism and petty corruption—there was hardly a case of gross corruption on the part of the military authorities during the whole of the War—grew rife.

Apart from that, some ill will was inevitable in the case of civil servants who were displaced, or who had to carry out orders where they had given them before. It was galling to a man who thought of his work as being a wholly necessary part of an organization that had been perfected through a long period of laborious effort and was admired throughout the world for its honesty and efficiency, to be told that any officer incapacitated for military service, or his non-commissioned subaltern with hardly a full command of German grammar (not to speak of the language of the law), could replace him at a moment's notice. The public—even those who were inclined to be opposed to military supremacy over the civil service—were apt to heap ridicule on those who had believed themselves indispensable for the maintenance of law and order, and who had been suddenly put out of court without any very terrible consequences. Bureaucracy must believe in the necessity of its labors. With this belief shattered, let alone the loss of public favor, it can hardly do its work as it should be done.

On the whole, it was more the system than the men who worked it which made the thing go wrong, and caused the aftereffects with which Germany has had to battle since the War. To my personal knowledge, which was acquired from contacts with two or three *Generalkommandos*, superior military commanders were almost without exception well-intentioned men, and in most cases very anxious to continue the administrative routine of the civil service with the least possible change and to observe the letter as well as the spirit of the law. Incompetence was chiefly noticeable in the censor's office, and in the censorship of private correspondence. The latter should have been left to the public prosecutor's office, and the former might have been entrusted to almost any civil servant versed in literature and newspaper editing rather than to officers or laymen who used their rank as reserve officers to offer voluntary service as heads of information bureaus, as railway station superintendents, commanders of prisoners' camps, and censors. In one of the districts which came to my special notice during the War the owner of a cheap bazaar who had risen to the rank of *Kommerzienrat* and captain in the militia by reason of his officious patriotism, succeeded in wrecking the domestic peace of his town by a few months' tenure of the censor's office; for he read private letters and used their contents to make those who had written or received them both suspect and suspicious. These were, happily, isolated cases. But even if there had been none at all, the system would have led to deplorable results in the end. It was bound to destroy the quiet relation of mutual respect and trust between the civil service and the public which forms one of the firmest bases of public order in a modern community.

There is one question of administrative detail which merits special consideration in this connection. Administrative districts in Germany have been formed by a very slow process of adaptation. In the Middle Ages they depended on territorial jurisdiction under the feudal system, and even in the late sixteenth and early seventeenth century the rule of *cujus regio cujus religio*—temporal control means spiritual control—had a wide application in many matters of government and administration besides the right of the lord of the territory to insist on the inhabitants sharing his faith and belonging to his church. With the growth of larger principalities and finally with the new régime resulting from the Napoleonic age, most of the old boundaries ceased to be of political importance, and in many cases a veritable *arrondissement* gave wider scope and better opportunity for efficient administration than the old territorial distribution of estates had permitted.

In all but a very few cases, however, the boundaries were fixed in conformity with real needs of life. Their origin may have been in feudal ownership, and this in itself meant a certain conservative tendency to maintain a self-supporting estate—rounded off by a long experience in efficient farming and in the marketing of its produce—in its organic structure and as an administrative unit, and to keep it from going to pieces by division among heirs. In any case, the size and situation of the district corresponded to political or economic or simply human and natural realities. The boundaries grew out of the soil; they were not drawn on a map by a man sitting behind a desk in his metropolitan office room. It was not self-government or local government in the technical sense—far from it—but it was not alien government either. The man on the spot, whether south German *Amtmann*—such as he has been immortalized in Goethe's writings, from *Werther* and *Wilhelm Meister* to *Wahlverwandtschaften* and the *Natürliche Tochter*—or north German *Landrat*, with his staff and his executive officers, was of the inhabitants' own kith and kin; and they could rely on his standing up for the needs of the district against all attempts toward centralization.

Here again, the War brought a tremendous change. For the first time in the history of the German people administration was ruthlessly rationalized without regard for tradition or regional independence. Germany, for military reasons, had so-and-so many army corps, each with approximately the same recruiting strength. Army-corps districts, with the passing of the executive to the military authorities, became provinces of administration. In some cases the district conformed with a state, examples being the Kingdom of Württemberg, or the Grand Duchy of Baden; in other cases, like those of Prussia and Bavaria, the kingdom was divided into several army-corps districts; in yet others, independent administrative units, like the smaller principalities in central and northern Germany or the Hanseatic free cities, were thrown together or combined with Prussian provinces. In all districts administration was centralized in the official residence city of the general in command, possibly the capital of a state, but in other cases simply a place of strategic importance, not even the seat of a civil governor. It needed only a very short time for those who had to deal with the *Generalkommando*, whether businessmen or industrialists, politicians or educationists, newspaper men, publishers, or ordinary citizens, to find out how much administration varied between one district and another according to the views and character of the general-in-command himself or his advisers, or perhaps even the members of his clerical staff.

I can recall one instance in my own experience. An article in which the principle of retaliation was severely attacked, and English, French, and German measures of retaliation in the case of prisoners' camps were condemned as making things worse and worse, had appeared in a Munich monthly, with a blank space in the place of every sentence which struck at a German measure in retaliation; an extremely silly proceeding of the military censor, for every intelligent reader could quite easily imagine what these sentences had been. A few weeks before, the matter contained in the article, had without mutilation, found expression in the form of a public lecture in a great town which was the seat of a Prussian *Generalkommando*. Some of the officers of the staff had been in the audience; and nobody had made any objection. Finally, a few weeks later, the article was inserted, with every sentence in its proper place, in a book which passed the censorship in Württemberg. The three districts were contiguous, and I happened to live in a fourth adjoining district where, to round the story out, I received a reprimand from the *Generalkommando* for having had the dangerous passages passed by the Württemberg censor. That happened during the first stages of the War. It was a stroke of luck that the publisher of the book had his printing office in Württemberg. Neither he nor I had known the censor in the capital of that state to be more liberal-minded or less strict than his colleagues of Bavaria. During the later stages of the War, however, the peculiarities of the different *Kommandos* became well known, and many people who had stronger reasons for soliciting a favorable decision than an author wishing to have his say about prisoners' camps, made very profitable use of them. They believed themselves entitled to do so because everybody felt the unreasonableness of the whole thing. It was the first attempt at bureaucratic rule proceeding from a central authority within a district, the boundaries of which were drawn on a map without regard to the special needs of local administration, and in which the authority was exercised by officials who had not been trained for the special functions of their offices. It was the first attempt to rule from above instead of administering affairs on the level of their own milieu, and coördinating the result of this kind of administration within a sovereign state, in so far as a certain unity of administrative rule was desirable.

In her recent book on German tradition, Ricarda Huch, who speaks of the intellectual history of her country with the twofold authority of a poetess and of a learned historian, enumerates the forms of government which are alien to German citizenship and those which it has always acknowledged as its own. The former are these: a unified State without social differentiations, despotism, or dictatorship of any kind whatever, and centralization. None of them has a place in the conscious memory of German citizenship. The latter are freedom, the finding of security by a voluntary union in a federal system, coöperative effort, the acknowledgement of natural differences, the composite and pliable, instead of rigid, system of government, and loyalty to the ideal of a German Empire. The World War destroyed the forms of government which more than a thousand years of civic life had helped to evolve in peace and which had survived the religious wars, the Thirty Years' War, the wars of the dynasties in the seventeenth and eighteenth centuries, and the disturbances at the time of Frederick the Great and Napoleon. It may be a matter of doubt whether the War alone destroyed them, or whether they were caught in the toils of the machine age and the new economic and industrial powers it has created; and in the light of recent events a detached observer may legitimately put the question whether those forms were, during all those centuries, only superficially imposed on a people that, through the War and its aftermath, has at last shaken them off and returned to type. But in any case the forms of government which the World War imposed on Germany were at the time felt to be decidedly alien to its traditional conception of the relation between rulers and ruled. It remains to be seen whether the War succeeded in bending or breaking the will which resisted its innovations.

CHAPTER IX

CENTRALIZING FORCES OF WAR

HAS Germany been united by a stronger bond, or perhaps even been unified by the War? If we are content to look at the centralized form of government, comparing the state of 1934 with that of 1913, the answer is easy enough. It becomes a matter of great doubt, however, if instead of administrative forms, we consider the union of will and coördination of effort among the masses of the people themselves. The intricacy of the problem is demonstrated by the fact that in theory the strongest partisans of a united Germany were liberals and pacifists; while those who—at least before they had lived through twentieth-century warfare—spoke highly of war, expressing the hope that in its furnace the red-hot mass of the whole people could be hammered into a hard, solid structure of the strongest steel, were, most of them, partisans of the old federal system. They were for maintaining the states in their sovereignty within the Reich, with enough financial independence both as to revenue and expenditure to keep their administration going and to provide for a liberal measure of higher education and scientific research; and they wished to leave the power of patronage, undiminished, with the state governments, each of which would have a certain share in the appointment of Reich officials. In 1919, after the monarchs had gone and the official flag of the German Empire had been changed to the black, red, and gold banner of the "Greater Germany" movement of 1848, those who had put their faith in war as the creative force of national unity clung to the emblems and colors of the states as to the last symbols of real national feeling and loyalty. The "unitarians," the partisans of centralized Reich government, after the War, were those who had opposed the war spirit, or at least submitted unwillingly to its reign.[1] They proved themselves fully as intransigent in

---

[1] The pre-war exception to this rule is well known to students of German contemporary history. The party led by Dr. Stresemann, National Liberal before the War and at that period one of the group of the *Kartell* parties— they consisted of the National bloc, voting for a strong army and navy and supporting the conservative régime and the class vote in Prussia against the Catholic Center, the left-wing Liberals, and the Socialists—and known as the German People's party since 1920, had from its beginnings combined cen-

their demand for a central government through a *Reichsreform* as their opponents had been in their praise of the manly virtue of war. Neither of them realized the discrepancy between their ideals and real life; they lacked the realism they pretended to admire and to see admired by foreigners as one of the great qualities of modern Germany. The War, as a means of uniting the people, was welcomed by those who did not really want to exchange federation for central government, while those who wanted the result abhorred war as a means of attaining it.

It is probably due to this strange contradiction between the ideal and the means to attain it that in spite of everything that the War itself, the way in which it ended, the abdication of the monarchs, and the Weimar constitution did to support centralist tendencies in Germany, the battle between unitarians and federalists was by no means decided in favor of the former. After twelve years of Republican single-chamber government from Berlin, a second revolution was needed to give at least a formal victory to the adherents of centralized power in the hands of president, chancellor, and executive government of the Reich.

At first sight this would seem almost incredible, if we consider all the circumstances which favored centralization. During the War, Bavaria, with certain remnants of sovereign rights in the matter of recruiting and military command, was practically the single relic of state sovereignty which seemed to live on. In all the other states monarchs were, except for duties of merely representative character, virtually suspended from their offices, and the general in command of the district became the actual sovereign in their stead. Those who had no military rank were lucky in being simply put aside and left unmolested if they abstained from any interference in political matters; others became technically subordinates of a Prussian general. The Supreme Command, in dealing with the different state governments, felt itself free from any considerations of domestic policy. The

tralist tendencies and the more pronounced form of political patriotism. Its members were *alldeutsch* and *grossdeutsch,* and a warlike nationalism matched with their avowed anti-federalism. "Petty state politics" was their favorite gibe at conservative loyalists, Guelphs, and Bavarian particularism; while their wish to see Germany one of the Great Powers of the world distinguished them from the Radicals and Socialists. That was a distinctive feature of their program; but, after all, they were only one of six great political parties in the old Reich.

first chancellor had, especially during the last ten years of his tenure of office and in two of his greatest speeches after his resignation, insisted on the voluntary character of the Federation which he was believed to have forced on Germany. After he had gone, the Emperor had several times proclaimed himself the superior in rank among the German princes and had experienced one or two rather sensational rebuffs, with public opinion almost undivided on the side of Wittelsbach, Wettin, or Lippe-Biesterfeld against any attempts at Caesarism. During the War the Emperor himself ceased to entertain any idea of personal protagonism. His ambitions were gone; he suffered terribly through such suffering as he was allowed to see; he submitted to the necessities of military rule as did his fellow monarchs in the smaller states, or the burgomasters in the Hanseatic towns. The Supreme Command was the sole authority—with one exception; and that exception is another striking illustration of the centralizing force of war.

Of the two chambers which, under the Constitution of 1871, had to collaborate as legislative bodies for the whole of Germany, the *Bundesrat* had almost completely ceased to exist. A free vote in the Council of the States against a proposal of the Prussian Government, dominated during the War by the Prussian War Ministry, would have been impossible. The federal influence was practically nil, and when it began to revive toward the end of the War against Russia, at the time of the proposal to create one or several Baltic states under German princes, it was quickly put out of court again, because of the rivalry between the reigning houses in that respect if for nothing else. In sharp contrast to the weak hold of the Federal Council, however, the unitarian chamber, the Reichstag, won real power, even in its relations with the military authorities. The Supreme Military Command coöperated with the Reichstag—and by no means only with the Conservatives and National Liberals, but with Catholic Centrists and Democrats from southern Germany and with some of the more ambitious or opportunist members of the Socialist party—in order to carry out its war policy, foreign and domestic, in the face of the Chancellor or of other civil authorities. If the War had lasted longer the great constitutional change in Prussia, the introduction of a general franchise for elections to the Prussian Diet, would have been accomplished through an arrangement between the Supreme Command and the Socialist and Center party leaders in the Reichstag, over the head of the Prussian Government and Parliament. Such was the decline in state and the increase in federal power, as brought about by the War.

The right to appoint magistrates and all kinds of officials had, it is true, remained with the governments of the states and with the municipalities; but during the War patronage in the matter of appointments did not count for much compared with patronage in the matter of military service. To an official as to any other man who was over the normal fighting age, the thing which mattered was whether the Government would be able to claim him for continued domestic civil service as one of the indispensables, or, if not, whether he would be sent to one of the war bureaus, be employed in the administration of the occupied territories, become a propaganda lecturer, a chauffeur, a Red Cross employee, or a staff orderly in the Etappe; and also whether his employment would be in the East, with great hardship and a certain danger of infectious diseases, or in the West, with relative ease and perhaps even the means of sending food back to his family and friends in the famished home country. Bavaria, and to a lesser degree Württemberg and Saxony, had retained the right to decide on the categories of officials and individuals which were to be spared military service if they were over a given age, and if the military commissions had judged them unfit for active service in the trenches or with the artillery. On the whole, however, every German and his dependents knew that his fate was in the hands of a central authority and its delegates rather than in those of the superior authorities of the municipality or the state to which he belonged and which, in peace-time, was his protector as well as his employer. There was nothing unpatriotic in this attitude: an overwhelming majority of these people would certainly have volunteered for service in the trenches if they had been allowed to do so. But volunteering for the front was, after the first months of the War, as strictly impossible as was shamming in order to escape service. Services were not asked for, but commanded.

The only place where non-officials who wished to obtain a record for war activity without entering military service could find opportunities to do so in any number was Berlin, with its multitude of war bureaus both ministerial and—in the case of the most important of them—independent. Employment in the capital, at the seat of the central government, became of an importance which had been quite unknown to German social and political life before the War. An employee of an industrial concern in the Ruhr or in Upper Silesia, or an inspector on an estate in East Prussia or Mecklenburg would, in former times, have looked down on Berlin as the seat of an officious bureaucracy which from time to time made the people who really did the work and lived the life of the country fill out statistical forms and apply for concessions, but did not matter very much otherwise. One of the reigning princes of southern Germany, a man of the highest patriotism and with almost fanatical sense of duty, was well known for expressions of genuine indignation at the mere suggestion of one of his *Landeskinder* entering the service of the Reich. Mobility among members of the civil service was in the main confined to the territory of the state, or, in the case of the bigger states, to a province; for the traditional dislike for Berlin was by no means peculiar to Bavarians or Swabians. Rhinelanders, Silesians, and Pomeranians had the same feeling toward the capital. The War, though it could not change the dislike felt by the provincials for Berlin, at least transformed their contempt for the fussiness of its bureaus into something like awe and respect. The "tempo" of government and, what is more, of political life in general, was set by the people in Berlin. Some of them were certainly rank profiteers or *Drückeberger*—people who tried to escape military service at the front. But they developed a capacity for work, and a spirit of camaraderie to boot, which few observers of the old administration would have thought possible.

Most of this centralization, during the War, went hand in hand with the policy of the military leaders which, though hardly conservative, much less Tory in character, may perhaps best be described as *autoritaire*, some of the members of General Ludendorff's inner circle having a rather hazy notion that giving a command for the sake of giving a command, irrespective of its actual merits, was a highly moral action both on the part of those who gave it and of those who obeyed it without questioning and discussion. The need of the Germans for "leadership," (*Führertum*), became a watchword used in sharp and hostile contrast to the "Marxian" system of self-government. It found favor with the industrialists; and the agrarian leaders, under the influence of men like the *Generallandwirtschaftsdirektor*—General Agricultural Secretary—Kapp, were led to ignore, or perhaps ignored of their own free will, the danger which these high-flown ideas of leadership in the heads of students and farming apprentices (*Volontäre*) involved for the quiet, long-enduring task of cultivating the soil. A generation of young men, each of whom was trained to think that as the future *Duce* he would be able to command not only cheap labor, chiefly of Poles and Wends, but also sunshine and rain, grew up tolerated and even adored by its elders, who should have known better what the peasant's attitude toward the things he cannot command must be. They became the shock troops of a movement which prided itself on being the first attempt to erase every remaining frontier line from the map of the Reich.

After the War, centralization, which had been fostered by the parties of the Right for the sake of the war spirit, became the open aim of the Democrats and Socialists.[2] They fought for and won the decisive influence in the Constituent Assembly which was to save the Reich. They showed themselves even better than their word by giving unstinted help and in some cases by even taking the lead wherever a plebiscite had to decide on the future national fate of a province. One of their intellectual leaders, a convinced pacifist in the best sense of the term, Dr. Köster, was the German Commissioner for the Plebiscite (*Abstimmungskommissar*) in Schleswig; and though at first he was regarded with some suspicion by the peasants and agrarian leaders, he was soon recognized as having high value for victory because of his enthusiastic faith in German unity, the faith of a Socialist who believed in the formation of as great a community of German-speaking citizens as possible.

With many of the Socialists who led and directed the great German effort of reconstruction and reparation after the War, dethronement of a prince who might have been a liberal ruler respected by all classes of the people did not signify an abstract preference for the republican form of government as opposed to a monarchist

[2]. Not of all the parties of the so-called Weimar Coalition. The Catholic Center, though the stronghold of federalism as a rule, at one time became rather inclined, under the influence of its trade-union wing, to join in the Centralist tendencies of the two allied parties. That was the reason why the Bavarian members formed a party of their own, the Bavarian People's party, which, after the downfall of the short-lived Communist and Socialist cabinets, formed the Bavarian Government and was frankly antiunionist, maintaining more or less openly the prospect of a possible restoration of the monarchy in Bavaria.

reign. They were men who had studied modern history and comparative constitutional law more closely than most statesmen of former times; they knew that democracy and "equal opportunity for all" might go with a constitutional hereditary monarchy like the British or Scandinavian, or with a constitutional elective presidency like that of the United States, as well or even better than with a republican régime manipulated by group interests; they knew, in fact, that the deliberate opponent of democracy—fascist government by corporative groups—has often proved more dangerous to monarchy or to hereditary aristocracy than to the *demos*. If the intellectuals among the Socialists united with the masses in forcing the German princes to resign and afterward imposed the republican form of state government on the whole of Germany by a provision in the Weimar Constitution, their object was not the demolition of a few thrones, but the demolition of the sovereignty of the states and the unification of government throughout Germany.

The same is true of the provision which imposed the electoral system chosen for the Reichstag on the smallest as well as on the largest states in the Reich. Proportional representation, in a form which places all electioneering business, the naming of the candidates, the choice of the platform, and the patronage belonging to it in the hands of the central party offices in Berlin[3] was selected as the best possible way for the people to express its will. This was, in part, for abstract reasons of justice and to secure the right of minorities to equal representation in parliament, and in part in reaction against the old electoral system which had served to arrange the constituencies to suit the Government or the party in power, and to favor the conservative agrarian section of the country against the towns. But more than by anything else the intentions of the politicians of the Left in 1919 and the following years were determined by the wish to see the old small constituency abolished in favor of a practically one-constituency scheme for the whole of the Reich. The business of elections and, before the elections, the nomination of candidates,

3. The Bavarian People's party formed an exception in that its headquarters was, of course, Munich; but in lesser scale Bavarian elections showed the same degree of party centralization in the capital as did German elections for the Reichstag. The members of the Bavarian Diet representing the Palatinate or northwestern Franconia had to be nominated by the party. They were not chosen by the constituencies.

was freer and more real under the old system than under the new. The candidate could, it is true, use his influence as a wealthy local magnate to secure nomination, but if he did so, it was a more or less open bid for the seat, and the voters chose to accept it, if they did accept, it, of their own free will. Candidates had to be known to be adopted, and almost everywhere a body of voters who put their trust in a non-party man as their favorite representative had at least a sporting chance of getting him chosen by one of the several parties in the field, or of having him contest the seat as an outsider.

In spite of all this, however, German radicals looked on the small constituencies in the agrarian provinces much in the same way as English radicals looked on pocket boroughs a hundred years ago. The single-constituency system, to them, seemed a bulwark of what the Germans call *Kirchturmpolitik*, the narrow viewpoint of a local politician who cannot see farther in politics than he could actually see if looking from the steeple of the parish church. Or, to give the word another explanation, it is the point of view of one who would be unable to find his way about except by using the church steeple as a landmark. He would, rightly, according to the new electoral system, carry a compass with him, and know how to read his direction from it; and the correctness and universality of the compass would in its turn be controlled by a central authority, a *Reichsanstalt* if not an international office at Geneva. Constituencies would be grouped not around a village church or the town hall of a small country town, but around an industrial area like the Ruhr, or Upper Silesia, or one of the giant municipalities like Hamburg or Frankfurt-Hanau or Berlin. The defects of the German system of proportional representation, especially the list of candidates for the whole Reich in addition to the constituency lists, lay in the inadmissibility of an elector marking his preference for one name on the list and his disapproval of another, the exclusion of by-elections, and the strengthening of party bureaucracy; and all of this today is conceded to be faulty or decidedly wrong even by the partisans of proportional representation as such. But these principles were in 1919 deliberately and wilfully adopted as a means of reinforcing centralization, that is, centralization through a single list of candidates who could collect the votes of the fragments of their party or their religious sect though scattered over the whole area between the Baltic Sea and Switzerland; centralization through voting uniformly for a certain list numbered 1 to 7 or 19 instead of voting for one of seven or nineteen human beings; centralization through the fact that an election had to be a general election or none at all; centralization through a party headquarters in Berlin managing the elections at its own sweet will; centralization, in fact, as the aim which could justify every means to attain it.

The slogan was: if the War has succeeded in bringing *Kleinstaaterei* to an end, Germany may still in a sense say that she has won the War, and that the ashes of devastation have sent the phoenix of national unity flying up to the sky. It is hardly fair to blame the system of proportional representation today for having done its task more completely than those who set it could predict, and for having brought into existence the National Socialist and the Communist parties, the first two parties in German history which could boast the whole Reich for their stronghold while all the others found their strength in regional connections. Under the old electoral system neither would probably have been able to elect to the Reich more than a dozen members each, for the first ten years of the Republic. Under the centralist election system of the Weimar Constitution they managed to elect nearly half of the members between them. That was a direct result of the centralizing forces of war.

The political views of the younger generation, irrespective of party ties and prejudices, show a marked predilection for what academic philosophers of our day like to call "*Ganzheit.*" It might be translated "integration" or "wholeness," or be described as the principle (in opposition to a mere state) of entity. It calls to mind in a pleasant way the mighty things pantheism has done for the emancipation of German thought and feeling from the classical scheme of a good and an evil principle disputing between themselves for the soul and body of man. For "*Ganz*" in German is the best synonym for "Pan"—much better than "All." It serves to strengthen the conceit of personality, in that integration and wholeness can be attained only in an ego, not in a multitude; and it works for nationalist views in politics, too, because it is almost a truism that only a man who is a hundred per cent in one way or another will be able to incorporate *Ganzheit* in himself.

In its application to national life it may mean racial fanaticism combined with a rather disgusting display of eugenics, such as is shown in the writings of one of the professorial members of the National Socialist movement, a man by the name of Günther. That is one of the aftereffects of the War peculiar at a given time and in a given place; but the utmost one can say about them, as far as the theory of government is concerned, is that all this depends on the moral and intellectual state of the country at a given time, and that every nation always gets the kind of parliamentary representation it deserves.

The main problem for all nations, at all times, is the relation between parliament—however good or bad—and the other powers which determine the government, a relation crystallized in the power of non-parliamentary forces to veto an act of parliament, or to dissolve parliament. This problem is not simplified, but on the contrary becomes highly complicated, where that authority is, like parliament, elective, deriving its power from the will of the sovereign people itself, and this, perhaps, in a more direct and unmistakable way than do the members of parliament themselves. From the point of view of that problem it is evident that a parliament with two houses, both representing the community, has a much stronger position than a single chamber can possibly have. The power of dissolution, which may easily under modern circumstances imply the threat of a dictatorial régime, is of necessity paramount over one house of parliament; it is obviously not so if it is confronted by the common intent and declared will of two houses of parliament. That is the more true where the constitution has to provide for a possible clash between federal unionism and separatist tendencies, for in that case one of the houses would embody the vote of the people while the other would represent the interest of the states. The president, according to the Weimar Constitution, could virtually override a vote of the house of representatives because his mandate proceeded directly from the people; and the authority of a party majority in the popular chamber could not possibly supersede that of the man who had been entrusted with the highest office in the state by the vote of the people themselves; but the president would have had to bear with the senate, because it derived its authority from the sovereign power of the component states.

The men who framed the German Constitution knew this well; they were acquainted with the working of the United States' Constitution and of the unwritten law which regulates government in the British Isles. They wanted honestly to establish parliamentary

CHAPTER X

MUNICIPAL IMPERIALISM

SPECIAL attention must be paid to the part the German municipalities took in the movement toward centralization, a part to which the War gave additional weight. Of old the leading municipalities were supporters of the Imperial ideal. In the time of the Holy Roman Empire they had been the allies of emperor-king after emperor-king in their trials of strength with the feudal power of barons and lords spiritual. They had also, occasionally, proved themselves staunch supporters of the reign of law and order against the peasantry. It is one of the peculiarities of German history that Roman law, renascent in the work of learned professors of jurisprudence in the Italian universities, and reshaped to suit modern life in the courts of the town republics and the principalities of northern Italy, was used as a means of simplifying and standardizing the practice of the courts in Germany. Roman law was to be the common law in the literal sense of the word, as a law known to few but applicable to all—except those living under the law of the Church—according to methods and rules elaborated in the sphere of thought untouched by the accidents and inconsistencies of daily life. The first to see the advantage of legal uniformity with its corollary of a greater certainty in the prediction of sentences were the citizen-merchants of the *freie Reichsstädte.* Good patriots that they were, they recognized, after a comparatively short period of diffidence and reluctance to introduce an alien law by decree of the sovereign, that what mattered was not so much the contents of a legal code as the widest possible national application of the law. The German poetry of the late fifteenth and early sixteenth century, written as it had been by independent burghers, clerks, and artisans, like Hans Sachs, bears witness to the haughty contempt the humanistic lawyers of the city courts felt for the rough and tumble practice of the *Dorfgericht,* where the town elders still gave their arbitrary awards according to tradition and their lights, trying to take their law from the facts of the case instead of from a *speculum juris,* or *tractatum,* or perhaps even a written code. Provincial and agrarian peculiarities of pleading and practice persisted to a remarkable extent through the centuries, and were still very noticeable when, in 1879, Germany adopted a uniform judicial code, for the first time in her history. Even today we encounter a Saxon, a Hanseatic, a Rhenish way of dealing with a civil case, especially in the lower courts. In one case it allows the fullest measure of oral pleading before the judge in open court. In another it enforces an elaborate, painstaking preparation in chambers, and relies on documentary evidence or a formal affidavit more than on examination of witnesses and parties, and the arguments of counsel. Even today, irrespective of formal unification, the provinces and the country at large keep to their old distinct customs while the larger towns try to evolve a method of "speedy justice" which satisfies the demand of the many hundreds of thousands of civil cases on the annual calendar of the German courts.

In many other instances the towns threw the weight of their influence in the Council of the Nation into the scale of Imperial unity. It is true that before the War, especially during the Bismarckian period, the importance of municipal policy in the constitutional equilibrium between federal power and the sovereignty of the states had suffered an eclipse. The *Reichstreue*, or loyalty to the Empire, of the upper middle class in the big towns and of its favorite party, the National Liberals, was taken for granted and there seemed to be no special need, from the point of view of the *ratio status*, to pay that attention to their wishes which had had constantly to be paid to the *desiderata* of the landowners or the great industrial trusts. In a possible conflict between the Government of the Reich and that of one of the smaller component states (a conflict between the Reich and the Prussian Government was, at that time, impossible, because the chancellor directed the policy both of the Reich and of Prussia), public opinion in the towns of such a State would have had no say. For instance, taking the case of Bavaria, public opinion in Nürnberg-Fürth or Augsburg would have had no weight. Nor, in the case of Baden, would that of Mannheim-Ludwigshafen or Freiburg. To take another case, the united or organized opinion of such townships as Frankfurt am Main, Cologne, Nürnberg, Leipzig, Magdeburg, Breslau, or Danzig—to name a few cities which had retained a conscious citizenship without having ever been the residence of a court— could not have exercised a real influence on the decisions of the Government, or even have influenced a debate in Parliament. During the whole of that period and far on in the reign of William the Second, it was a typical phenomenon that the lord mayors of some of the largest cities (some indeed with populations far exceeding those of certain of the smaller German principalities) who had seats, ex officiis, in the Second Chamber, the *Herrenhaus*—or the *Ständekammer*, in the case of one state—or who had been called to sit in them by the royal prerogative, as exercised through the nomination of members, never came to possess anything like real parliamentary power and influence, either singly or as a body.

A slight change had come through William the Second's predisposition in favor of technical progress, and a development of resources which expressed itself in outward munificence. Official statuary, the construction of public buildings he liked to encourage and in some cases to superintend, the founding of new high schools for the natural sciences and other kinds of research work, the lending of his countenance to social welfare institutions and hospitals, historical pageants and musical festivals with competitive part-singing for male choirs—all this brought the Emperor into close and constant contact with almost every city in Prussia, and most of the German towns outside his own kingdom, and made him ready to listen and to talk to the men in authority in municipalities like Hamburg, Frankfurt am Main, Munich, or Cologne. The curious—because entirely voluntary, non-military and non-feudal—special link between the sovereign and his subjects in the larger cities of the realm had begun to reaffirm itself.

A change of greater importance, however, was due to the War and to war administration in the homeland. From the military point of view, war cannot be said to forward the interests of the population of a big town. Peasants and farmhands are the best soldiers. The provinces have to provide the workingmen employed in war industry. Youths from the smaller university towns are the most ardent volunteers; whereas in such metropolises as Berlin, Hamburg, or Frankfurt-Hanau the masses of the younger workingmen and employees incline to political radicalism, and many of them are both physically unfit and intellectually overeducated. In addition to that, a town is much more difficult to "comb" than the country. It gives many more opportunities for escaping active military service to those who wish to do so than a place in the country where everybody knows everybody else. If the War had been waged as a purely military affair, towns would have had no chance to strengthen their national positions by the part they took in it. As soon, however, as the War became a twofold business, on the one hand one of strategy, military technique, and battles, and, on the other, one of physical endurance for the civilians, propaganda, and destruction of public morals, the importance of war administration through the municipalities became self-evident. Most of the war bureaus had their central offices in the capital of the Reich; and the task of coöperating with them soon made the military authority of the district of Berlin, or the *Generalkommando in den Marken,* one of the most important political bodies in the Reich. Food administration, it is true, could not be centralized in Berlin. Even the most convinced advocates of strong central leadership for the whole of Germany had to own that when it came to the milking of Frisian cattle, the digging of potatoes and beet roots in Saxony, and the egg laying of Swabian poultry, it would hardly do to attempt to put such things under the control of a war food bureau, a *Kriegsernährungsamt,* none of whose officials had ever milked a cow or plowed a field or even poked his nose into a poultry farm. It was difficult enough merely to get the farmers to agree to any control at all, even by one of their own people, their prefect (*Landrat* or *Bezirksamtmann*), and to permit their surplus produce—after they had subtracted the precise official quantities of food due themselves—to go the way of forced sale at official prices, plus the cost of a distributing bureau and its staff as well as the usual middleman's share. The task would have been enormously greater if the bureau and the staff of the bureau, both in themselves hateful things to the farmer, had had its seat in Berlin or Munich or Stuttgart instead of in the nearest town, to which in normal times he carried his produce and where he put it on sale in the open market.

Thus, at least, during the first half of the War, while some kind of food could still be produced in Germany or obtained from neighboring neutral countries in sufficient quantities to allow of a certain administrative freedom in handling it, the Central Government was well content to leave the responsibility of maintaining a certain standard of subsistence to the local authorities. Civil administration, so far as it was in the hands of the states themselves, was more or less put aside by the handing over of all the essential services to the local military commanding officers. Municipal administrations had experienced changes in personnel; for all officers of reserve had had to join their regiments at once, and they had known a very heavy death rate during the first months of the War. Otherwise, the governments of towns and cities remained comparatively unchanged. They were outside, or beneath, the sphere of political activity reserved for military administration. The fact that municipal government was independent of the ordinary civil service helped, in this contingency, more than anybody could have expected.[1] While bureaucratic routine suffered severely from the interruption of its administrative reign, town clerks and even lower-grade officials took a new pride in the importance of their functions. They developed a group feeling not unlike that of trade-union secretaries or unofficial leaders of the Youth Movement. They had been overshadowed by the omnipotence of the civil service in normal peaceful times; but during the War they assumed, or believed they were now assuming, their due share in the management of national affairs. They had one advantage over both the ordinary civil servant and the officer of a *Generalkommando*. Theirs was a more modest social standing and, therefore, a closer contact with the economic condition of the people in their daily life. Their mental attitude was more like that of employees in private banks, or tobacconists, apothecaries, officials of public utilities companies, building contractors, or other middle-class tradesmen than that of officers, whether civil or military, who have to hold aloof from the daily round of gossip, humble pleasures, and the petty struggle for life. They were familiar with the byways of trade, and those little applications of *do ut des* which make every unofficial administration run more smoothly than any official bureaucracy ever can, because of its healthy abhorrence of anything even distantly savoring of bribery. Theirs was an easier way of taking life, a touch of *nihil humanum a me alienum puto*, that is, of broad humanity. In middle and southern Germany, at least they possessed a greater capacity to get out of fixes they had got themselves into. They could do it by making a joke about their own failings, perhaps warning a man who had cheated them that next time they would get their own back again by means of the lesson they had learned

1. The following sentences do not apply, of course, to the administration of the three Hanseatic city-states. Hamburg, Bremen, and Lübeck differed from inland towns like Frankfurt, Nürnberg, or Leipzig in that the administration of the municipality, in the former, was merged in the civil service of the state.

from him. And, by possessing such resources as this, they were incomparably better organizers of war economics, of *Kriegswirtschaft*, in its smaller details, than their colleagues of the army or the civil service.

During the later stages of the War the confidential relations between the Supreme Command and the other central authorities and the municipalities continued, though they changed in nature. Under a genuine scarcity of food, and in many cases with the complete disappearance of certain kinds from the open market, recriminations between the townspeople and the farmers of the surrounding district every day became more bitter, most of all in the case of the provincial towns of medium size which up to 1916 had had normal open markets for vegetables and had been regularly provided with dairy products, even under the card system. Relations between the older citizen families of the towns and the peasants in the neighboring villages were in many cases of a standing that went back centuries. Since time immemorial the farmer's wife, after having sold her heads of lettuce or cabbage, or her bundles of asparagus, peas, and beans in the weekly market, had gone to the same shop, one generation after another, to buy household articles, glassware, or clothes; while domestic servants in town houses were, as a rule, taken from the country district around the town. And beneath the superficial varnish of nineteenth-century fashions, life was still making an extensive use of its old connecting links, its *Bindemittel*, of family relations and personal friendships and loyalties. By 1917 even those connections had been either broken or, if they continued, had to be concealed in order to escape fines and confiscations. On the main road, where the gates had stood in the Middle Ages, there was a picket of gendarmes whose duty it was to search vehicles and even pedestrians who seemed of too portentous a size; for they might have been picking up a few eggs or a piece of bacon from their old friends in some village two or three hours from town, or might be carrying a sack of potatoes in the baby carriage, with the baby fast asleep on top of the precious load. At that time town and country were distinctly hostile to each other, and it was now the turn of the central war bureaus to help the municipalities by allotting to them food and victuals which had been taken from the peasants and landowners, or had come in from allied and neutral countries.

Still the union, or at least the close coöperation, between central and local government remained a strong element of centralization. The physical existence of each human being, and food and housing for his family, depended, like the existence of the nation itself, on either the central government of the Reich or on the ability of the local authorities to find the necessary provisions, whether by making direct demands upon producers or by securing ample allotments from the central office. And, after they had found the needed provisions, they had to be economical with them. The Empire and its towns governed Germany between them, while the civil-service administrations of the component states became of less and less importance. To a casual observer it almost seemed as if they were, all of them, "people who could be dispensed with," or who were *abkömmlich*, as the technical word for cannon fodder expressed it. They could not feed the people, they could not house them or help them mend their clothes; and as for regulations and bylaws, the Central Government issued so many emergency decrees on questions of administrative detail that even in that respect the field for state activities was very restricted.

Looking back on the development of local government during the War—from the point of view of 1934—it seems difficult to say whether the material growth of the burden and responsibilities of local government led, in a logical sequence of events, to the present difficulties of municipal administration and the financial distress of most of the greater towns in Germany, which was such an important factor in the economic crisis of 1930, or whether, if the War had ended otherwise and the transition from the pre-war standard of life to the present condition of war indebtedness and general economic distress had been smoother, the municipalities might not have proved equal to their greater task.

It is certain that during the last two years of the War, even apart from the difficulties of food and the shortage of coal, the towns were the first to experience some of the hardships from which the economic and political constitution of Germany had to suffer in the later period of the Republic, and it seems equally certain that the nervous tension which makes the task of the Central Government and of the administration of the great towns in Germany more difficult than even unemployment and destitution would explain, is in the main due to the comparisons people are constantly making between their present-day condition and the traditional conception of what a well-ordered community should offer its inhabitants in the way of public-health service, cleanliness, education, opportunities for recreation, social welfare, protection against all kinds of abuses, and general security of life. This traditional view of what one should expect from municipal government goes much farther back, of course, than mere pre-war times—to a time, indeed, which has no links with modern life. It was built up in the course of at least five centuries, during which Germany, while she never had a center like Paris, Rome, London, Vienna, or Moscow, always had a dozen or more cities of stronger individuality, wealth, and self-reliance than any provincial town in other countries except Italy in the early Middle Ages; and Germany also had a corresponding number of universities and other seats of learning which, like the Free Towns, felt a direct allegiance to Germany as a whole and, at the same time, put the demands of the middle class for higher education, and a well-ordered and even an easy life, at higher levels than those found in other countries of greater wealth and older civilization.

Germany had no doctrinal notion of the political value of local government as a ferment of national culture and as a means of education in politics for squirearchy and bourgeoisie alike, until the liberal reformers about the middle of the last century introduced the English system of government to their countrymen in Central Europe. But Germany's tasks in local government, quietly (if proudly) fulfilled by municipalities throughout German-speaking areas, had a history that went farther back than those of any other European country. The municipality had to be responsible for all public utilities, for hygiene and sanitation, for hospitals for the poor, for almshouses and *Spittel*, or, as Bavaria calls them, *Ehehaltenhaus*, for high-school education, public libraries, assembly halls, civic theaters; for recreation grounds, gardens and woods, city planning, which was one of the chief activities of *Bürgermeister* and *Magistrat* long before the term became familiar to English readers; and, if a river ran through the town, the municipality charged itself with the public baths and waterfront. It controlled the police, and was the overseer of weights and measures, even of public morals. In the case of a university town, the municipality used to provide part at least of the buildings and institutions—the hospitals, museums of fine arts, and historical collections—and it likewise furnished the housing facilities both for professors and students, though the universities themselves, up to the end of the War, were state endowed and, financially at least, did not depend upon the exchequer of the town.[2]

It is evident from a mere glance at the catalogue of municipal activities that the power and responsibility of local government was of the first magnitude in the German cities, and this not only in the case of the *Grosstädte* (those of over 100,000 inhabitants), but in most of the cities of 60,000 or more, and even of certain smaller ones, notable for their historical associations, or as seats of universities, or as the towns nearest to some rising industrial area. The mayor and the town councilors, of whom some used to be appointed, others elected, and most of whom drew salaries of only moderate size, had to decide on the allocation of public money, raised by independent city taxation. They could try to make their towns resplendent because of their educational institutions, or their possession of some famous playhouse or museum of continental fame such as that at Mannheim—a typically industrial riverside town. Or one might cite Essen, with its *Folkwang*, or Nürnberg, with its German Museum. Or they could likewise make their town a model because of its social welfare institutions, or its system of traffic regulation or sanitation. They could foster a change from provincial sleepiness to industrial activity by offering an undeveloped area in the vicinity for factory building, and by promoting steam and electric power development in connection with its waterway. Or they could choose to make their municipality a garden city, attractive to those numerous well-to-do pensioners, retired army officers, judges, or government officials who were free to select a domicile in such a German beauty spot and so contribute to its sources of taxation. Fortified walls might be razed if the relations of an ambitious and energetic mayor (*Stadtoberhaupt*) with the military authorities were friendly enough for him to gain permission; and city planning on a large scale might follow. Or the mayor might perhaps put himself at the head of a movement for the building of a canal that would connect his town with one of the great river systems of Germany and therefore with the sea.

2. Of the three German universities which have been opened since 1914, one, that of Hamburg, is a normal public university endowed by the State of Hamburg, which is a city-state whose state territory and municipal area are almost completely identical; the other two, in Frankfurt am Main and in Cologne, belong to a new type, one with mixed state and civic support and control.

The freedom to adopt a policy tending toward any of those goals gave the heads of the local government a position far above that of a cabinet minister in most of the German states; and in the nineteenth century the spirit of liberal competition between the Residenz, a seat of government like Karlsruhe or Schwerin or Dresden, and a free township in its neighborhood like Mannheim, Stettin, Leipzig, or Magdeburg—or, to recall the famous rivalries of the classical period, between Goethe's Weimar and Schiller's Jena—went far to foster civic independence and self-reliance.

The War bereft them of the best part of this freedom. Up to 1914 the diversity of interest and temperament in the different regions of the Reich had been allowed free play, thus permitting each community to feel that it represented in its own peculiar way an essential trait in the German public character. Freedom made for unity, while the unity won with the fervent support of the towns in 1870 visibly protected the free development of municipal activities. A war of brief duration might have made little change in that respect, or might even have brought the Central Government and the city administrations into still closer contact and mutual dependence. When the War dragged itself out, however, some of the most important functions of city government, in the fulfilment of which the leaders of German self-government had delighted, had to be abandoned for new tasks giving them much less chance for initiative than they had had under the old régime.

The most urgent of the War's demands upon municipal authorities was for the provision of, at first, temporary, and later on, permanent abodes for the civil population that had had to be evacuated from areas threatened by actual trench warfare or by devastation, either from bombardment or because of strategic advances or retreats. No previous war had presented this problem, that of quartering the population of whole districts and provinces upon a few towns in the remaining part of the country, with the same magnitude as did the Great War; and, from its very beginning, this held true in Belgium and northern France, in East Prussia, in the Polish territories of the three Empires and Galicia, and in Alsace-Lorraine. It is essentially a problem of modern warfare, and we may assume that it will be with us always. In future the mobilization plan of a country which has to defend an unprotected frontier against the offensive movement which the enemy will probably make during the first two or three weeks after the beginning of hostilities will consist, to a considerable part, in providing amply for the evacuation of the area exposed to the first wave of enemy invasion, and for distributing those who have been ordered away, especially women and children, among the more distant provinces, or, if war is threatened on two frontiers at the same time, among the central provinces of the country. It will have to be a systematic *Einquartierung,* or billeting, such as had been practiced for many years on the occasion of major army maneuvers; and special care will probably be taken in future to quarter as many fugitives as possible on the smaller villages and to try to use them as farmhands and domestic help during the course of the war.

No provision of that kind had been made when the War broke out. The General Staff had been concerned only with the military technique of mobilization and with keeping civilians out of the way during the mobilization period. Staff officers had, most of them, a terrible way of shouting, "I am not to be disturbed on any pretext," at anything and anybody which presented a case unforeseen and not arranged for in the mobilization plan. They had, moreover, been educated to believe, first of all, in the superior merit of attack as such over defense as such—the pernicious result of the ill-considered and much abused maxim which says that attack is the most efficient means of defense. When the fugitives reached German territory, behind the range of guns and enemy patrols, during those first months of the War which saw the Russian invasion in the northeast and the battles in southern Alsace, such fugitives were seen to have left their homes in disorder and panic. During their days and nights of irregular flight most of them had gone through sufferings which at that time still seemed the most cruel the present generation had experienced; and, in spite of the fact that everybody was ready to show them hospitality and to pity them as the first victims of the cruelty of war, they felt helplessly stranded and lost. No organization, except voluntary patriotic or charity associations, was ready to take moral and social care of them, to settle them as far as possible in at least temporary work, or to find them some new chance to maintain themselves as active members of the community. The majority of the fugitives, at any rate during the first period, came from the country, from villages, or small towns. They were the families of lower-grade officials, of clerks, shopkeepers, artisans, and peasants; and only a small percentage of them found new homes or occupations in surroundings either of the same standard or similar to those they had left. Even in the case of the families of landed proprietors in the east whose manorial seats had been ransacked or burned down, only a few found a refuge in those great estates in Pomerania, Brandenburg, or Silesia, which enjoyed immunity from all the direct ravages of war that existed nowhere else in Germany. They were extremely unwilling to accept their change of fortune as something final, something to be put up with and to be overcome by a resolution to begin life afresh. They fomented opposition to the Government for its being, as they saw it, slow and slack in carrying on the War and gaining that decisive victory which would reinstate them in their former possessions and compensate them for their losses. They advocated the most drastic measures of retaliation against the enemy, eye for eye, tooth for tooth, looting for looting. In short, not from any special malice or ineptitude, but because they were out of social gear, they did exactly the things best calculated to lessen every chance of winning that victory which, they claimed, was due them.

During the later stages of the War new batches of fugitives came in, mainly repatriated Germans from Great Britain and the British Dominions, from Africa, from the Far East; and in probably still greater numbers, there were also Austrian, Polish, and German Jews or people of Jewish descent from the eastern provinces of Germany and Austria, southwestern Russia, Rumania, and Bessarabia. In the case of the former, the change in their social position was simply appalling. Many of them had been very prosperous as merchants, farmers, or traders in the colonies. They had been accustomed to administer large estates. They had built up plantations or factories, or were handling whole shiploads of precious raw materials; and they had lost practically everything. For their savings had been invested in securities in their adopted country or deposited in its banks and thus sequestrated as enemy property. They had, most of them, suffered the humiliation of the white man who is destitute, and perhaps, in addition to that, who has been sent to prison, put to forced labor or even beaten, with the Negro or Malay workers of his former domain—with Chinese or Japanese coolies standing by and looking on. As enemy civilians, they had smarted under the special grievance of war measures which had come as a complete surprise to them, every German having been inoculated with the firm conviction that the first law of war was to have men in uniform belonging to the regular armed forces fight out the war alone, leaving civilians, and even the private property and the business affairs of soldiers, entirely outside the range of the war's activities. These *Auslanddeutschen*, "outlander Germans," as they came to be called, also drifted into the towns, and waited for the fortunes of war to change. They claimed indemnities from the Reich, and cursed the countries from which they had to flee the more heartily because, in many cases, they had loved those countries more than the country of their birth, and had honestly done their best to contribute to their national wealth and well-being.

As for the Jewish immigrants, most of them were townspeople and had been accustomed, in pre-war times, to live under conditions appreciably worse than those they found in the poorer quarters of German towns. And an additional source of irritation and constant complaint between the native citizens and the newcomers lay in the fact that the habits and business codes of the latter were different, and, in the opinion of Germans, distinctly inferior to those of German traders, or even peddlers. The Jewish newcomers were accustomed to bargain for the sake of bargaining. They offered fantastically low prices for the things they wanted to buy, and asked absurdly high ones for anything they had to sell. A German, however, is inclined to assume that things have an absolute value dependent on good or bad workmanship or quality, and that to try to set prices which do not recognize this value means to cheat either the buyer or the seller. Moreover, the eastern Jews, Ukrainians, Poles, and even Russians, regarded a more or less open bribe as an ordinary part of a business transaction; whereas in Germany bribetaking or giving, at least among the great mass of small officials and among the lower middle class generally, was a degrading thing, something to be shunned by a man who had any self-respect. As for the higher walks of business life, if it was not unknown in them, it tried at any rate to hide itself under the form of some special fee or bonus. The Jewish middleman, particularly during the last two years of the blockade, served the German food administration extremely well by finding hidden supplies, getting the peasants to sell their corn, and by smuggling provisions through the lines, in fact, by doing all those things that the military administration would have been unable to do even if aid in the shape of the best civil experts in agriculture and forestry had been sent to the occupied territories. The same things, however, when done by these Jewish peddlers and agents in Germany, worked like madness in the brains of those German politicians and economists who had exulted over the organization of the food supplies brought from the Ukraine during the War.

Besides being so many elements of instability and irritation in German politics the newcomers proved a real and enduring burden on municipal government. The situation, as it had developed in most of the German towns of middle size, and in all the large cities, was certainly peculiar to this war. It could arise only in a country which was blockaded on every front as Germany was, except to a certain degree on the extreme southeast. There some leakage at least occurred up to the end of the War. But on the other hand, the frontiers dividing Germany from her small neutral neighbors came to be almost hermetically sealed under the system of Allied surveillance. No such situation could have developed, at least to such a degree, in a country like France or Russia, because neither has anything to compare, in numbers or in wealth, with the German communities in foreign countries, or *Auslanddeutschtum.* Moreover, in the towns of France and Russia, the population is less dense than it was in those of Germany even before the flooding back into the Reich's present-day area of masses of people from Posnania and Alsace-Lorraine. Finally, the change would not have affected France or any other western country as violently, because they are not exposed to a direct inflow of what was practically a torrent of Easterners who swamped every kind of petty trading, and had a great influence on Germany's organs of publicity as well. Other countries might also have been better able to cope with the new situation as it arose. Germany, in this matter, again showed a marked inability to meet a surprise development, or—to put it on a lower plane—to make the best of a bad business. On paper it seemed that war must of necessity diminish the existing overcrowding difficulties in the towns. For millions of men, a huge proportion of them single men, were on military service in foreign countries. Hundreds of thousands had been killed. More hundreds of thousands were prisoners. There had been an exodus of practically all foreigners who had lived in the country at the outbreak of war. And all this, taken together, should have left abundant housing space, and certainly enough mere vacant rooms to accommodate those whom the War sent back to Germany from foreign parts.

On paper, yes. But in reality the facts were quite the other way. In the second year of the War a shortage of housing became perceptible. In the third year, when the return flow of Germans and their families from England and the colonies began in earnest, stock was taken of all available accommodation, and compulsory billeting began. Even in a small university town, where the lower middle-class population in peace-time had in part made its living by letting rooms to the few thousand students during the college terms, rooms and sleeping space became scarce, though the number of actual students had dwindled to one or two hundred during the last war-time terms; and such students were, most of them, the incapacitated sons or daughters of the townspeople. Compulsory billeting is a very unpopular thing. In Germany it often meant a complete dislocation of the life of apartments and small houses, if they could not be divided into separate apartments. Kitchen, scullery, and cellar, sometimes even the lavatories were used in common by various groups of people living on the same floor or at least in the same house. As in so many other war-time instances, moral deterioration set in almost before physical conditions became intolerable. "Middletown" is everywhere prone to scandalmongering and to sitting in judgment on the behavior of the family next door. In the smaller German towns the friendly *Kaffeeklatsch*—gossip over the afternoon coffee—had been one of the familiar elements of provincial life. Indeed, on the whole, it was inclined to be good-natured gossip, and, if anything, it made for regularity and thrift. But war, always a terrible incentive to spying on a neighbor's patriotism, was given a double and treble chance of setting people of different habits and opinions against one another when a family of lower social standing, or belonging to another faith, or perhaps only to another part of the country—with another conception of cleanliness, outspokenness, and moral courage —was quartered on the occupants of a house of seven or eight rooms. From the first it fell to the lot of the municipal authorities to bear the responsibility for the allotment of rooms to the *Wohnungssuchenden* and the *Wohnungsberechtigten*, those in need of rooms and those entitled to have rooms allotted to them; and it was a responsibility far heavier than any imposed on them by such important decisions as they had been called upon to make, on their own judgment, in pre-war times. Then, when a *Bürgermeister* or town councilor made a wrong decision, he might have had to resign, or might not have been reëlected when his term was over. But such cases only occurred perhaps once or twice in a lifetime. During the days of the special housing board, with its compulsory billeting and its requisitioning of any available room, the chances of making decisions which might arouse furious criticism, complaints of bribery and favoritism, and endless worry for the officials responsible occurred by the thousand.[3]

3. One of the most important factors in the economic development of the post-inflation period in Germany, the imposition of a special tax on occupied buildings, the proceeds of which should, in the main, serve to lend support to the building trade and allow it to build great blocks of cheap flats in the suburbs of the big cities, is at least indirectly connected with the war developments mentioned above. It is directly due to the effect which inflation, on the scale of 1922 and 1923, had on mortgages. All mortgages on German real estate had, according to law, to be in terms of German currency; and therefore with the value of the mark, the value of such mortgages disappeared completely, to be, a few years later, revalued at some 25 per cent or less of their former value. The profit accruing to the owner of a house through this elimination of indebtedness (representing in many cases a considerable proportion of the purchase price) was, in the case of a house left on his hands, diminished to some extent by the loss he suffered through the rents being paid in paper marks—that is, not being paid at all. With the stabilization of the mark, however, he was able to collect rents again, though not beyond a maximum, and legally fixed, ratio to pre-war rents. There were now two irrational distinctions which seemed unjust to the bulk of public opinion. One was the distinction between the leaseholder of an old (pre-inflation) house or apartment who paid only a moderate "peace rent," *Friedensmiete*, and the would-be leaseholder who had to find himself an apartment in one of the new buildings, and had to pay as much as the owner asked for it. The other injustice was the difference between a building which had been mortgaged and had retained its value while the mortgage was automatically and without any merit of the owner reduced by at least 75 per cent, and a building which was not mortgaged, and on which inflation, therefore, had not been able to work the same kind of miracle. The *Hauszinssteuer*, or house-rent tax, was thought to be a remedy for both these injustices at the same time. It took the form of a tax which was roughly calculated on the basis of the interest the mortgagee would have been obliged to pay to his creditor if inflation had not freed him of his debt. This explains why the man who lives in his own house has to pay a housing tax of the same rate as the man who lets his house. It is not the rent of the leaseholders which forms the basis of the calculation or justifies the tax, but the former mortgage, and the interest on that mortgage that has to be paid by the owner of the house whether he inhabits

MUNICIPAL IMPERIALISM

A second matter in which municipal government began to overreach itself during the War was social welfare and public charity control. It is extremely difficult to say with any certainty or even to make a near guess at the primal origin of the state of things which prevailed from 1925 on. At the beginning of the War, the Red Cross organizations went to work in every town; and if they had succeeded in uniting all efforts to help the families of those on active service, support widows and orphans, and find work for the disabled soldiers irrespective of class, religious belief, and party politics, it is evident that the welfare officialdom which in Germany had arisen many years before the War and had almost gained the victory over the old forms of private charity,[4] would have experi-

---

it himself or not. (It is one of the strange consequences of the housing tax that the owner can free himself from paying the tax by letting the house remain empty.) So far the tax is a preventive against unearned profit for the owner. Its main justification with public opinion, however, was—and still is —the help given to people who had to find apartments after the War or after the inflation. The proceeds of the tax, one of the few sources of independent income remaining to municipalities, had to be used to reduce the cost of new buildings, and, consequently, the amount of rent paid for those buildings. The history of the *Hauszinssteuer* in Germany, from 1925 to its gradual abolition in 1932, forms an important chapter in the history of post-war attempts to continue that socialization in Germany which the War had begun. It is beyond the scope of this part of the Economic and Social History; for without inflation, this kind of municipal tax and direct levy on a form of old capital in order to allow for the easier formation of new, on the same lines, would not have resulted from the War and from the extension the War gave to the functions of city administration. Even inflation need not have been of the special kind which justifies almost any measure of compulsory redistribution of capital. On the other hand, there can be hardly any doubt but that the trend of events which led to this result began during the later stages of the War, when lack of foresight (as distinct from, and sometimes the opposite of, planning and fixing the formal competence of administrative bodies) led to misdirection of the stream of immigrants and reëmigrants, and assigned to the city administrations a new set of powers which were beyond the natural scope of their activities.

4. One of the protagonists of standardizing charity, Dr. W. Polligkeit, head of the Private Charity Center, the *Zentrale für private Fürsorge,* in Frankfurt am Main, gives an interesting description of the general uncertainty which prevailed as to future development of welfare work at the end of the War, in an article in the *Handbuch der Politik* (3d ed., 1921) III, 146 ff. He ends with the demand for centralization through the creation of *Wohlfahrtsämter.* "In this respect, it is of interest to note the rapid growth

enced a serious setback, and a really efficient, impartial, warm-hearted, and decidedly coöperative administration of charity, poor laws, and *Arbeitsbeschaffung*—labor bureaus—(including the widest facilities for the adoption and encouragement of every honest attempt at non-political communism) could have outlived the end of the War and the constitutional changes which resulted from it. Instead of that, Red Cross activities themselves became part of the official overorganization which, in the end, stifled individual efforts and, in the case of the civilian victims of the War, helped to transfer their entire care to the Government, which, in its turn, shifted part of this responsibility to the municipalities.

In the case of social welfare policy, the municipalities were close associates of the Central Government in those centralizing tendencies which largely coincided with the social policy initiated during the first years of the reign of Emperor William the Second. The number of towns with more than 10,000 inhabitants had, between the census of 1895 and that of 1910, risen from 28 to 48, and in fact, since a few towns came very near the 10,000 mark, had practically doubled. At the same time, a comparison of these two censuses from the standpoint of employment, shows that industrial urban workers had increased by a total of almost 50 per cent, and by almost 100 per cent in the cities with more than 10,000 inhabitants. The increase of urban areas, the drawing of smaller suburban towns and villages into the swiftly increasing and rapidly circling orbit of the metropolis went hand in hand with the industrialization of the country at large. It came as a more or less natural result of this traditional union of imperial and municipal policy that when unem-

of the movement for the establishment of public welfare boards, to permit of local welfare work being centralized and standardized according to a general plan. Such boards are to be found in towns and rural districts, in the provinces and in central state departments. They are, at present, voluntary organizations of the most varying type, even though they are called by the same name. It is less for the sake of a system than for practical reasons that a coordination of the different branches of welfare work under a unifying control is advocated." The last sentence should not be taken too literally; the school of thought to which Dr. Polligkeit belongs has long advocated centralization *Zusammenfassung* on systematic grounds. Another popular essay by a member of the Frankfurt organization is that by Dr. Chr. Klumker on "*Die Organisation der Fürsorge für hilfsbedürftige Jugend*" ("Charity Organization for Deserving Youth"), in *Frauen-Vormundschaft* (Stiftungsverlag Potsdam, 1917).

ployment insurance (within the general system of social insurances) was introduced, and when—as experience seemed to demonstrate the insufficiency of the method primarily adopted—had twice within six years to be reorganized, the municipalities and the districts, but not the states, had to share the responsibility with the Reich.

The Reich, at first sight, seemed to take a considerable burden off the cities and towns. Until unemployment insurance was introduced under the poor law, they had to deal with at least some of the worst cases of unemployment, those where the savings of better times and the possibilities of family support or private organizations had been exhausted. Looking at the problem from this point of view it seemed only fair that after a first period of provision for the maintenance of the unemployed during which the central authorities (with the Reich as guarantor in case of a deficit) were solely responsible, and after a second period of joint responsibility by both the Reich and the local administrative bodies (this only in case of abnormally prolonged unemployment because of an economic crisis which, as the initiators of the scheme thought, was certainly not to be expected but might possibly occur) the local bodies should finally take care of those apparently very improbable cases where unemployed persons—apart from those disabled by sickness or accident and old age—after being helped by the two stages of insurance benefit, in the strict sense, and by "crisis aid," as well, should still be unemployed and without means of subsistence. The calculation on which this reasoning relied was speedily belied by the facts; it had omitted the difference between the old kind of poor-law assistance and the new, the claim of the unemployed to be compensated for the loss of labor, and, more than that, to be maintained by State aid, till they got work again. Poor-law assistance is given solely on satisfactory evidence, not only of individual poverty, but of the non-existence of other persons or organizations that could and should assist the one in need; and the administrative body from which assistance was to come was practically a judge over its own case when it was a question of the absolute need for help. Regulations and the actual administration of the poor law could be made more rigid or relaxed according to the means at the disposal of the authorities concerned. Above all, they were expected, and in any case were certainly entitled, to work in the closest coöperation with the churches, with the guilds, trade-unions, and other sources of money and also with the regular charity organizations. There were cases, and quite legitimately so, where the policy of the responsible administrators of a large city was consciously directed to obtaining as many pious and charitable endowments and foundations as possible from wealthy citizens, in order to relieve the ordinary budget of the town from the demands of poor-law assistance. Criticism of such a policy, which had seemed rather doctrinaire, was strangely justified at the time of the inflation; for endowments legally obliged to subscribe to State and communal loans were harder hit by the depreciation of the currency than any other kind of investment except trust funds for widows or orphans, which were condemned by the investment regulations to vanish into nothingness, along with the value of the mark. On the whole, however, the poor-law payments could always, in some way or other, be adjusted to the general economic situation. Those who earned their living by hard work and paid taxes on their incomes could feel sure that the authorities looked very closely and conscientiously into the cases in which assistance from public funds was to be given, and that whatever was given as public alms constituted the discharge of a real obligation. All that changed, of necessity, with the adoption of the insurance plan. It is of the very essence of that plan that the payments made to the unemployed are not what in England is now called a dole, or an alms, or a charity, or indeed any sort of protection from distress and destitution, but the fulfilment of a legal claim, based on a contract of labor, a collective agreement, *Kollektivvertrag*, between every individual worker and the community which, in theory, was obliged to find work for him. He himself and his employer have paid premiums; the relation between the premium paid and the insurance money has been calculated by actuaries on the basis of averages taken from millions and millions of cases. This means that no single case can be dealt with on its own merits, that is, on considerations based on the special need of this or that man or woman and the possibility of meeting that need in any other way. It means, further, that an error in calculation is charged against the insurance company, in this case the State and, in the last resort, the municipalities. They cannot alter the amount nor can they investigate the conditions of the insured. If the insured can show that he or she has an insurance contract and is out of work the insured must be paid the weekly or monthly sum fixed by law.

The effect on the budget of the German local units which had to provide for this third group of the unemployed, the *Wohlfahrtserwerbslosen*, was terrific. We take the latest statistics from an article in *Tagebuch*,[5] showing the yearly gross deficit—that is to say, the expenses which are not covered by the revenue that goes with them—and the part of social welfare expenses in the budget:

Year	Total Net Expenditures	Social Welfare	The Unemployed	Personal Expenses	Other Expenses	Taxes	Receipts from Other Income
1913	1804[6]	290	2	888	626	1503	278
1925	3876	1090	114	1624	1162	3203	412
1926	4346	1383	200	1691	2270	3584	643
1927	4682	1306	...[7]	1902	1474	4090	507
1928	5160	1470	150	2200	1490	4400	621
1929	5500	1790	268	2200	1510	4350	621
1930[8]	5600	2270	595	2200	1130	4150	590
1931[8]	....	....	1040[9]	1950	....	....	...

Another table appearing in the same article shows the development of expenses in the budget of 41 cities (excluding Berlin, Munich, and Cologne).

Year	Total Expenses	Welfare Expenses	Schools	Boards	General Cost of Administration	Amount Paid for Salaries only
1929	1914.3[6]	334.9	364.9	166.9	140.3	603.3
1930	1938.9	412.8	357.5	170.6	134.6	601.5
1931	2053.0	610.3	329.2	147.5	132.0	565.8

5. Dr. Leopold Heinemann, "*Der Zusammenbruch der Städte*" ("The Collapse of the Cities"), August 22, 1931, p. 1320. And the expression "the *collapse* or *breakdown* of municipal government" was one which at that time was freely used in Germany.

6. All sums in millions of marks.

7. In 1927 the *Reichsanstalt*—the Imperial Fund—for unemployment insurance was established in order to take the burden of the 200 million marks, which seemed excessive, off the municipal and other local budgets. The rise in personal expenses in the same year, and in 1928, was due to a general increase in salaries, not to an increase in the number of salaried persons.

8. For 1930 and 1931 the expenses and receipts are those in the estimates, while for the earlier years the actual figures have been used.

9. The number of the unemployed on the pay list of the local units rose from 155,000 in 1928 to 650,000 in 1930, and to well over a million in 1931; while the number of other poor persons in need of assistance rose from 1,689,000 (i.e., either as individuals or couples, or as whole families) in 1928 to 1,986,000 in 1930.

During the same period receipts from taxation and other public income not only ceased to rise in proportion to the increase in expenses but declined more and more rapidly. During 1931 this decline was at such a rate that it could no longer be explained by the natural loss a more general and even distribution of property always means to the Treasury. It was evidently tantamount to a general inability to pay taxes on the part of the commercial community. In fact, the taxpayer was following a kind of policy of passive resistance. This is a condition which is commonly found where, as in Germany after the War, a central government assumes more and more direct control over all taxation. In the German case the component states of the Reich were the first to suffer. The financial reform which derived its name from Erzberger, the Minister of Finance and leader of the Catholic Center party, centralized the administration of public finance and thereby took away certain sovereign rights of the states, as maintained by Bismarck. Politicians in the town councils may have rejoiced at the weakening of powers in the state governments: they seemed to have on their side all the arguments that could be taken from German history when they believed that a strong central power in the Reich also meant a strengthening of the influence of the Reichsstädte. But their turn came a few years later; and now not a trace of financial, political, or cultural sovereignty is left to the municipalities.

Centralization, in the matter of taxation as in other things, means that it is impossible for the man in the street or the ordinary citizen to know anything about public affairs, and permits only a few members of high ministerial boards, or still fewer members of parliamentary committees or party caucuses to take an active part in them. During the War this effect of centralization was welcome to those responsible for its military conduct, for under modern conditions such people are the opposite of what a great commander or warrior had to be in a more heroic age. They have to move unseen, and inaccessibility is one of the main conditions of their success. Public discussion is shunned, decisions are given without reasons or explanation, and the individual citizen is told that the only way he can help the common cause is to obey orders, keep out of the way, and refrain even from talking or thinking. It is not the accumulated public effort of millions of men and women which carries the leader of modern warfare to final success, but the concentrated energy of a silent bureau in which a few men work under such nervous tension that their plans might be disturbed by the mere possibility of other people outside G.H.Q. or the War Office saying or doing anything on their own responsibility. Government, whether in peace or war, is always more or less of an oligarchy, except, perhaps, in cases of pure despotism; but an oligarchy can either claim to be self-sufficient and self-supporting, or it can, like Fascism, rely on continuous, popular, democratic approval and support, making the nation feel that the best intelligence and the strongest material power it has at its disposal has placed itself voluntarily at the command of the national government and is ready with constructive advice and help. The former method is that of war, and in that respect it is true to say that war is the enemy of democracy; the latter is certainly the best method—almost Utopian in its perfection—for peace-time. In Germany the former method had become almost synonymous with the rule of Berlin. It coincided with the rapid growth of the influence of parliamentary parties and their caucuses in the Central Government during the last two years of the War. It culminated, after the War, in Erzberger's measure of financial centralization already mentioned, and in the proposals (in 1932) for an association under the strong leadership of the President of the Imperial Bank of Germany, Dr. Luther, the association to be called the *Bund zur Erneuerung des Reichs*, "the Union for the Renewal of the Reich." It is one of the inherent weaknesses of this method that, while it claims to be an autocracy, its success must necessarily depend on the constant reinforcement of the oligarchy in power by competent men from the ranks of the bureaucracy and the parliamentary parties, who possess the confidence of the masses. Such men act as a bulwark against the often very bitter criticism of those who have had to resign office and make way for the members of the oligarchy. During the first ten years of the Republic such outstanding leaders came for the most part from municipal governments in the provinces. The mayors of cities like Nürnberg, Dortmund, Essen, Magdeburg, or even smaller places such as Constance, were drawn, one after another, to Berlin; and a few prominent corporation lawyers and directors of industrial combines also rose from their provincial spheres of activity to occupy seats on the central boards in Berlin. On the whole, however, the circle of the ruling oligarchy rather narrowed down. Parliamentarians were discarded; municipalities grew restive under the growing burden of the deficit which became more difficult to explain, even to the initiated, from year to year and from month to month; and, from the beginning of 1931, the Brüning chancellorship tended to become more and more a one-man government, almost strictly absolutist in character. Though the Chancellor himself was a model of conscientious and impersonal service, his government seemed to be firmly resolved to take public opinion into confidence merely in so far as to let it know that there must be the strictest economy.

Economy and thrift, however, call much more for a moral than for a material effort on the part of the nation that is to practice them. If this policy is not simply to be forced upon them, but is to be resolutely and freely adopted and carried through by them, it needs one thing above everything else, and that is exactly the thing which the centralizing method taught by the War could not give. People must know and be able to see wherein the lavish spending they have had to bring to an end was wrong or, in other words, to what end their savings, if they can save, will be applied. They must understand government, political and economic, and take their part, every one of them, in public affairs. To attain this ideal state they will have to unlearn everything the War seemed to have taught them about government. They will have to recognize that peace, just as it calls for more real courage than war, also calls for a greater efficiency in the individuals who make up a nation if they are to cope with its demands and requirements.

It was for a nation bewildered alike by the unexplained lavishness of spending from 1927 to 1929 and by the equally unintelligible application of the "ax" since 1930, a nation ignorant of the causes of events as well as of the merits of the cure to be applied, a nation lacking all the smaller units through which it might acquire a sense of politics, it was for such a nation that a sublimation of centralization was proposed in 1933, the "totalitarian state" proclaimed by the leaders of Germany's National Socialist movement.

CHAPTER XI

THE STRAIN OF WAR AND THE REVOLUTION

CHANGES in the substance of government and in the attitude of the people toward government, such as the War brought to Germany, cannot but affect the form in which executive government is exercised. The fact that the Weimar Constitution, framed under the direct impact of the War in its closing stages, lasted only ten years—its vitality had been destroyed by overdoses of emergency decrees years before it was virtually suspended in 1933—cannot free us from the necessity of regarding it as one of the most important pieces of evidence that bear on the effect of the War on government. It is too early to judge of the degree and character of the influence that the Constitution of 1919, and governmental practices based on it from 1920 to 1932, have had on the formation of single-party government in Germany and on the new attitude of the executive since 1933. Opinions are sharply divided both among apologists for, and critics of, the Third Reich. Was the Republic of 1919 an aberration *in toto*, and as such should it be completely erased from the history of the nation, much as the record of a felony and subsequent conviction is deleted from the papers of a man who has shown that his crime was due to a passing mental affliction or was committed under compulsion? Or, on the other hand, was the Third Reich a preparatory stage in the political education of the people? Even the adherents of the former conception, however, would certainly agree that the new Germany of 1933 arose out of the War, which means, of course, not merely out of July, 1914, but out of the experience of the four and a half years that led up to the winter of 1918–1919 and the fateful spring of 1919.

What took place in October and November, 1918, has been described as a revolt, as a revolution, and as a purely negative collapse. At the time, in Munich and Berlin, it was regarded as a revolution, and that is how the heads of the new government in the two capitals described it in their official statements. In the provinces it resembled, according to its local traits, both revolt and collapse. But I doubt whether, viewed at long distance, it should not be considered merely as having been a simple registration of the existing state of things, alike by the electorate and its representatives, by the army and the civil service, and by most of the former reigning princes as well. Apart from the change to the republican form of government which in most cases took the form of abdication by consent, the only radical and formally unconstitutional innovation was woman's suffrage, in so far as both men and women took that for granted, and the women voted in the elections for the constituent assemblies.

A comparative survey in detail of the events of November, 1918, in the various sections of Germany would, in my opinion, confirm this view. We must confine ourselves here to a few observations upon the immediate effects of the War in the democratic south and to a somewhat fuller account of the so-called November revolution in northern and central Prussia.

German thought, shaped by the German language, owes much of its energy and liveliness to its birth in, and its constant revitalizing by, the two patois languages, those spoken by the peasants and the working population and likewise cherished by the poets and musicians in the north and south, the low German patois of the Lower Rhine, the Frisian coast, the Hanseatic towns, Holstein and Mecklenburg, and the Alemannic dialects of German Switzerland, the Black Forest, and Southern Alsace.[1] At the same time Slav and

---

[1] It was the fashion among a section of German philologists and folklorists, filled with a nationalist predilection for the aboriginal, to disparage the importance of the southwestern influence in the formation of the new German language during the fourteenth and fifteenth centuries because it was suspect of being imbued with humanism and the Latin spirit. They extolled—as evidence that there were precursors of Martin Luther other than the Swiss and Alsatian—certain fragments of Bohemian prose of an earlier period, notably an anonymous dialogue between Death and the Plowman. I pointed out the doubtful character and possible spuriousness of these pieces in the *Zeitschrift für Bücherfreunde* as long ago as 1913. The eulogies on them have to be carefully sifted for the political elements they contain before they can be accepted. The contribution of German Bohemia consists in a pathos and heaviness of expression which sometimes amounts to a sadistic worship of the darker side of life; and because of that peculiar idiosyncrasy it fell in with the predilection of modern German nationalism for magical signs, secret meetings, and "feme" judgments. The influence of Bohemia on German literature, as voiced by the Silesian poets of the Baroque period and the hymns of the Moravians, is not to be denied. But neither can it in any way be compared to the parts which southern, western, and northwestern Germany have played in the formation of the German mind since the Middle Ages.

Wendish customs have had a strong influence on the peasantry of the east, and Latin and the Romance languages in the southeast; while the Franks, Thuringians, and Saxons of Middle Germany have served more as a melting-pot for southern and northern, western and eastern modes of life than they have lived a life and spoken a language of their own.[2] The north-northwest and the south-southwest were the two districts where old customs and ways of life and the traditional attitude toward the daily round of duties and bonds of family, as opposed to the great moral earthquakes of history, wars, and revolutions, had been handed down in an almost unbroken line for many more centuries than human beings are able to recall even in their books of national history. In the southwestern part of the Holy Roman Empire, ranging from Lake Constance to the Swiss Juras and the Vosges, tales and songs in the modern German language had been told and written down and printed for more than half a century before Luther stamped that language with the seal of his translation of the Old and New Testament. Under the constitution of the Second Empire, Bavaria with the Allgäu and Bavarian Swabia, Württemberg with the Friedrichshafen air dock and the

2. Not that a full share of the glory of what is best in German poetry and literature could be denied to Franconia, Thuringia, and Saxony or Silesia. Frankish realism and the ability to appreciate the good things of life peculiar to the people of a sunny, wine-growing country are still as great an asset to German culture as they were from the time of Willibald Pirkheimer, Ulrich von Hutten, and Hans Sachs to that of Goethe, Rückert, and Jean Paul Richter, and, in our own days to that of Dauthendey and the "Räuberbande" of Leonhard Frank. Saxony and Silesia, in the wake of the Lutheran faith, produced most of the hymns—Paul Gerhard's, Flemming's, and Benjamin Schmolck's—which, learned in the Sunday service and memorized in school for generation after generation, have sunk deeper and deeper down into the inner recesses of subconscious thought and inherited ways of speech. The two greatest provinces, however, from the point of view of German literature, are the northwestern, from the Harz Mountains down to the sea, through the heath to Hamburg and to Holstein, with Klopstock, Lessing, and Johann Heinrich Voss, Mathias Claudius, T. H. Campe, and Gottfried Bürger, Grabbe and Hebbel, Annette von Droste, Fritz Reuter and Wilhelm Busch; and the southwestern with Sebastian Brant and Johannes Fischart, with Geiler von Keisersberg, Tauler and Wickram, with Zwingli, Reuchlin, and Melanchthon, with Albrecht von Haller and Johannes von Müller, Hegel and Schelling, Schiller and Hölderlin, Uhland and Mörike, Johann Peter Hebel and Hauff, Jeremias Gotthelf, Gottfried Keller, and many others in the first rank of poets and prose writers.

old Tübingen Foundation, the principality of Hohenzollern-Sigmaringen, Baden with the left bank of the Rhine from Constance to Schaffhausen and Basle and again to Breisach and Mannheim-Heidelberg and the Alsatian Reichsland—all these had their essential parts in this stronghold of German peasantry and citizenship, of stubborn conservative democracy[3] and extremely proud regionalism.

The Southwestern Kingdom and Grand Duchy, Württemberg and Baden, had both been most loyal supporters of the Bismarckian policy since 1870; and, in spite of their marked sympathy with the first Chancellor of the Reich after he had been exiled from office, they were still undoubtedly *reichstreu*—loyally imperialist—under William II. But they had felt the change from a reasonable measure of self-government to the war régime more acutely than the other German states. Bavaria, also a democratic country ruled by her own chosen officials and by the clergy recruited from the old peasant and bourgeois families of the land, kept her self-government almost intact, at least in appearance, during the first years of the War. Prussia had, in the east, never been accustomed to anything other than an administration of more or less feudal character, the *Landrat* taking his powers from and representing the central authority to which the resources of the district were, after a moderate deduction for local needs, devoted and directed in a constant movement from the outward provinces toward Berlin—something unimaginable in either Württemberg or Baden. Moreover, civil administration and the military career were much more closely interwoven in Prussia. In it there existed the unwritten law that reserved special privileges for crack regiment officers on reserve, for former members of the select student corps who were looking for the higher places in the civil government, and for the nobility, who had equal access to both army and civil service. In the southern states army and civil administration were less closely knit, and privilege counted for less. There, Roman Catholic opposition to dueling, even among students, made itself felt; and even the higher posts of the civil service were open to Catholic or Liberal Protestant sons of bourgeois families, young

---

3. In lower Baden a strong liberal and "unitarian" element had succeeded in getting hold of the administration of the Grand Duchy, in spite of the drastic way in which the revolution of 1848 had been put down. But regionalism remained always a strong and living force in Baden's Alemannic party, made up of those nearest to Switzerland and Upper Alsace.

THE STRAIN OF WAR AND THE REVOLUTION 157

men who were quite unconnected with the army, and whose association with a theological or philological students' club or an *Akademischer Gesangverein*, a university choral society, was their only title to a career of ease.[4]

In both sections, however, the people never went beyond grumbling about the "Prussian" manners of this or that officer in a *Generalkommando;* and grumbling about the pompousness and conceit of officials had always been a favorite Sunday pastime for those who lived about Lake Constance, in the Black Forest country, or in the Swabian highlands. Baden felt too close to the theater of war, with its low, ceaseless thundering of gunfire from Alsace and, at times, its bombing raids on her towns, to make much of the petty troubles or chicanery of the day. As for Württemberg, it had an overwhelming majority of homebred officers in the *Kommandos,* many of them well known for their harsh language and the severity of discipline they liked to enforce, but always in the orthodox manner and in the best patois of the country, more "*grob*"—blunt—than "*schneidig*"—insolent.

Moreover, both Württemberg and Baden felt the tie between reigning house and people to be a very strong and natural thing, something to be defended, in peace-time, against any attempt on the part of the Prussian court to lord it over them. Both King and Grand Duke were respected and even loved in a homely way by the great mass of the people. For they were men devoted to the duties of their office, of signal modesty and even plainness, but of real dignity of behavior and possessed of a real sense of responsibility. They would have made model constitutional monarchs.

Both in Württemberg and Baden the Revolution was, for these reasons, bound to be non-violent. The course of events has been described with great detail and in the plainest terms by men who, either as the last ministers of the monarchy or as leaders of the constitutional opposition, were eye-witnesses of what happened in

---

4. Ministers and other high officials in Württemberg and Bavaria bore, almost without exception, the title of nobility, "von." But in most cases it was a personal favor conferred upon them by the sovereign, similar to English knighthood, and only became hereditary if it had been given to three successive bearers of the same name, who had all three been equally distinguished in the civil service. A real distinction in that case.

the capital,[5] and later had access to the best unpublished material on the subject.[6] Students of the historical relations between the new German Constitution and the Bismarckian Empire as it had been transformed by military government during the War, should give special attention to the case of the two southwestern states—the *Musterländer* or pattern states, as they used to be called by the wits of Berlin.

1. *Prussia*

THE effect of the War both on the constitutional and on the *de facto* position of the State of Prussia within the Reich is difficult to describe. At one time, and from the military point of view, Prussia seemed to have swallowed up the rest of Germany. The command of the war forces in the homeland, apart from a few not very important matters of administrative routine and the conferring of medals and honors, had passed to the Prussian Ministry of War. The general-in-command of the central district of Prussia (*Generalkommando in den Marken*) was *primus inter pares* among the generals who wielded supreme executive power throughout Germany. War industry was almost exclusively reserved to the great industrial areas of Prussia, northern Thuringia, and Saxony, and this in itself seemed enough to strengthen the industrial superiority of northern and western Germany over the south and the east, in a way that lasted far beyond the period of the War itself. Military rule ended and civil administration took its place again, with perhaps a remnant of war-time centralization during the next few years. But the supremacy won for industry by the decisive increase in power of production, and acknowledged by the public privileges which, by the provisions of the National Service Law, the commonwealth had

---

5. Minister of State Dr. Ludwig von Köhler, *Zur Geschichte der Revolution in Württemberg* (ein Bericht) (Stuttgart, 1930), published in reply to General von Elbinghaus, *Memoiren,* and to Karl Weller, "Die Revolutionstage in Württemberg," 1918 (in *Schwäbische Merkur* of October and November, 1928, and as a separate book, *Die Staatsumwälzung in Württemberg 1918–1920* [Stuttgart, 1930]); Wilhelm Blos, *Von der Monarchie zum Volksstaat* (Stuttgart o.J.); and A. Remmele, *Staatsumwälzung und Neubau in Baden* (Karlsruhe, 1925).

6. Two memoranda, by Ministers von Soden and von Weizsäcker, *Ueber die Vorgänge im Wilhelmspalast am 9 November 1918,* and by the Minister for War Von Marchtaler in the State Archives at Stuttgart, are not as yet accessible.

conferred on the workingmen employed in war industry, had embodied all the elements of a lasting change in social values. It had also raised the wages and the standard of life of the whole population in these industrial areas to averages far above those in other provinces of Germany where agriculture was the predominant industry.

On the other hand, however, in the field of politics Prussia was in striking contrast to all the other states. For Prussia had retained, for the popular chamber, the system of indirect elections by three classes of voters grouped according to the amount of taxes they paid as shown in the property census. They were arranged in order of wealth. The first class was made up of a few landowners or capitalists of the district who alone paid a third of its taxes. The second class consisted, in like manner, of those who paid the second third of the taxes in the constituency; and the rest of voters, thousands and thousands of them, formed the third class. Each class had the right to the same number of electors; and the electors chose the representative of the constituency by majority vote. The votes of the members of the first class were worth several hundred or even thousand times as much as those of the third, and in some cases a man with a conspicuously unearned income might carry ten or twenty times the weight of the vote of a cabinet minister or of the Chancellor himself if he went to the polls where he held office instead of where his estate was, in the country. The justification was, of course, to be found in a superlogical application of the principle from which the power of Parliament had emanated in the early times of British constitutional law, when the King asked the Lords and Commons for means and supplies, and those who paid the taxes had the right to vote them or refuse them. But such considerations did not mean anything to the German people in the throes of the War. The system stood for all that seemed reactionary and unfair to the growing political importance, and to the intelligence, of the great mass of the working-class population in Prussia. It was a slight on the north German worker in comparison with his fellow trade-unionist in Württemberg, Bavaria, or Saxony. Above all, it seemed to assume an almost grotesquely out-of-date character when the War took constitutional and economic development into its own hands. For the War distributed munition factories and other centers of war industry throughout all parts of Prussia. Through the National Service Law, it gave the Prussian workingman a social position and a political influence, entirely apart from Parliament, which far outweighed anything in the way of a direct contribution to the Exchequer made by this or that wealthy taxpayer in accordance with the vote of his representative in the Diet. In fact, as we may note in passing, this was one of the underlying causes of the easy success fascist ideas were to win a few years after the War, when people began to realize what had happened.[7] They came to see that there had been no reasonable and adequate interdependence between political power and parliamentary expression of the will of the electorate for a long period before the War. Both the military leaders and the soldiers, who did everything that was to be done, and the workers in the *lebenswichtige,* or "key," war industries in the homeland were unrepresented in Parliament and, so far as they concerned themselves with the matters dealt with in Parliament, even felt themselves to be misrepresented by the parties in power. The Diets of the smaller German states were not expected to occupy themselves either with international policy, the conduct of the War and the question of war aims, or with social legislation and the representation of working-class interests in the council of the nation. When the revolution made the Diet supreme in Bavaria, Saxony, Württemberg, and Baden it was not so much a break in the traditional working of government as it was in Prussia. The stubborn resistance of Prussian conservatives, or rather of the ruling class in Prussia, under the leadership of Secretary of State Von Loebell (afterward president of the anti-socialist Civic Union, or-

7. The downward permeation of an idea from the narrow circle at the intellectual surface of a nation where it originated to the wide depths of public opinion became a much more rapid process in Europe after the War than it had been during the preceding hundred or two hundred years. In the sixth volume of the *"Handbuch der Politik"* (*Urkunden zur Politik unserer Zeit,* 1926) the editors made an interesting experiment when, as a preface to the series of documents of each period they inserted a few extracts from writers and orators whose thought dominated the preceding period, for instance from Rousseau, Herder, Humboldt, Kant, and Goethe for the documents of the first two decades of the nineteenth century, and from Lassalle, Carlyle, and Treitschke, for the period from 1870 to 1890. The period during which the opinions of an individual become transformed into an inbred popular sentiment grows shorter and shorter, till, during the War and in the period that followed it, it dwindled to a few years.

ganized to keep the Socialists out of the Government and the higher posts of the civil service), had done a great and lasting disservice to constitutional government in Germany. Prussia was held up by the reformers, and indeed by many conservatives who wished employers and employees to take part in government, as the deterring example of a state machinery which had to be replaced by completely new equipment. The relation between the Central Government of the Reich and the Prussian Government, with the same capital housing the ministerial departments of both in the same quarter of the town, and only a few minutes' walk from one another, is necessarily a close, if delicate one. Up to the War it had always been the main source of administrative strength for the Government of the Reich to be on good terms, or perhaps even allied by personnel, with the Prussian Cabinet, having the Prussian vote in the Federal Council at its disposal, and being able to exchange officials with Prussia by way of mutual favor and patronage. Prussia could dispose of the highest prizes in the army and the civil service; and the Reich could do the same for diplomacy and the Imperial Court at Leipzig. At the end of the War it was almost the reverse. All the important political decisions, except of course on military questions, were taken in close consultation between the Imperial Government and the leaders of the Reichstag parties; and among them, the two parties which in the Prussian Diet had been (the one in almost constant and sometimes very bitter opposition,[8] and the other almost entirely and automatically) excluded from Parliament were now in strong ascendency. For their support in the business of "seeing it

8. Foreign students of the differences between pre-war and post-war conditions in German parliamentary life should always bear in mind the first-rate importance of the fact that the Catholic Center in Prussia had to play the rôle of an opposition which was said to be disloyal to the national cause. The Center protected the Polish minority in Prussia against the domineering policy advocated by Hugenberg and his associates of the German settlement commission in Posnania; it complained of the preference given to Protestants, to members of fashionable students' organizations, or to officers of reserve over Catholics who, forbidden to engage in duels, were therefore excluded from these influential organizations. Much of what was to happen in Germany after 1919, and especially the readiness of the Catholic Center to coöperate with the Socialists is to be explained by the resentment of the Center against the old exclusive Prussian administration, based on treatment received from it in the past.

through" had to be won by at least admitting them fully to the council of the Government and keeping them busy giving and getting information. "National" parties, as such, in Germany and elsewhere, have to be content, as soon as war has been declared, with war service as a matter of principle; it is inherent in their program, together with armaments, annexations, and antisemitism. They cannot ask for anything more than the state of war in itself gives them. German nationalist activities, moreover, had exhausted themselves when, during the first two years of the War, they demanded the suppression of the last remnants of the supremacy of civil power and of "*Zivilcourage,*" the courage of independent political opinion in civilian offices of state. And, in particular, they had demanded the removal of the Chancellor. To that must be added their manifesto of May 20, 1915, protesting against premature negotiations for a separate peace with one of the enemy powers, and calling for the economic annexation of Belgium, northern France and the iron-ore fields in Briey. To do that was to strike at the Chancellor and the policy of the Foreign Office. And it left them with nothing else that they could demand. The Center, the Democrats, and the Socialists were the parties which might be expected to be propitiated by the political gifts the Government had in its power to give. Association with Prussia, where the Socialists were still regarded as untouchables, began to be a hindrance rather than a help to the Imperial Cabinet; and during the last stage of the War nothing would have better pleased the chancellors and secretaries of State, struggling against terrible odds for the maintenance of some unity of purpose in Imperial politics, than to be able to offer the Center and the Socialists a bill for an adult franchise in Prussia, on the one-man-one-vote basis, in return for their support in the Reichstag. The influence of the defenders of the class franchise in Prussia was so strong that it could not be done. As late as the summer and early fall of 1918 they had been able to oust the chief of the Emperor's Civil Cabinet, his trusted personal adviser in all matters of state other than military affairs, who did not side with *jusqu'au boutisme;* and they had replaced him with one of their own leaders. It became their declared policy—a policy which played a fateful rôle in the days when the abdication of Emperor and King came up for decision—that if, in a final military or political débâcle, the Reich went down, Prussia must still remain the *rocher de bronze* of monarchy. Driven back

THE STRAIN OF WAR AND THE REVOLUTION 163

into her own sphere of national strength and relying only on herself, she could win the War, if not for the Rhineland or at Berlin, then in East Prussia and Silesia, with Königsberg as the legitimist stronghold. With such views prevailing in official Prussian circles it was almost inevitable that on the other side, in the Reichstag and deep down in government circles, the opposing view came to be taken: "Let us save the Reich," it said, "and if Prussia stands in the way Prussia will have to go." The chancellors of the last war cabinets and their successive collaborators came from southern Germany. Count Hertling belonged to the Bavarian Catholic Center; Prince Maximilian was a member of the reigning House of Baden, allied to the Guelphs, and by his mother a descendant of the Napoleonic Leuchtenbergs; Vice-Chancellor Payer had been the leader of the Württemberg Democrats, and the President of the Württemberg Diet, a countryman of Deputy Erzberger who was one of the most influential members of the Standing Committee in the Reichstag. While Stresemann represented Saxony, Ebert came from Baden, Gröber was another Württemberger; and a few others, none of whom had a definite interest in Prussia or the Prussian Parliament, came from south or central Germany.[9]

Furthermore, Prussian unity had to submit to the central and eastern provinces in their strenuous opposition to the policy of the Prussian Government, an opposition which had led to a situation where Prussia's various provincial groups in the Reichsrat[10] were

9. There was more than one link between this group of politicians and the post-war school of political thought which tried to further the reform, or, as they preferred to call it, the "renewal" of the Reich, a rejuvenation, almost a rebirth of national government, more closely united and at the same time in more real touch with independent local organization. It was not an abolition of Prussia as a separate state that they proposed. It was something which meant a voluntary abdication of Prussian sway over the Central Government, a merging or *Aufgehen* of Prussia in the Reich, so that their relationship might be something not unlike that of England in the British Government and the Parliament of Great Britain, as compared with Scotland, Wales, and Northern Ireland. That is, the constituted counterparts of the latter would be found in Bavaria and the other South German states.

10. All other states that were members of the Reichsrat gave their vote as a unit, even if they had more than one actual vote. Prussian votes were divided into the votes of the Central Government of Prussia and the votes of the autonomous provinces. Some of them were predominantly agrarian, monarchist, and nationalist, instructing their representatives accordingly, even if

repeatedly found voting against one another or against the Government on important questions of domestic and sometimes even of foreign policy.

In spite of all this—and it is difficult to explain it—Prussia kept together during and after 1919, and was still the greatest single source of administrative power within the Reich, stronger in everything than the Reich itself—except that Prussia had no control over foreign policy or over the army. In education, the Weimar Constitution provided for a uniform system of elementary teaching, the abolition of private schools, and the admission to high-school training by examination tests without any class distinction. But education was still under the control of the Prussian Government. Its Department of Higher Education and the Arts exercised sovereign power over eleven universities and a score of technical and commercial *Hochschulen*, of which the Reich possessed none. The churches were officially connected with, and owed their public standing, their rights, and privileges to the State of Prussia, though the papal nuncio is accredited to the President of the Reich, and the German Penal Code protects religious bodies against blasphemy, libel, and disturbances of divine service. The courts and the bar, with all their traditional influence on public opinion and parliamentary life, remained under the domain of the State, that is, of Prussia, after the War as before it; and even in matters of Imperial legislation, especially the drafting of bills, the Prussian Ministry of Justice had an influence equal to and sometimes greater than that of the Ministry of Justice of the Reich. The latter appointed only the judges of the Supreme Court; and here also the states possessed by custom the right to submit nominations. The police which had to protect the President of the Reich, the Central Government, and the Reichstag itself were Prussian police, acting under the orders and on the responsibility of a Prussian Minister of the Interior. The State of Prussia had not chosen, in its constitution, to create a presidential office such as the South German states had done; but the Prussian Prime Minister was, next to the President of the Reich, the outstanding representative of political power and influence in German policy, a true director of the fate of his subjects, while the

the majority of the Diet and the Government belonged to a coalition of parties of the Left, a coalition republican and favoring a conciliatory policy toward the Western Powers.

Chancellor of the Reich could not pretend to be more than a trustee or a political adviser of the nation.

The Prussian revolution had found its best diarist in the man whose rough strength of will, when aided by the prudence of President Ebert and the quiet reliability of Field Marshal von Hindenburg, was chiefly instrumental in restoring constitutional life in Germany, and averting the danger of a radical revolt by Right or Left between November, 1918, and March, 1920. I refer to the Socialist deputy, Gustav Noske. During the revolutionary period he was successively Military Governor of the Port of Kiel, Minister for Defense, and then, after his enforced resignation in 1920, Lieutenant-Governor of the Prussian Province of Hanover. And he was one of those men for whom the only canon of action is necessity. They seem to recognize necessity more clearly than other men do; and having recognized it, they are ready to act on it as if there were no other law, either human or divine. Whether the necessity is that of moving an obstacle out of the way, or of removing an opponent, they are never beset by doubts or feel the need for justification, even when, many years afterward, they write the story. Necessity gives an order and one obeys it as one answers one's name when the roll is called. No question or doubt can arise, let the action be right or wrong, just or unjust. For the point is here: While a man *ought* perhaps to do what is right and fair, he simply *must* do what is necessary. Upholders of a kind of justice which, in the absoluteness of its rule, is quite as much outside the domain of logical defense as is necessity itself have attacked Noske's apologia for his rôle during the two critical years as being an unashamed confession of a ruthless use of armed power against a people demanding full political rights. Critics have instanced the way he wrote of the murders done by officers of the army on the leaders of the Independent Socialists, Karl Liebknecht and Rosa Luxemburg, while he was in supreme command. But he was not to be moved by such criticism, and his knowing it would come would not have changed a single word in his memoirs. It may be said more truly of Gustav Noske than of the military leaders themselves that he was a man of war. He wrote his book in the spirit of a man who believes that might is right because he had had the might, had felt the necessity of using it, and by so using it had brought about those things which it seemed necessary to bring about, if national life was to go on. The man and the book could not have come to be without the War. The War had, to men like him, the fascination of an organized mass movement in which both the fighting and sufferings of individuals had alike become considerations that were minor and hardly worthy of mention at G.H.Q. In like manner the revolution was also a process in which individual feats counted for little. Mobilization had been three-quarters of the War, and revolution was going to be a kind of demobilization.

Noske's contention, as he formulated it in a speech at Brunswick on Sunday, November 3, 1918, the eve of the week of revolution, was that Germany needed far-reaching reforms but no revolutionary violence; that could only add further misfortunes to the sufferings the German people had had to endure. The German Socialist movement, he said, had always refused to use force in a revolution; it was ready to call itself revolutionary and to give the usual three cheers for the liberation of the peoples by the "social democracy in revolution." But that meant a mental revolution, and a corresponding change in the economic situation that would bring it into line with the new attitude of mind. No violence. The shots fired by the sailors at Kiel seemed "objectionable"; but Noske found support and comfort in an experience which he himself had when traveling next day from Berlin to Kiel. A functionary of the Socialist party in Kiel, who had been sent to Berlin to obtain official support against the radical wing of the Kiel revolutionaries and, with Noske and Secretary of State Hausmann, was returning in their first-class compartment, was held up by the ticket collector and ordered to get out of it because he had only a third-class ticket. Such was the spirit of law-abiding orderliness and the observance of rules and regulations without fear or favor on the first day of the revolution.

The rising at Munich and the régime set up by Kurt Eisner in Bavaria went as much against Noske's grain as did the behavior of the mutinous sailors at Kiel. Eisner was never a mere party leader. He was an individualist of the purest water. Viewed from the standpoint of the official Socialists his political ideas must have seemed to belong to a vague romanticism entirely out of keeping with the sturdy *Lokalpatriotismus,* or regionalism, of the Bavarians. Nor did the doubts of the Berlin leaders as to the reliability of Eisner's politics grow less when he began to play on the traditional federalism of Bavaria and the dislike of Munich for Berlin. He was certainly, together with Liebknecht and Rosa Luxemburg, the born leader of a revolution which, in Brunswick parlance, was to be intellectual rather than any material upheaval, with barricades, looting, and the guillotine. But all three of them met violent deaths at the hands of their political antagonists, who realized that dreamers and speech-makers might be more dangerous to their plans to return to power than men of the type of Noske and his collaborators.

At Kiel, and later on in Berlin, Noske tried to maintain a working agreement with officers of the army and navy who were known to him for their ability in war administration, or who seemed to promise to be helpful in carrying out his plans and orders. One of them was the governor of the fortress, Vice-Admiral Souchon, who had won fame in the early days of the War by one of the few actions sanctioned by the Supreme Command in spite of its desire to keep the Grand Fleet intact. As commander of the ships in the Mediterranean when the War broke out, he took them to Constantinople; and, by the successful execution of this move, he gave a new turn to the War's political course. Since then he had been condemned to comparative inactivity at Kiel. When the revolt came, he was unable to put it down singlehanded, as might have been within the powers of a great general, or of some battleship commander who had for long enough been bound to his men by the solidarity of battles. But Noske tells a good story that brings out Souchon's personal courage and his sense of duty and honor. The Sailors' Council, in the days of excited ignorance as to what would occur next—when everybody still believed that something was bound to occur—had heard of the beginnings of a counterrevolution, which, according to rumor, was being planned for the following day by a group of officers and subalterns who were that night meeting in a copse outside the town. The sailors were about to raise a general alarm and to launch an attack upon the supposed nest and meeting place of the conspirators, an attack which would almost certainly have resulted in desultory firing, a panic, and the killing or wounding of the wrong people. But Admiral Souchon offered to go, alone and by night, to the enemy's camp and, by parley with them, persuade them to disperse. The sailors believed him. He went, found that the whole thing was an invention or a mistake, returned, and was again believed. That is, by so doing he halted something that was pure folly, folly, too, that would have meant loss of life. And in doing so he exposed himself to greater danger than officers of his position are usually exposed to during war. For at the time everyone knew that flags of truce were little respected by those who held their foes to be either traitors or hired murderers in the pay of tyranny.

On the morning of November 7 there came confirmation from Munich of the report of the proclamation of the Bavarian Republic, and from Hamburg of a sailors' revolt and a march on the town hall. For Noske, and for his colleagues in the Soldiers' Council, of which he was now the chairman, this meant that the revolutionary movement was more than any mere expression of local dissatisfaction, and that it would spread to Berlin and all over Germany. He records:

We sat down, six or seven of us, behind closed and guarded doors in the waiting room of the railway station, and deliberated on our next move. One thing seemed to be clear, that nothing, at this stage, could stop the revolutionary movement. The time for shilly-shallying was past; the *mot d'ordre* must be to take the reins firmly in hand and direct the revolution's course. A proclamation was arranged for. According to its terms the Working Men's Council established itself as the provisional government for the province of Schleswig-Holstein. I was opposed to proclaiming the republic in the province.

Noske let the leader of the radical wing of the Socialists, a man by the name of Popp, who quickly disappeared again, take the responsibility as head of the Soldiers' Council, while he took the military power in his hands as Governor, in the place of the Admiral with whom he had collaborated. The latter now quietly and with remarkable dignity facilitated the task of his successor. In Berlin, Stiller von Mann, the Imperial Secretary of State for the Navy, willingly gave formal confirmation to Noske's appointment; he knew that the elected Governor was the only man to keep the sailors in hand.

The events at Kiel, seen at a distance, seem a very local affair. The port, the town, a few half-dismantled ships, the office of the Governor, a third-class waiting room at the principal station, a small wood near the town, said to contain a nest of conspirators but which proved to be empty as soon as a courageous man entered it—all that makes a surprisingly small story for the beginning and initial success of a revolution in a country like Germany. That impression, however, would not be a correct one. The big cities and the

THE STRAIN OF WAR AND THE REVOLUTION 169

military centers, like Munich, Hamburg, and Kiel, merely came first. And there was no need, neither would there have been a chance, that any such capital as Paris or Moscow could, by sending forth its revolutionary alarm, impose its will upon a reluctant country, and electrify its lagging march into the future. In the first days of November, 1918, the change of the old system of government in its outward form was overdue. The provincial, or country town, the smallest hamlet even, was only a few hours, or a day or two, behind Munich, Berlin, or Breslau; and the course of events was everywhere so much the same that the Revolution appears as an almost inevitable consequence of the moral state of the nation as a whole, much more than as the result of this or that event which caused the first stones to be thrown or the first shots to be fired. Throughout Germany the same things occurred almost in the same sequence: the organization of Soldiers' or Workingmen's Councils, or both, or of Citizens' Councils to try to quiet the hotheads; gatherings in the market place, and proclamations drafted and posted by whosoever was able to pen the few necessary sentences; perhaps a few wild rumors, originating in some momentary renewal of loyalty and fervor among the youngest subalterns or lieutenants, in whom there remained more faith in the monarchy than was left in the generals-in-command and the military city governors; a few isolated acts of assault upon officers in uniform or some old army surgeon who had made himself unpopular by returning invalids to the front, or insulting the unfit at a medical examination of recruits. And then, after two or three days, everything settled down again into its old rut, with the small things once more seeming to be much more important than the great affairs of state. All this held true whether it was a case of the workers in the great cities, the people of the smaller towns, or the peasantry in the country. That the demand for the abdication of a monarch was raised first in his capital and that the revolts of soldiers and sailors took place in the town centers of the military districts from which they wanted to escape were characteristic instances of the sober matter-of-factness of the German revolution. It was not planned in security by conspirators who went out from their hiding places to start the fire where they thought the fuel was driest; it sprang up from the soil. One might almost say that it was part of the routine of daily life.[11]

11. For the story of the events in Berlin and the abdication of the Em-

In Schleswig-Holstein the province promptly followed the capital, with little difference between the country districts and the commercialized areas near Hamburg and Lübeck. The response was slower only in the Danish section of northern Schleswig, which, not having experienced the whole terror of the War, was less prepared for this outcome of it than was the rest of Germany. The garrison towns were the first to offer assistance to their new commanding officers, who were glad to be assured of their loyalty to the new order, in case the Kiel sailors should be tempted to try a more radical form of proletariat rule. They found in Noske a man of their own kind, who spoke and understood their language. He was able to impress them with an unconditional belief in the necessity of maintaining the authority of the State and a powerful government. In a few weeks he became a really popular leader who looked on election to office as something in no wise superior to an officer's commission, or being appointed by the monarch. And all this was only due recognition of his being able to fill his office by reason of his personal gifts.

In pointed contrast to his appreciation of the support which many civil servants and officers of the old army gave to his efforts, Noske passes severe judgment on the officials and employees of the two big government industries, the Imperial Docks and the Marine Clothing Department (*Marinebekleidungsamt*). He begins by blaming the former régime for the bad spirit prevailing among the officials, staff, and workmen in these industries. It was the pre-war system at which he caviled, a

miserable system, which [he says] has resulted in the downfall of those who had profited by it. Openly to profess oneself a member of the Social Democratic party was not without its danger in the above naval establishments. If the people at the head of the establishment regarded a

peror compare: Popp and Artelt, *Ursprung und Entwicklung der November-Revolution;* Ernst Eichhorn, *Ueber die Januar-Ereignisse* (1919); Emil Barth, *Aus der Werkstatt der Revolution* (1919); Heinrich Marx, *Handbuch der Revolution in Deutschland* (1918–19) (Vol. I, 1919); Karl Liebknecht, *Politische Aufzeichnungen* (1921); Prinz Max von Baden, *Erinnerungen und Dokumente* (1927), pp. 615–647; Alfred Niemann, *Revolution von oben —Umsturz von unten* (1927), pp. 269–320; Hermann Müller-Franken, *Die November-Revolution* (1928), pp. 41 ff.; Philipp Scheidemann, *Memoiren eines Sozialdemokraten* (1928), II, 287–350; Eduardo Labougle, *La révolution allemande de 1918* (Paris, 1928), pp. 45–54, 103 ff.

man as being what they called an agitator they put him out of his job on some pretext or other if, at the moment, they did not like brutally to dismiss him as a measure of discipline. Even membership in a trade-union organization had been a thing suspect for many years. The worker was bound to his work by the prospect of a pension from special funds and by the welfare benefits he was to enjoy, all of which made him particularly afraid of dismissal. Spying on other working men had become a favorite occupation, and many of the employees had been inoculated with the spirit of time-serving, sycophancy, and servility toward superiors.

Noske does not mean to accuse militarism or universal service. Far from it. He would be the first to recognize that on a warship or in barracks any confession of the Socialist creed, or any agitation against the reigning system, could not be tolerated. He knew that freedom of opinion had its limits in any organization which had to keep great numbers of human beings so well in hand that, at any given moment, it could deal a blow with them as with a weapon. He further knew that neither in the army nor in the navy was the system, which his last bitter sentence castigates, in force before the War,[12] that it would not even have been tolerated for a moment, and that the place-hunter was the last man to get on in the Prussian army, whatever its faults in other respects. His words struck at the semi-military establishments, which employed civilian workers. Nor does he spare the workers of the post-war period. It is their general attitude towards labor and service that he tries to make clear in a picture of the state of things before the War.

As soon as this high pressure was removed, workers swung from one extreme to the other. A raving hatred of their superiors and the officials of the plant broke out like wildfire. No man in uniform could be tolerated in the factories. Many officers and officials were simply driven out at a moment's notice; and a few, who had made themselves especially unpopular, were carried out bodily on wheelbarrows and set down in the open street. In the torpedo factory at Friedrichsort the

12. The same thing cannot be said with the same certainty for the period of the War, at least from 1918, on. The thing called "obtaining military information," practiced under the protection of General Ludendorff's staff, contained at least a trace of the terrible curse of party sycophancy, that policy of acquiring favors by expressing approval of the conduct of the War —a curse which since the War has worked havoc in public life in Germany.

admiral in charge was declared to have forfeited his office, and an elected board, which as first constituted contained only a few radical workmen, was provisionally entrusted with the control of and the drafting of new regulations for a factory plant in which thousands of workmen and employees were occupied. For the torpedo factory and for the docks a Central Works Council was established which sat almost continuously.

There were, further, councils for the several departments of the works, and committees of delegates for employees and officials which sat sometimes jointly, sometimes separately, and often differed in their conclusions. The officials thought they could manage very well without the higher grades of employees. The employees for their part felt themselves capable of doing the work of the officials, and opposed them. Their opinions were above all divided as to the amount of pressure to be put upon the smaller groups within the factory and the details of their work. In the torpedo factory I had to act as arbiter in one of the meetings of the Council because they could not agree among themselves. The Admiralty in Berlin was hardly in a position to intervene in the affairs of the Kiel Works during the first period of the Revolution; my own responsibility was therefore the greater. The workers firmly refused to perform any war service. The adoption of an eight-hour working day had little meaning under these conditions, for there was practically no real work done at that time.

The less they worked, however, the more they talked. Discussion was endless. Committees of workmen, office staff, and technicians were commissioned to draft a plan for changing the naval works into an industrial establishment to produce peace commodities, with all-round socialization. Another committee was entrusted with the task of getting large orders for the new kinds of goods which were to be produced. It cannot be said that the actual result fully corresponded to the zeal with which the discussion was carried on. Those who believed themselves to be the greatest experts in practical administration and had grandiose plans ready to be put in execution proved to have a really deplorable lack of world wisdom and an ignorance of the elementary economic facts as to conditions in Germany. To change those enormous establishments with their semimilitary routine into ordinary industrial plants seemed an easy undertaking to them; and they talked glibly of orders which would come in, amounting to fantastic totals.

The quotation is interesting from more than one point of view. It shows the mind of the organizer who has first of all to be able to command obedience in order to create order afterward, and who does not care for enthusiasm and utopian conceptions of a millennium of prosperous peace. It shows, on the other hand, a state of mind which was common among those in Germany who welcomed the end of the War and believed in peace, not as a period of purgation for the sin of war, but as a cure for the sufferings they had gone through. Germany, except for the few monarchists who had remained true to the old order and had begun to denounce the peace enthusiasts as traitors, lived in a mystical belief in the influence and the intentions of the President of the Central States and the treaty of peace he would dictate. The central idea of this peace dream was that the hundreds of thousands or even millions of men who were now to be dismissed from the ranks of war should enter the service of peace; and they would rebuild the towns they had been forced to destroy, restore the devastated regions to fertility, and generally turn swords into plowshares. It was partly a sincere feeling of commiseration for the victims of war devastation which was uppermost in the mind of the simple soldier returning from France and Belgium, and even a real wave of pacifist idealism which created this desire to make good what the War had destroyed. Combined with this there went a naïve conviction of the ability of German industry and of German workmen to do better, through their newly won freedom from munition work, than they had ever done before. They would make the French villages and provincial towns models of town planning, with public gardens, up-to-date equipment and sanitation. In fact, they would have done all the things they did in Germany after the inflation, when the credits began to flow in. They would teach the Russians the use of machinery, electric power, engineering on the grand scale, so as to get ten square miles' worth out of one. They would build up a network of railways and canals between the Atlantic and the Black Sea, linking the Central States with Central Asia—all this in a fever of planning that would keep them working day and night. The economists could have told them, then and there, that international economic relations consisted not in supporting a foreign country but in excluding its imports and in dumping one's own exports into it, in closing the frontiers against the immigrant who could offer cheap labor, in complaints of unfair competition, and in forcing unemployment upon one country through the efficiency, thrift, and hard work of another. Economists, however, had been silenced; their prophecies about the economic consequences of war had so often been falsified by the event that they were no longer listened to even when they told the sober truth.

Men were blinded by their faith in the healing power of peace, in that turn for the better which everything would take as soon as life again became the ruling principle instead of death. There would be no more bombing of cathedrals, nor cutting down of woods and orchards. The morass of the trenches would be dried up and the shell holes filled in. Again, there would be plowing, sowing, and reaping. No one cared to think, at the time, of the old truth that peace demands stricter discipline and greater sacrifices than war, simply because in war the obligation to act together is forced on the man in uniform by superior command, while in peace it has to be willed and accepted as a moral obligation. Nowhere was the necessity for this voluntary resignation of freedom of action more difficult to realize than among the workmen in the government factories which had been organized on strictly military lines during the War, and had now to shape their lives on lines of their own. The judgment which Noske pronounces on the Kiel labor men may have been colored by a sense of having met with unfair treatment where he might have expected gratitude for his loyal devotion to the task of restoring order and keeping the naval station in being. Accordingly, he may have painted things too blackly. But, after every deduction on that score has been made the substance of what he says still remains terrible evidence of labor conditions during the first post-war years.

Order [he says] could not be restored on the Kiel docks in spite, or perhaps because of, the great number of committees trying to perform this task. On May 28, 1919, the day of my last visit to the place, crowds of workingmen were standing idly by while I went through the workshops. In one of them, after I had passed, a few ultraradicals jeered behind my back; but when I turned and passed them again they sat silent and cowered over their work. In March, 1920, I had to issue an order for military measures that would bring about the closing of the works, because, within a short time there had been four hundred cases of theft.

One conclusion emerges very clearly from these remarks. If[13] administrators of the Noske type—for there were a few others of

13. I am aware of the objections to the use of sentences beginning with "if" in a work dealing with past events, and on principle I concur in these

THE STRAIN OF WAR AND THE REVOLUTION 175

similar character—had been able to rely on organized labor and had met with a real response from the great majority of the working class, Germany would, then and there, have been reconstructed on the lines of a National Socialism in many respects different from the system under which the country has been governed since 1933, but resembling it in its tendency to create unification secured by strong, single command. As it was, a man like Noske had, consciously or by instinct, to fall back on the officers and the civil servants who were willing to support every promising effort for the maintenance of law and order, from whomsoever it came; and that, in its turn, led, temporarily at least, to a recrudescence of state sovereignty. The loyalties as well as the small daily habits and manners of the men in the army and the civil service were connected with one of the states, not with the Reich.[14]

2. Württemberg[15]

WÜRTTEMBERG enjoyed, in its relations to the Central Government, an independence of administration—absolute in the case of local government, police, education, forestry and waterways, and some minor matters—which was the more pronounced as it could be based on the fact that, financially, Württemberg was practically self-supporting. In the last budgetary period before the War, expenditures amounted to about 120 million marks, of which 114 millions were raised in Württemberg itself while the Reich had to contribute the odd six millions. The taxes imposed by the Central Government were, under the old régime, assessed by the financial administration of the states; and in a country like Württemberg, where the districts with relatively small peasants' estates form the backbone of

---

objections. But in the case of the sentence in the text the temptation, for once, proved irresistible.

14. This also is true of the change in Bavaria after the collapse of the communist government which had followed the assassination of Kurt Eisner. The officers of the old army and the civil servants who were the mainstay of the new government—formed by the Bavarian Catholic Center party—acted as loyal Bavarians. The new régime was marked by a distinct tendency to apply to the citizens from other German states police measures designed for the control of undesirable aliens.

15. This section is a fragment of a larger survey of various sections of Germany, which the author had intended to complete. Work on it was delayed however by his exile. EDITOR.

the economic body, assessment of taxes means more than the law and the amount of taxation itself. In addition, Württemberg—in contrast to the Grand Duchies of Baden and Hessen-Darmstadt, though less so than Bavaria—had retained the right of keeping her military organization separate from that of Prussia. It had occasion, during the War, to feel proud of its contingents. The Württemberger was disliked because of the rougher characteristics in his make-up, both by the enemy and by other German fighting men. In particular the Bavarian and Saxon regiments used strong expressions in barrack song and war story about their Swabian fellows. But the Württemberger was able to point to his record of sacrifice during the War. Where twenty-four of every thousand Württembergers under arms paid the price, twenty-three was the figure for the Prussians, including the Baden and Hessian regiments which had suffered terribly in France; twenty-one for the Saxons, and twenty or somewhat over twenty, for the Bavarians. The peasants who had to suffer the largest part of the loss were very bitter about it. They became more hardened and more self-contained than ever.

They had the more justification, for the Government of Württemberg had always stood for a sensible policy of peace, and the encouragement of international intercourse and trade. Of the bigger German states Württemberg was the only one with a naturally neutral frontier. No French, Belgian, Danish, Polish, Russian, Czechoslovakian, Hungarian, or Italian menace or rivalry or memory of past feuds, invasions, or counterinvasions had had a disturbing influence on the minds of the people of Friedrichshafen, who look across the Lake of Constance to the Swiss shore of St. Gall, or travel for half an hour through Baden territory to Schaffhausen and Zürich. They feel akin to the German-Swiss democracy alike in its sincere desire for peace and in its appreciation of military training and good marksmanship. The common sense which distinguished the representatives of Württemberg in the deliberations of the Federal Council's Committee on Foreign Affairs had been proverbial from the time of Prime Minister von Mittnacht. It had an excellent spokesman in the last Prime Minister of the Kingdom of Württemberg, Freiherr von Weizsäcker. His father, in his Department of German Theology, was one of the finest scholars possessed by the University of Tübingen in the nineteenth century; and he himself was a man of the highest intellectual qualities and great firmness of character. During the War it was the voice of Württemberg that made itself heard for moderation, and for a due regard for peace whenever the various governments were consulted, even during the fiercest contests of the War. It was the representative of Württemberg who opposed the plans for a partition of Alsace-Lorraine among Prussia, Bavaria, and Baden, and threatened the partisans of this fantastic project with Württemberg's formal veto, if they tried to proceed with it. Minister von Weizsäcker was the only member of the Federal Council who opposed unlimited submarine warfare on the ground of endangering relations with the United States, a critical view which was shared by many others who, however, could not muster the courage to stand up against the combined forces of the supreme Military Command, the patriotic associations, and the industrial interests behind the policy of *jusqu'au boutisme*.[16] The Minister was supported by the King. But the party leaders suspected him of a certain lack of respect for Parliament, and he himself, with all his strong sense of duty and responsibility to the community, was not a Parliamentary Minister, but a *Fachminister*, a civil servant qualified for high office by his intimate knowledge of affairs, his administrative abilities, his loyalty to the Crown and country without distinction of party. It is the sort of loyalty which in Württemberg is in one way really akin to the strong bonds of some all-civil-service fraternity; and in another it is like the feeling of the peasant for the land which has been in his family from time immemorial, and that makes him call his country by his chosen diminutive term of endearment *unser Ländle*.

The relations with the central authorities in Berlin, and especially with the various war bureaus in which the annexationist group of industry and shipping was extensively represented, were of course handicapped by the fact that the Prime Minister and the Cabinet held independent views as to war aims and foreign policy. Minister von Köhler says:

Government and Parliament at that time [1917] often had occasion to complain of attempts now to muzzle and now to slight them. They

16. Cf. *"Württembergische Erinnerungen," Deutsche Revue*, XXIV, 97 ff.; *"Zur elsass-lothringischen Frage im Weltkrieg," Deutsche Revue*, XXV, 193 ff., both articles by Freiherr von Weizsäcker himself. Confirmed by Dr. von Köhler, *Zur Geschichte der Revolution in Württemberg*, pp. 18 ff. See

also had to complain of Berlin's want of tact and psychological insight into the special needs of Württemberg, when there was no satisfactory excuse for it, in the difficulties of the general situation or in the special cases which came up.[17]

And Von Köhler quotes a speech setting forth the economic interests of the country by a member of the First Chamber, the head of a great piano-manufacturing company, Privy Councilor Schiedmeyer.

He, in a report on behalf of one of the standing committees of the House, had this to say:

We had to learn to our regret that the authorities in Berlin quite often decided to do exactly the opposite of what would have suited our needs; and in a good many cases we had occasion to see how urgent was the need that the highest authorities should be better informed as to our condition—of how things stood with us.

Another writer, also quoting from personal knowledge of Württemberg and Baden industry, says:

The industrial works in Württemberg could not at first get any orders from the military authorities; they had to be content to obtain them from middlemen. It was only after prolonged negotiations that the representatives of Württemberg attached to G.H.Q. and to the War Ministry and staff succeeded in obtaining consideration for the special interests of the country in the ordering of provisions for the army and the distribution of supplies of prime importance for German industry. They ended by having Berlin agree that a fixed quota of all army contracts should be allotted to the Württemberg factories. An *Ausgleichsstelle* between the federal states was set up as a kind of clearing-house for orders: it had to see that contracts were distributed throughout Germany according to the productive capacity of the states. The fact that Württemberg had a War Ministry of its own contributed essentially to the maintenance of economic activity in our country during the War and, by keeping industry and trade alive, to the avoidance of serious disturbances in the relations between employers and the working population.[18]

also Von Köhler, p. 13, on the proposal for closer coöperation between the three South German states.

17. *Ibid.*, p. 17.
18. Weller, *Die Staatsumwälzung in Württemberg*, p. 46. Cf. E. Gäckle and H. Blezinger, *Die Familie Blezinger. Biographisches und Geschichtliches aus drei Jahrhunderten* (1928), p. 164.

And Minister von Köhler adds:

> Among our people the unfair treatment Württemberg experienced in the matter of coal deliveries and food control had aroused great indignation; and this was only intensified by the fact that Württemberg had loyally fulfilled its obligations toward the Reich in the matter of food deliveries. We had, moreover, a feeling that in Berlin the decrees and their execution were sometimes meant only for show, and were far from being observed in Prussia with the same conscientiousness and exactitude as in the states of southern Germany.[19]

Such things will happen in a war; they are only examples of a general feeling of insecurity, of injustice without redress, and of the total eclipse of everything which in normal life is regarded as an obvious course of cause and effect—in fact, the cessation of causality. The individual compared his own efforts and sacrifices of self and property with those of his next-door neighbor, and in many cases believed himself entitled to complain of the other man's comparatively easy or even entirely unmerited gains in wealth and influence and honors. As for himself, he had slaved for his country and seen his family ties broken, his hopes were gone for a well-earned reward in future, and he went unnoticed or perhaps was reprimanded by the authorities for some technical error of conduct. Similarly, the German states, and, on a still larger scale, the Allies watched each other's efforts and the results of those efforts, and

---

19. *Ibid.*, pp. 17 and 205, quoting, from the archives of the Ministry of the Interior, instances of the impertinent behavior of Prussian supervising officials in the case of flour mills, unreasonable demands for fodder deliveries from Württemberg and unfair treatment, instanced by compulsory seizures of stocks of fruit and cabbages.

Of course, there were also instances of the contrary. A few towns in southern Germany which lived on specially good terms with the country people around them had one or two confectionery shops going with fairly good pastry, and genuine cream on a cup of chocolate long after Berlin and the whole of Saxony had had to forego all those things and to feed on substitutes for them. Bavaria gave her people a portion of good cheese once a week long after Prussia had none. Families living dispersed all over Germany learned, after some time, to find out all about these different petty advantages of the "war emergency kitchens" (*Kriegsküchen*) and gave one another the benefit of it. I remember traveling from Würzburg to Frankfurt once holding an egg in each hand which I had been able to find in Bavaria and wished to take to a friend in Frankfurt who was ill.

they compared them with their own condition, in which they saw so many cruel injustices of fate and whims of fortune. In peace they knew—or they thought they knew—that there was an inexorable law of reward for the civic virtues and accomplishments of a nation which could be diminished and injured by bad government policy, but never, in the long run, entirely lost. The better people would reassert themselves. It was the courageous, the long-suffering, the practicers of self-abnegation, those who were ready to put the commonweal above private interest whom Peace was certain to crown with final success. It was the opposite in war. The utmost courage, heroic suffering, and a superhuman effort for victory might only serve to make worse the fate of a nation doomed to lose, and, to complete this picture of logic reversed, a government weak or bad might, in war, do away by its incompetence or vainglory with everything that had been won by the stoic bravery of its subjects and by the military deeds of its army.

During the last year of the War, the Democratic group in the Württemberg Diet had tried to find a way to parliamentary government and the *Volksstaat* by persuading the King, who was always willing to listen to well-meant advice from that quarter, to make a change in the Cabinet, and replace three or four of the five civil servants and the general who then composed it[20] by members of the popular chamber. They were to be parliamentary ministers who would be appointed, as before, by the monarch as the head of the State, just as the President of the United States appoints the members of his Cabinet. But of course they would have to be chosen from the parties forming the majority in the Chamber, on which the Government relied for carrying through its bills and getting its budget voted. The leader of the Democrats, Konrad Haussmann, was especially eager to see this step taken, in order to bind the Socialists still closer to constitutional monarchy and ease the transition to the new state of things, which, he clearly foresaw, would come about after the War. He went so far as to use his influence in the Reichstag, where he and his friends had been among the staunchest supporters of the political truce between Right and Left during the War, to bring that change about. He may have hoped that southern

20. Prime Minister, in charge of foreign affairs including relations with the Reich; Minister of Justice, Minister of Education and Ecclesiastical Affairs, Minister of the Interior, Minister of Finance, and Minister of War.

Germany would lead Prussia on her way to a new electoral system and to parliamentary rule. All these efforts, however, were frustrated by the stubborn opposition of the Württemberg Catholic Center. As late as the summer of 1918 the leader of the Center made a formal declaration to the effect that his party, in complete accordance with the Conservatives and National Liberals, would resist all attempts to introduce parliamentary government, which was not suited to German political ways; that the royal prerogative of appointing the ministers in whom the confidence of the King was freely placed, must remain unaffected; and that, while, in the administration of the districts, it would be a good plan to have more men of general political trustworthiness and a recognized standing with the public,[21] Parliament should not have the power to impose upon the monarch as ministers, men from its own ranks.[22]

It was only on November 8, 1918, after the events at Munich had there led to the quiet proclamation of the Republic, but before they were known in Stuttgart, that the Government was constituted as a partly parliamentary, partly civil-service Cabinet. The King wished

21. The Democrats of Württemberg had been the majority party supporting the Government for so many years that their use of administrative patronage had become a general source of complaint with the other parties. The demand of the Catholic Center that a fair quota of civil-service appointments be reserved to Roman Catholics, which, in the States as in the Reich had been consistently put forward, directed itself against the National Liberals in Baden or the Democrats in Württemberg as well as against the Prussian Conservatives. All these parties were predominantly Protestant, with this difference: that the Center's members and those it protected were supposed to be zealous and sincere members of the Church, practicing their faith—taking part, for instance, in southern Germany, as in Austria, in public processions, especially on Corpus Christi Day. But the other parties, even the Conservatives, did not concern themselves with the real, as distinct from the merely formal, adhesion of their members to one of the denominations of the Protestant Church.

22. One of the reasons for this attitude was the personal antagonism between the leaders of the party in Württemberg and Erzberger, the most active member of the party in the Reichstag, who was himself a Württemberger. He had put his stake in the Reich and his ambitions certainly went far beyond a seat in the Stuttgart Cabinet. But his example, that of a disturbing element in the councils of the party and the nation, as they thought, was always before them. In the Reich, the Center party consistently upheld the claim of a parliamentary majority to suggest ministerial nominees to the head of State or the Chancellor.

to retain the two ministers who had been chiefly instrumental in keeping the political and economic administration of the country in good order and who were both liberal-minded men who, without any party ties, possessed the confidence of both Chambers of Parliament. The Minister for War had to be an officer who could, if necessary, represent the Sovereign with the Prussian authorities as the titular head of an army of his own; and as each of the four parties which promised to support the new Cabinet presented one minister, it remained to add a seventh member to the Cabinet. A Department for Demobilization was created and allocated to the Socialist minister, a lecturer in the Technical High School at Stuttgart. The ministries of Foreign Affairs, Justice, and Education went, respectively, to the Center, the Democrats, and the National Liberals, a Democrat being made Prime Minister.

The new Cabinet issued a proclamation to the people of Württemberg, signed by the King and all the members of the Cabinet. A mass meeting of the radical Socialists had been announced which might have led to a demonstration against the King. He felt so confident in the loyalty of his people and trusted so much in his own conscience, for it told him he had done his best to protect the Constitution, that he would not have thought of leaving the capital. He would have wished to speak to the leaders of the crowd, a risk his ministers were anxious to avoid. The proclamation shows that on November 9 there was every prospect of monarchy in Württemberg being preserved—and the same was true of Baden—as a constitutional monarchy with parliamentary government.

The new Cabinet [it said], which rests on the confidence of the elected representatives of the people, has been formed and has taken office. The King, conforming to the will of the new Government, has ordered that a Constituent Assembly of the country shall be called together. The franchise for the Constituent Assembly will be general and equal, the ballot secret, the election direct, and every national of the State of Württemberg over twenty-four years of age, without distinction of sex, will be entitled to vote. The Assembly will be summoned to give our country a constitution which will satisfy the needs of the new era, on a democratic basis. The majority of the people of Württemberg will, by this measure, be able to decide for themselves on the future form of government. The King has stated that his person will never stand in the way of a step which is desired by the majority of the people, and that he has always held that his sole task is to safeguard the well-being and the legitimate wishes of the people. We address ourselves to the entire population with the urgent demand and exhortation to use discretion in these days of the Fatherland's direst distress and to uphold peace and order. It is only by doing so that we can save our people from utter misery, from the danger of starvation and from the invasion of the enemy.[23]

The proclamation introduced only one principle which was entirely new and alien to the law and practice of the old Constitution. The lines dealing with the position of the monarch himself, which he signed, together with a Socialist and two other members of the Opposition, had nothing new to tell the people. They knew their King for a man who had honestly tried to act in everything as one of themselves, and who had always tried to use his prerogative of choosing his cabinets for the best interests of the country. He had chosen men who were loyal not only to him but to the country and to Parliament. No elected president could have acted otherwise when exercising his public functions. Such criticism and opposition as had been directed against the King arose from court factions and personal intrigues that involved him, but not because of any part he took in public affairs. It was the same with most of the other announcements in the proclamation. Württemberg had been a democratic commonwealth for almost a century; the representatives of the people were elected by secret ballot and general franchise, and the State of Württemberg had been conspicuously free from the influences by which, even with such a franchise, Government, Church, associations of employers, guilds, trade-unions, and the owners of large estates know how to turn elections to their own benefit in other countries. For the peasant and petty bourgeois Württemberger is well known throughout Germany for his "good solid Swabian head" and the keen resentment with which he can meet such undue influence as some wealthier or in any other way would-be superior individual, or official character, might attempt to exert upon him. The First Chamber of the Württemberg Parliament which, in the proclamation, was quietly dropped and had ceased to exist, had for many

23. *Staatsanzeiger für Württemberg,* November 9, 1918. W. Keith, *"Wie sich in Württemberg die Revolution vollzog,"* *Schwäbische Tagwacht* (1919), No. 261, Supplement; Von Köhler, *"Bemerkungen zu den Memoiren des Generals von Ebbinghaus,"* Special Supplement to *Staatsanzeiger für Württemberg* (1928), No. 12, pp. 249 ff.

years—as in practically all German states with the exception of Prussia and the Mecklenburgs—exercised the functions of an advisory Privy Council. It had never attempted to intervene in questions of finance or the budget except for an occasional, and very general, warning as to lavish expenses and high taxation. Not that, in Württemberg, even the Socialists had leaned too much toward extravagance or waste.

The only material innovation of the last Royal Decree in Württemberg was the vote given women on the basis of complete equality with men. Many women had accomplished extraordinary things, during the War, not only as models of moral courage and perseverance in a peculiarly difficult situation. A woman rises almost without fail to situations that threaten immediate danger and demand physical aid. But this was a case where women had to sit still and do small things, and could not even learn what was happening to the men "out there" in the trenches. And, furthermore, they had to take the places of the men. We grew accustomed to seeing peasant women plowing and felling trees, the wife or mother of a landed proprietor directing work in the fields, or superintending the stables and keeping the books, the *Hausfrau* of a tradesman serving the customers in the shop, while caring for her children as well; women assistants carrying on the work of their chiefs in hospitals or laboratories, in the barrister's office or the labor-exchange bureau. The writer remembers a case of a widow who had been a keen supporter of the movement for equal rights for women long before the War. Without means of her own she had managed to send her children, a son and three daughters, to the best schools of the provincial town in which she lived. The son, an ardent pacifist, was killed in the first weeks of the War; the eldest daughter, who had been one of the most active leaders of the *Wandervogelbund,* threw herself into the study of foreign languages and international law. She earned her living and helped the family by day work in the bookkeeping department of a brewery, and gave lessons to other girls, her academic courses and studies being confined to evening and night work. At the end of the War she was able to obtain her degree of Doctor of Laws and to enter upon a career of lawschool teaching and research work in international law. The two sisters whom she helped to bring up have both become musicians of merit. The memory of their brother had transformed itself into a call to the duty of helping to overcome the evil of war, even as he would have answered the call if he had lived. Every German knows of cases like these; exceptional as they may seem, they became almost an understood thing during the War.

Another case is that of an old lady, a professor's widow with a name honored all over the world for the rôles some of its bearers have played in science and the arts. She had done voluntary social work in the great organization for women's welfare work which had been created in Baden by the Grand Duchess Luise, the daughter of the first Emperor, the *Badische Frauenverein*. She was nearly seventy years old when the War broke out, but returned from Saxony, where she had lived for some years, to her native town in Baden to do Red Cross work and take up her former duties as well. She lost all her savings by her subscriptions to the national loans. At eighty-six she was living in a flat, doing housework herself, without a servant. In her case also, war, by bringing about woman's suffrage and equality of the sexes in public affairs, had added to the German electorate and the political forces of the country a vote for peace and the will to overcome the effects of war.

The proclamation of November 9 came too late to influence the course of events; the revolts both in Kiel and Munich—the first the direct result of the conduct of the War at sea, the second the natural sequel of the Austrian collapse which had opened the road to Bavaria for the Allies—had proved to be much more than local affairs; and just as Westphalia and Brunswick, Berlin and the Saxon cities were flooded by the revolutionary tide which came up the Elbe and Weser, the Bavarian movement spread to Württemberg and, a few days later, to Baden.[24] Still, the manifesto remains a valuable piece of

24. It must be said, however, that Württemberg itself had seen a kind of military revolt not unlike that of Kiel, on October 26 and the days following. On the twenty-sixth, the workmen of Friedrichshafen, on Lake Constance, had assembled for a public demonstration in the cause of peace. They had carried red banners and had cheered an orator who asked for the abdication of the Emperor and a republican constitution for the Reich. The Württemberg police and the official of the district who had to report to the Minister of the Interior put the blame for these occurrences, which at the time did not seem very serious, on the many North German workingmen and sailors among the employees of the Maybach Motor Works connected with the Zeppelin dock. The marines were evidently the first to strike at the rules of military discipline. The military police at Friedrichshafen agreed with the civil authorities that the best policy was to meet the wishes of the men so far as possible. The factory council, which the moderate Socialists dominated, had

evidence and shows the continuity of public life even under the trying circumstances of these November days. The new Cabinet, which was formed on November 10 and consisted of six Socialist representatives of the people in revolution together with two ministers of the old Cabinet, a Democrat and a Catholic,[25] renewed the proclamation for a constituent assembly; and it used almost the same words used in the manifesto of the last Cabinet of the Monarchy, and proposed the same mode of election.

In the capital of Württemberg the news of the revolt at Kiel and the rumor of a republican uprising in Berlin and other German capitals had led to several attempts on the part of the leaders of the Independent Socialist party to arrange a big open-air demonstration. On November 5 the Independents had formed a Workingmen's Council against the wishes of the majority Socialists, who hoped to be able quietly to succeed to parliamentary and ministerial power. The Council had proclaimed a general strike, and had sent emissaries to the military barracks to ask for the formation of Soldiers' Councils. The highest military authorities, the General-in-Command of the Army-Corps District of Württemberg and the Governor of

asked for the closing down of the factory on the day of the demonstration, as they would have to take part in the meeting and the procession, and by doing so would be able to keep the hotheads from causing too much disturbance; and the authorities accepted this demand at once. On the other hand the central military authorities—evidently without any knowledge of or regard for local conditions—had ordered a combing out of the men in Friedrichshafen and about two hundred factory hands had got *Gestellungsbefehle,* a measure similar in its effect—though of course on a much smaller scale—to the Kiel plan of ordering the fleet out for a last high-seas battle. A new demonstration was announced at which there would be open incitement if the orders to join the army should not be canceled. The director of the Zeppelin Works, Colsmann, sent an urgent warning against the dispatch of troops to Friedrichshafen. This policy of conciliation proved the right one. Friedrichshafen calmed down, and it was only after the disturbances at Kiel, on November 5 and 6, that a Soldiers' Council was formed. Even then an official sent by the Ministry of the Interior was able to have four of the radical leaders arrested by the police on November 7. They were released on November 8 on the promise of the workmen to return to their jobs. It was only after the events in Munich and Stuttgart that the Republic was proclaimed and the red flag hoisted at Friedrichshafen.

25. The former Minister of the Interior, Von Köhler, resigned but remained at the disposition of the new Cabinet in order to safeguard continuity of administration. It was the wish of the King that he should do so.

Stuttgart, were doubtful whether their men would obey orders in case of a workingmen's demonstration that could not be handled by the police. The King, though convinced of the loyalty of his people and his ability to come to terms with them if he could meet them eye to eye, was anxious to avoid street disorders and possible bloodshed. The bodyguard at the palace gate consisted merely of a lieutenant, two non-commissioned officers, and eighteen men, and the ministers felt that if they were overcome there might be rioting that would put the King in danger. The only thing everybody seemed to agree on was that military power was completely ended and the only people who could possibly quell a revolt were officials of the old administration, now in mufti, who spoke the language of the people and were known to them as their companions in suffering during the War. A deputation of sailors from Kiel was held up by railway officials on November 8 for failing to produce their military permits for shore leave. The day before, the Minister of the Interior had given orders to arrest the two radical leaders, Thalheimer and Stöck, who had gone to the fortress of Ulm to call out the garrison. But the military governor of Ulm was afraid to hold them, as his jurisdiction did not seem to cover such an emergency. And the local police took them to Tübingen and put them into an ordinary cell in the district courthouse, along with fifteen Spartacists who had been arrested in Stuttgart. Indeed, with the leaders of the radical wing put away, and the moderate Socialists honestly endeavoring to coöperate with the civil authorities, in the capital, public demonstrations planned for November 8 and 9 might have passed off without any violent change but for news from Munich whither, on the seventh, the King had fled, and where Kurt Eisner, an uncompromising radical, had formed a revolutionary government. On the evening of the eighth, the members of a conference called by the Minister of the Interior decided that they would let things take their course, and that each would try to avoid bloodshed in his own way. The Mayor had informed the conference that it might reckon on the proclamation of the Republic. The ministers had asked the generals whether they could prevent the masses from marching on the palace and the official buildings and occupying them by force. The military commanders had replied that this was a task for the police, that their men—insufficient in number in any case—would probably refuse to use arms against the people, and, finally, that they "had not ten men they could rely upon."[26] As a result of this declaration and the King's statement before his Chief of Cabinet, Baron Neurath, that he meant to avoid any conflict which might lead to the spilling of blood, the conference resolved that it would not resist the popular movement. By order of the municipal council, next morning saw the posting of a proclamation to that effect.

Citizens [it said], the working population of Stuttgart will assemble this morning on the Schlossplatz and the squares near the palace so that they may be informed of the domestic situation by their competent leaders. Such a gathering will serve to promote a peaceful and orderly transition to a new constitutional régime. We ask the entire population to preserve order and tranquillity. In that way a citizen can best serve his town and country.

On November 9 orators proclaimed the Republic at these public meetings. Part of the crowd got out of hand, made a rush for the palace, disarmed the few guards who were still on duty in the center of the town and the dozen or so soldiers in the palace entrance hall, replaced the royal standard by the red flag, and made an attempt to force their way into the royal suite. When the King's physician and a few old servants told them, however, that the King ought not to be disturbed they thought better of it and went quietly down the stairs and out of the palace. Somebody told them that machine guns and munitions were hidden in the castle yard, but while they were on their way to seize them, a technical-school student arrived by way of a side street,

climbed the railings and, in the yard, by a few simple gestures and shouted directions, succeeded in getting the crowd out and back in the street. They had good naturedly obeyed him because they mistook him

26. Von Köhler, *op. cit.*, pp. 136 ff. Professor Weller maintains his belief that "in spite of a few mutineers no military formation in Stuttgart was so little to be relied upon that the officers, who were all of them loyal, could not have held it firmly in hand if they had shown the necessary energy." That may be true, but it cannot be proved, and the responsibility of the officers in command for the turn events took, both in Stuttgart and Munich, would only become more evident if it could be proved. It has since been said that a sufficient number of officers or former officers or perhaps engineers would have been ready to form shock troops themselves. I was told at the time that in Würzburg, the seat of a Bavarian *Generalkommando,* a number of artillery subalterns sent a deputation to the General-in-Command, asking for permis-

for one of the Socialist leaders. He stationed a few soldiers and workmen picked from the crowd, at the doors, and had them protect the building, which they did with much zeal. There was no looting.[27]

In the barracks no serious resistance was made when the people entered to call on the soldiers to fraternize with them, and even in the case of the premises of the military Supreme Court which might have been expected to stir the Radical Socialists to special fury, the only damage done was to the records which were thrown from the windows. In the evening of November 9 the King and Queen drove from the capital to their castle at Babenhausen, an hour or two away. For escort they had two men chosen by the Soldiers' Council, but there was no one to molest them. It was only on November 30 that the King formally abdicated. In a public proclamation the provisional Government thanked him for having to the last let himself be guided by his love for the country and the people. The castle in which he lived for two more years without seeing the silver lining to the clouds over Germany, he, of all German princes, should in justice have been spared to see, is shown by the people of Württemberg to visitors who pass through the lovely country around it, with a sympathetic word of respect for their former sovereign and almost with a kind of awe for the fate he suffered.

The provisional Government which, as first composed, consisted only of Socialists of both party wings, was at once forced into a conflict with the Spartacist group whose aim was a dictatorship based on the Soldiers' Councils; for the soldiers had proved more radical than the workmen and peasants. By the evening of November 10 the two ministers of the bourgeois parties who had agreed to keep their old posts in the new Cabinet had been enrolled, and the assistance of practically the whole civil service had been secured. The attitude of the King, which was well known, helped monarchists among the civil servants to overcome their conscientious opposition to a republic which, at least in its first stage, had every indication of being of a strongly socialist character. The Workingmen's and Soldiers' Councils were legalized by a law of December 14. Their

sion to fire, and that he ordered them to get back to barracks and offer no resistance to the Soldiers' Councils' orders. It may have been the same in Stuttgart. No call for resistance nor even permission for independent action by subalterns was given by any officer in high command.

27. Weller, *op. cit.*, p. 109.

functions remained advisory, and they never wielded real executive power. Public order and security was maintained by fifteen *Sicherheitskompagnien* ("security militia") approved by the central Soldiers' Council, which did their duty impartially and on the whole efficiently, though their task was not without difficulties, for some of the service units on their way back from the trenches were rather unruly. It is a remarkable fact that demobilization, which, even in a victorious country with a well-established government and no restriction on supplies or means of transportation, is one of the most difficult administrative problems, began and proceeded during the winter months of 1918–1919 without any considerable disturbances or hitches, if with great loss of public property. This in a country shaken to its depths by defeat, under conditions of big-city food supply which amounted almost to starvation, with the railways practically out of business, and with no civil or military executive that could rely on silent and blind obedience to the orders it gave. It was an instance of how much can be done without a plan and even without an organization in an emergency that appeals to the common sense and good will of the whole people, without distinction of class or party. The thing could only be done by a great human effort in the strict sense of the word, and, in this way, with all playing the part of simple human beings whose one wish was to get out of the War and back to peace.[28]

The *Sicherheitskompagnien* were able to put down a communist rising on January 9 and 10 without more loss of life. The ministers chosen from the left-wing Socialists had to leave the Cabinet, and

28. It is true that, as intimated above, demobilization under such circumstances as prevailed in Germany at the end of 1918 and 1919 meant a great loss of public money and a terrible waste of material. Profiteers could buy stocks for a small fraction of the amount they would normally have had to pay to the commissariat after the demobilization. One must not forget, on the other hand, that mobilization and War, though planned and carried out by a government with the completest executive power, always lead to profiteering on a great scale. The difference in the two cases consists mainly in this, that the profiteers, in normal cases, have to share with bureaucracy and legitimate trade the gain they make at the common expense, while in the case of a sudden and unorganized breakdown like that of 1918 they are able to establish a kind of monopoly—with the corresponding risk of being robbed of their gain or even summarily hanged for it, whereas in normal times their smaller takings are supplemented by titles and decorations.

THE STRAIN OF WAR AND THE REVOLUTION 191

the "Majority Socialists" retained ostensible command. The elections to the Constituent Assembly gave only 40,634 votes to the Independent Socialists. The Communists boycotted the elections, branding the attempt to legalize the revolution by a vote of Parliament as a betrayal of the people. The governmental Socialists obtained 452,699; the Democrats, reinforced by the bulk of the National Liberals, 328,689; the Catholic Center, 273,200; and the coalition of the three parties of the right, all of them more or less avowed monarchists, as many as 209,223. The task of drafting a new constitution was at once attacked with great zeal, the chief merit of its success falling to a professor of Roman civil law at the University of Tübingen, Wilhelm von Blume, the descendant of a Prussian family which had given many distinguished members to the old army and the Protestant clergy. He himself had been a fellow worker with Friedrich Naumann and Rudolf Sohm in the old National Socialist movement of the Nineties, and a National Liberal.[29]

29. Cf. Max Rümelin, *Wilhelm von Blume, Archiv für die zivilistische Praxis* (1928), pp. 129 ff.; O. Koellreutter, *Die neue badische und die neue württembergische Verfassung, eine vergleichende Gegenüberstellung. Archiv des öffentlichen Rechts*, XXXIX (1920), 437 ff.; V. Bruns, *Württembergs künftige Verfassung* (1919); and W. von Blume, "*Wesen und Aufgabe der Parlamente*," in *Handbuch der Politik*, I (1920), 336; "*Volksvertretung in den Ländern*," in *Handbuch der Politik*, III, 77.

PART III

EFFECTS OF THE WAR ON INDUSTRY

CHAPTER XII

POLITICS AND BUSINESS IN WAR-TIME

War-time politics and the attempts of constitutional law to make itself heard and felt under the reign of war seem incoherent enough, as the preceding chapters have shown. In one respect, however, a deliberate movement in the direction of a new condition in public affairs can be traced with sufficient distinctness. We may even assume that in considering this movement we have now left the peculiarities of the German situation behind us and have entered the realm of modern great-power war as such. War, when it takes a great country with all its implements of mechanized life in its grip, exercises a definite influence on the value which, in the balance of governmental power in such a country, is given to politics in the wider sense of the term on one side, and to industry and finance, also in the widest sense of the words—that is what Germans mean by *Wirtschaft*—on the other.

The War brought politics into discredit and disrespect; it allowed business to overestimate its own importance in the life of the nation, and seduced public opinion into joining in this overestimation. War is, in the Nietzschean sense, a great "smasher of old tables of valuation," but it is perhaps a greater danger to healthy national life when it sets up new tables than when it destroys old.

There is no war that does not find the people accusing, more or less articulately, politicians, members of the cabinet, parliamentarians, and diplomats of a carelessness or incapacity which makes them appear responsible for the sufferings of those whose well-being had been entrusted to them, for the death and mutilation of millions of soldiers, the misery and starvation of millions of women and children, the general breakdown of economic life, and the destruction of property. The politicians should have been able to prevent the war —or they should have been convinced of the impossibility of preventing it and should therefore have made more careful preparation for it. The politicians had spoken too glibly of war, "painting the Devil on the wall," until, one day, it sprang, alive and fiery, out of the picture—or, by their pacifist declarations, they had lulled to sleep the good people who had warned them of the Devil. The politicians had given too much rein to their general staff and to the bureaus in the Ministry of War. They had allowed the generals and colonels too much latitude in arranging with their military *confrères* of another power for a common offensive against a third, or in drafting mobilization plans which involved the violation of neutral territory. They had winked when their chemical works had invented forbidden gases and explosives; or those same politicians had refused the same generals and engineers and chemists the necessary funds to play their strategic games, to finance their laboratories, to construct tanks or submarines or bombing planes.

Some such charges can be brought against politicians with a show of justification, and generally with a great display of moral indignation, whenever war has broken out and has not led to the overrunning of a weak enemy country and the forcing of peace on it within a few months. It did not need any formal outlawry of war to show that war as such was always a terrible item when on the debit side of a government's political accounts.

In modern times most of the Great Powers and many of the smaller ones have entrusted the leading positions in cabinet and parliament to lawyers and administrators trained in the law. It was against them that popular ill will used particularly to be manifest during the War. The Roman adage of *"inter arma"* is still freely quoted with lively satisfaction wherever two people with an old grudge against the law or the lawyers meet in the street after a declaration of war. The God of Battles silences Justice and her servants; he boasts of being the Lord of Deeds while the Law could only talk—a preposterous claim, as the nuisance of noisy talk and the shouting of mobs is as common in war as in peace, but still a plausible claim in the eyes of the masses. During the first stages of a conflict, while peace must not even be mentioned, the lawyer is compared with the active soldier to the former's great disparagement. To the man who wields the sword, the scribe or *Federfuchser* of many cartoons, with pen and ink as his only weapons, contrasts very badly indeed in public opinion, which during a war is largely formed by women adoring the manly virtues. The sword has become the symbol of the Lord of Heaven Himself, the instrument of Fate, while the Pen serves only the despicable group of men who try to evade responsibility for a deed of courageous lawbreaking by laying it upon others and by inciting passions without daring to give vent to them.

Looking back at the War as it really was, we now see the Quartermaster General sitting in an office, talking through the telephone, drawing plans of attack or retreat on the map and discussing his schemes with the Emperor or King or President as the case may be, or with politicians from whom he wants parliamentary support—all this while the person the people admired was some man of action who carried a sword, charged the enemy lines on a fiery horse, or bore the colors to victory at the cost of his own life. We now see the administrators, lawyers, and scribes in feverish action from morning till night. They go recruiting. They find the provisions for a beleaguered town or a blockaded area. They maintain the life of the nation from which the great sacrifice of war is being exacted. And they do all this with their bodily strength because mere pen and paper could never do it. Later on, if confidence in a military victory is on the wane, the lawyers and politicians are by no means reinstated; their only comfort, if it is one, consists in seeing the unsuccessful generals and the officials in the War Ministry sent to join their old opponents in that wilderness where scapegoats end their miserable lives.

By then the time has come for the forces that call themselves, succinctly, if perhaps not modestly, economical—*wirtschaftlich*—and that by then alone are thriving amidst the general misery and distress. It is their time to address the people. Why, they ask, did not the nation listen to the advice of business instead of following incompetent bureaucrats or soldiers of fortune? Why did it fail to recognize that business and not armaments is the real power in modern life, and that in business, and not in politics or in the law lies true good sense? Had not the politicians or the lawyers, even while they were protesting to them about their peaceful intentions and their ability to steer the ship of state between the rocks, thrown them headlong into war? Had not the generals—although the people had voted them everything they had wanted, for year after year, and although victory had been anticipated even to the fixing of the exact date for it in the mobilization plans and the arrangements between the General Staffs of the Allies—had not the generals had to acknowledge defeat or at least military stalemate? Business, on the other hand, if one listened to its prophets and advertisers, was entirely innocent of any bellicose intentions. It was merely a power of peaceful international intercourse which knew debtors and creditors in their mutual dependence, but was ignorant of a state of things in which two subjects battled one with the other, equally armed and each with equal intention of overcoming the other as completely as possible, or even of destroying him forever.

Business had maintained its position, amidst the violence and lawlessness of war-time, by its own standard of ethics, had made a profit out of the gain and loss of the belligerents and thereby, to a certain degree, had mediated between them. And after both the civil government and military leadership had had to acknowledge their inability to cope with the situation, it was only right and fair that the direction of affairs should now be entrusted to businessmen. They would undertake to repair the damage and reconstruct the House of Peace provided the nation was willing and ready to pay the cost of the War and the reparations which the business experts had calculated.

For four years after the War had been formally ended the politicians and their military advisers tried to maintain their hold upon national and international government, at least in the capitals of the victorious Powers. By the year 1923, however, almost the whole of Europe—except, of course, Soviet Russia, where politics reigned a little longer before giving way to the New Economic Policy and the Five Year Plan—had begun to put hope only in reconstruction that could be brought about by the advice of the business experts. The last attempt to carry out a definite policy by political means—aided by military sanctions—had failed ignominiously, having been met by a radical measure of economic resistance on the part of the country which was to be its victim. Inflation, carried through to the vanishing-point of the German currency, had shown the futility of further political sanctions by demonstrating the economic interdependence of creditor and debtor countries.

One remembers the general relief felt in Europe when people were told that a body of experts with an American citizen as chairman had been invited by the governments of the creditor countries to report to them upon the economic situation in the matter of the German war debt and the means of obtaining payment of as much of that debt as Germany, in the opinion of the experts, could pay without disturbing the equilibrium of the German budget and endangering the German currency. A sound, sober business account of the remaining assets and their eventual use in the reduction of the debts was to take the place of social utopias and political ambitions; and nothing short of a speedy recovery from the years of distress and destruction was expected from a faithful observance of the recommendations the experts had made. In its outward form the Dawes Plan was not more than an opinion offered to the governments which had called for it, but in substance it voiced a dictate which, supported as it was by public opinion in both hemispheres and by the most powerful financial interests in the creditor as well as in the debtor countries, could not have been ignored even by the strongest political power in the world.[1] When the tribunal, which later on had to decide on questions of differences of interpretation of the Plan by the debtor and creditor governments, heard the arguments of counsel, all of them learned members of the British, German, French, or Italian bar, both sides rested again and again on these points: that the Plan had not been formulated by jurists with their strict sense that justice must be done at all costs, and their conception of the twin character of right and remedy, or *droit et sanctions;* nor had it

1. It must be borne in mind that the situation in 1924 or even in 1928, before the Dawes Plan was changed by the second experts' report into the Young Plan, was entirely different from the situation in 1926, when the French franc was stabilized by the intervention of an American group, and the French Government, Radical Socialist up to that time, had to make way for a Cabinet headed by M. Poincaré, and entirely different from 1931, when combined action on the part of the American group and French banking houses was called for to support the British currency, and a Conservative-Liberal Coalition Cabinet emerged from the crisis in the place of the Labor Government. In both cases accusations that national independence had been sacrificed for the benefit of international finance were freely made. We may quote the opinion of a Swiss paper well known for its western sympathies and its moderate liberalism, the *Journal de Genève,* on the latter case (September 3, 1931, Edition du matin) : "The American financiers seem then to have made it clear that if the British Government did not take every energetic means to balance its budget, make an end of waste, and restore public confidence, it seemed to them to be useless to go on throwing money into the abyss. Have they exacted reforms? Have they been made a part of British policy? Have they brought pressure that was irresistible? It is useless to play upon words. Being in a position either to grant credit or to refuse it, they have made plain on what conditions they would advance their money. That is all." That shows the root differences between the experts' reports containing the Dawes and the Young plans. The only thing they have in common is that in every case the politicians have to submit to the opinion and will of the economists speaking or acting for international finance.

been formulated by politicians who must regard it simply from the standpoint of boundless sovereign power demanding obedience and admitting no plea of *ultra posse*—that a debtor can pay only according to his means. It had been drawn up by experts in international finance who knew the just and reasonable relation between creditor and debtor, and how to obtain security and release.[2] Everybody believed in the ability of the experts to cure Europe of her post-war illness, crediting them with possessing the secret of a certain treatment which would restore the debtor's health by keeping his wounds open and letting the blood of payment flow from them at regular intervals.

There is no need for insisting on these things; they belong to a period of recent world history which has been widely discussed in international literature. The change in the relative importance of business and law or politics is less obvious if we turn to domestic affairs. The difference between the international and the domestic influence of *Wirtschaft* is striking. The term *Wirtschaft*[3] itself seems objective and real enough, but behind it we find two entirely different groups of men planning, calculating, acting, and speaking their mind on international and on national affairs. The leaders of *Wirtschaft* in its international aspect are, first of all, the heads of the great banking houses of the world and, in the next place, the men in charge of public utilities, industrial, transport, or agrarian concerns to which the big banks stand in close connection through credits given and taken, their spokesmen being the corporation lawyers, or syndics, or, in some instances, the editors of periodicals, or the professors of statistics or social science. The leaders and spokesmen of *Wirtschaft* in its national aspect are a different class of men. The

2. Cf. M. Schoch, "*Politische Wissenschaft*" (1926–1929), Heft 2, 3, 9.

3. In German the term is used very freely in political conversation and in literature with a semblance of definite meaning which is in striking contrast to the differing applications of the term in composite words like *Staatswirtschaft, Privatwirtschaft, Volkswirtschaftslehre, Reichswirtschaftsrat, Wirtschaftspolitik, Wirtschaftsführer, Wirtschaftssachverständiger, Wirtschaftspartei*. The nearest synonym to *Wirtschaft* is the loan-word *Oekonomie* which has fallen into disuse except in the official term for the University Chairs of Economics, "*National-Oekonomie.*" In southern Germany the term *Wirtschaft* has a special meaning, at least in colloquial language; it means simply a tavern, while "*Oekonom*" is a semiofficial title given to the wealthier class of peasant-owners.

retail trades and the big associations of commercial employees, the house owners, especially the owners of apartment houses and the local butchers, bakers, tobacconists, or barbers, owners of book- and newspaper-stalls, apothecaries, proprietors of local hotels and restaurants, craftsmen and artisans of all kinds, architects, electricians, plumbers, and a host of other tradespeople and members of the liberal professions form the bulk of a party which, since the War, and in direct consequence of the effects of the War, has steadily grown in numbers and influence and has styled itself the *Wirtschaftspartei*, to indicate that in its program economic interests took precedence of everything else. During the seven critical years in which the German Republic was to be either made or marred, from 1921 to 1928, the *Wirtschaftspartei* took hundreds of thousands of votes away from all other bourgeois parties, most of them from the Democrats, who at the time of the elections for the Constituent Assembly had, next to the Catholic Center, been the strongest bourgeois party throughout Germany.[4] Their appeal to the electors consisted chiefly in their claim that the State lived by them; it throve on the goods they produced, by the taxes they paid, by their savings, which went to form new capital, and by their contribution to the steady increase of demand and supply, causing as it did an ever greater speed in the circulation of money and thus meaning prosperity and the accumulation of national wealth. Look at the budget, they said, and you will find that everybody else, most of all the civil servants, figure on the side of expenses, while we alone, together with the *Landwirtschaft*, form the assets.

Disappointment at the result of combined leadership by professional politicians, lawyers, generals, and their academic advisers during the War led, almost inevitably, to overconfidence in the economic forces which, as their partisans were quick in declaring, had

---

[4]. In 1930 the Democrats chose the name of *Staatspartei* in direct challenge to the *Wirtschaftspartei,* claiming to represent the common interest of all, and not the economic interest of a group, an *Interessentenhaufen*—a crowd of people anxious to safeguard their special interests—as one of their leaders called it, which should dominate in political considerations. The *Wirtschaftspartei,* in reply, claimed to be foremost in loyalty to the country. National strength, so far as town life was concerned, stood in direct relation to their own strength in the nation. In other words, while the State maintained the army, the judiciary, and the civil service, they, the active members of the *Wirtschaft,* maintained the State.

been neglected or even wilfully kept down by those who had proved unable to stand the test of the War. Though it did not develop its full power as an organized party until about 1925, the *Wirtschaftspartei* with its allied organizations—for instance, the *"Technische Nothilfe,"* the *"Deutschnationaler Handlungsgehilfenverband"* and some of the freak groups that had organized themselves after the inflation with a view to obtaining a 100 per cent revaluation of their papermark notes and claims—were directly traceable to the War; and it was the War, which, through the agency of this comparatively small group, wrecked the German Constitution during the critical years that followed. It was this group and the interests represented by it which prevented the formation of a clear majority either of Left or Right in the Reichstag and in the Prussian Diet, and which led to the parliamentary bickering and the final deadlock in the Reichstag in 1932. Having attained so much, it suddenly collapsed and left the electors to choose between a return to the methods of government which, though they had meant prosperity and prestige to pre-war Germany, had failed in the War, and the despotism of one party which had risen to the first rank in pure party politics, and now felt strong enough to monopolize public administration in every walk of life. Later, the rank and file of the *Wirtschaftspartei* became followers of the National Socialist movement which, in its turn, lays the greatest stress on the close interdependence of a united economic body and a centralized, or totalitarian administration.

That is the main point we have to consider if the relation between the War and industrialism is to be assessed at its real worth. War and industrialism are allies in their need for mass organization and centralized government and their abhorrence of individualists and democracy.

Warfare on a modern scale and industrial production are, in many respects, as much akin to one another as up-to-date warfare is opposed to craftsmanship or to small farming. Both war and industry ask for mass production of standardized goods. Both delight in an acceleration and increase of production, which is only possible if the products are used up so quickly that the demand for them remains unsatisfied. Both are socializing forces in this sense. They take practically all the able-bodied men of the nation, and they group them together for common work, either for so many hours a day that their rest hours go wholly to a hasty supper, followed by bed; or, in the case of war, they group them for so many months, and perhaps years, of uninterrupted service, that family life, which goes so well with a peasant's or artisan's or teacher's work, is almost of necessity destroyed, even aside from the chance of illness or death taking the man off before his time. Both war and industry, apart from agriculture, can go on only by constantly destroying their own products and results. They both serve death, in the literal and in the metaphysical sense, and not life. It, on the contrary, is made to serve their ends by the sacrifice of all that makes it worth living. Life is individualistic *à outrance*, and everything which serves life, from the highest work of art or the religious conviction in a human soul down to the smallest piece of woven cloth or scrap of natural food, is constitutionally opposed to standards, statistics, and centralization. It is death which claims that all men are equal before him. Even against death, human individualism tries to maintain its love of the individual, if only by embodying a memory in the inscription on a wooden cross or in the flower on a grave. It is war and industry, both alike, which have the mass cemetery, with its millions of nameless sacrifices, for their final goal.

In a system of politics we may call the prevailing tendency in the development of national industries—agriculture always excepted—"industrial imperialism." The tendency is toward the largest possible scale of production and consumption.

The term economists use for the area of consumption, "market," has been borrowed from the primitive usages of the village or the smallest kind of town. Today it is used for an area which may range from a territory like Russia, Central Africa, or China to a continent, or to the whole world. There is hardly any relation left between industry, human individuals, and natural facts; a huge structure of organizations and combines is what remains. And while in the primary condition of an exchange of goods money is used as a subordinate means of facilitating the valuation of the goods which are to change hands, in the present condition of industry and trade goods have come to be an expression for the value of money which, in its turn, is handled on the international exchange on the largest possible scale. The value of the currency of a country determines the value of the goods bought and sold by it, not the intrinsic worth of the goods nor the amount of labor which went to produce them.

It is obvious that this tendency toward imperialism and centralization existed before the War. In Germany tollgates and custom houses have been the objects of attack ever since the period of industrialization began. The demand for national unity came later on; but the liberals and future socialists who advocated it, the vanguard —whether they liked it or not—of Bismarck's German Empire, took a great part of their strength from the trading community, from far-sighted industrialists in the Rhineland and in Württemberg and Saxony. Progress seemed to mean a change from extreme federalist tendencies glorying in the very narrowness of territorial and spiritual orbits, of *"Kleinstaaterei"* and *"Kantönlisgeist"*—the attitude of small state or canton—one of the chosen objects of adverse comment in the Forties, Fifties, and Sixties of the last century—to a great nation, able to form an economic autarchy, a *"geschlossener Handelsstaat"* or to force its superfluous products on other nations by the weight of its military and financial supremacy, as the case might be.

When German national unity had been obtained and, except for a few remains of particularism in Bavaria and of irredentist opposition in Alsace-Lorraine, all barriers to uniform trading within Germany had been done away with, industry asked for a larger area of trade. An overseas domain for the supply of raw materials and an overseas market for the preferential sale of homemade goods had to be acquired in order to place German industry on a level with that of France, Belgium, Holland, and Great Britain. Colonial policy, with the German people, originated in this demand for economic imperialism in the face of the safer advice of professional politicians and the German people's innate lack of familiarity with the outside world; the flag had to follow trade. The same economic forces have been at work, at least since the Nineties of last century, to redress the political severance of Austria from Germany. Under the influence of Bismarck, Germany tried to keep out of Danubian associations with the Near East, and apply all her energies to the strengthening of her position in the regions of the Atlantic and the Baltic Sea. A realistic conception of Germany's industrial strength was content to base it, in the main, on its strongholds in the Rhineland, Westphalia, Saxony, and Silesia, that is to say, roughly, the country between the Rhine, the Elbe, and the Vistula. But it was industrial imperialism, in open contradiction to the code of Bismarck's foreign policy, which staked its claims in Constantinople,

Baghdad, and Basra as well as at Casablanca. The Alliance of the Three Emperors in the Seventies, and the Triple Alliance between Germany, Austria-Hungary, and Italy, which, for the sake of friendlier relations with England through the medium of Italy, had replaced the older alliance in the Eighties, were political alliances devoid of and even working against commercial interests. For through the Triple Alliance Germany had intended to proclaim her disinterestedness in the territories, Balkan and Asiatic, southeast of the Austrian domain, and in northern Africa southwest of the Italian sphere. Bismarck's own design was not only to restrain German policy from any intervention in the affairs of those regions, but even to keep the Allies from extending their own activities in that direction. They must not be allowed to entangle Germany in any Bosnian or Tunisian adventures. Rumania was added to the Triple Alliance partly on dynastic grounds, partly for military reasons. There was never even a hint of either a cultural or an industrial *pénétration pacifique* of the Rumanian ally at that time. The political conception of an alliance between sovereign states implied a promise of mutual regard for all the susceptibilities which a sovereign cherishes in the case of his own territory, especially its economic independence. Propaganda, pacific penetration, or an attempt at actual hegemony, which seemed permissible or at least tolerable if they were directed against a neutral or an adversary, were forbidden between Allies. In the post-Bismarckian era the rigid rules of international courtesy which he liked to observe were relaxed. Side by side with the Chancellory and the Foreign Office, in which, in the great Chancellor's time, the direction of affairs had centered, other departments, such as the Prussian Ministry of War and the *Reichsmarineamt* had developed to an independence of administration and political conduct which at times amounted almost to overruling the intentions of the nominal head of the Cabinet.

And, in like manner, the semiofficial organizations of the shipping trade and of industry had assumed a leading rôle in public life instead of remaining boards of experts entitled to give advice on technical questions without professing political opinions of their own. In the Nineties and during the first years of the present century neither Austria, with its system of bureaucratic rule, nor Hungary in its pride of economic and administrative autocracy could have been subjected to a German campaign of peaceful penetration. But their territory could at least be made a link with the Near East. This program of economic expansion which is connected with the names of many an important leader of German finance and industry in the history of that period—with the Siemens, the Helfferichs, and the spectacular rise of the Deutsche Bank—triumphed over the traditional policy of the Wilhelmstrasse. Industrial imperialism had won the Emperor to its cause, and since the Chancellorship of Prince Bülow it had conquered even the Foreign Office.[5] The need felt by the big banks for new outlets for capital, the need which the industrial world had for new markets, and the general expansiveness of trade and commerce accomplished something which it would have been impossible to accomplish even by the most extreme forms of political imperialism. The Emperor and his military and civil advisers looked down on the professors, tradespeople, houseowners and industrialists of the smaller provincial kind in the camp of the Pan-German imperialists with a mixture of contempt and distrust that they were hardly able or willing to conceal, while the relations of court and government circles with high finance, leading industrialists, and shipping magnates became more and more cordial. The preference of the Emperor for the sciences—the leading representa-

5. It was a coincidence—if a very important one—that the program of expansion in the Near East became intimately connected with Pan-Germanism. The demand for a political link between the mother country and the German settlements in Croatia and Servia, in Transylvania, and in the Crimea fused itself with the demand for economic autonomy. The *"geschlossene Handelsstaat,"* a favorite conception of amateurish nationalism, seemed suddenly to be nearer its realization than those who made speeches about it to patriotic meetings had dared to think. In spite of the terrible pace of modern mechanical inventions, which seem to dissolve the very substance of a territorial reign, changing the relation of human beings to the soil into magics of electricity, feats of flying through the air, and the making of wireless connections with far-off continents, a new vista of a real, territorial empire, founded on a coherent chain of German settlements along the Danube and perhaps along the German-built railway through Asia Minor, opened itself to the ambitions of nationalist dreamers. But they could not have achieved it by themselves; and though many of them, even at that early time of what is now called *Nationalsozialismus,* would have been loath to be linked, for the purpose of this task, with the promoters of international finance, they had to realize that something more substantial than the Pan-Germanism of the provincial Middletownish bourgeoisie was needed to make German foreign policy budge from its traditional position.

tives of which were in their turn closely allied to the industrial world by personal and material bonds—helped to accentuate this policy.[6]

Economic forces and the influence of business leaders were, furthermore, put to good use to favor the policy of a great navy, one able to hold the sea in a future war, and the policy of acquiring naval bases in distant seas, especially in the Far East. The least that can be said in this respect is that the leaders of industry and commerce and the economists must bear a full share of responsibility for having stood aside when this policy was initiated, and for allowing its promoters to take advantage of the Emperor's interest in the sea and in shipping and so further their plan. Some of them possessed constant access to the Privy Council of the Emperor. They could have

6. To appreciate the motive power behind the policy of the last period before the War one must pay close attention to the details of the connection between engineering, science, and Big Business—using this term without any critical antipathy to the undue influence attributed to Big Business, but simply as a designation for a group of leading industrial and commercial enterprises. The technical high schools, which enjoyed the special favor of the Emperor, and which he liked to single out to praise for their achievements in contrast to the humanistic high school and university, had a strong, active, nationalist element among both the teachers and the students. They were filled with an almost fascist energy at a time when the universities were complaining about the lack of interest in politics among their students. The technical high schools and the research institutes, which were also under the special protection of the Emperor, had won the recognition of scientists all over the world; and there were millions of people who supported the policy of encouraging the *Realwissenschaften,* the practical sciences, even at the cost of neglecting philosophy, ethics, history, and the law, because they were justly proud of the world-wide reputation of German engineering and science. The German people have a profound respect for, almost a worship of *Leistung,* "achievement," and sometimes they are inclined to take the applause of the world for such a national achievement too seriously. On the other hand, scientists and technicians fully recognized the fact that their work, experimental and laboratory, as well as the fruits of research and the exploitation of the new processes they had discovered, were inextricably bound up with the capitalist system and with a public order which acknowledged social differentiation. The disciples of science were as loud in their claim to social leadership as the officers of the army in their demand for social prerogatives. The fact that Soviet Russia today rivals Imperial Germany for the way in which engineering and technical sciences are put above humanistic learning should not blind us to the other fact that in Germany nationalist politics of the fascist type found their first abode with students of the technical high school, and with engineers and scientists employed in industry.

represented to him with great force the adverse effects on Far Eastern trade and on relations with China which the venture into the French, British, and Russian competition for territorial concessions on the continent of eastern Asia would necessarily have for Germany. Others, as we have since learned, through the disclosures of the War, were aware of the danger to Anglo-German relations and to peace which sprang from this systematic rivalry in shipbuilding. They were afraid to speak out, while their compatriots in the Hanse towns acclaimed as a welcome sign of the Emperor's far-sightedness every new development resented by Great Britain, hailed his naval policy as a decided improvement on Bismarck's rule,[7] and praised him for his truly businesslike, his *wahrhaft kaufmännische*, ability to make use of the national resources.

Negotiations between businessmen and departments of State for the most part escape written documentation. But it is common knowledge today that such diplomatic enterprises of German policy as the Moroccan ventures in the time of Secretary of State von Kiderlen-Wächter were decided upon after prolonged negotiations between the Foreign Office on the one hand and, on the other, those industrialists who had the greatest stake in the economic development of transport facilities for the Moroccan mining industry and seaports, especially the Mannesmann brothers and their banking consorts, Messrs. Warburg of Hamburg. It is one of the most significant cases of undue preponderance of economic considerations over those that are purely political. The Moroccan affair had been liquidated long before the conflict which actually led to the World War had taken shape, removing, by its solution at Algeciras, the political activities of the Great Powers from northwestern and central Africa to the Near East and the Balkans, a still more dangerous

---

7. There is a story that Bismarck in his later days was invited by the Senate of Hamburg to inspect the harbor at a time when one of the big new liners was lying there, and that Germany's Grand Old Man said, a little reluctantly, that this was all new to him, an embarking upon greater adventures than he could have dreamed of. It filled him, he was reported to have said, with awe and wonder. The story was probably invented or improved upon in order to please the Emperor, and to confirm him in his good intentions for the development of the seaports. It is not without value, even if entirely *trovato,* in showing in a popular form the natural conflict between the conservative territorial policy of a great country squire and the liberal imperialism of "princely merchants."

nidus of war bacilli. At the time, however, the German claim for equality of opportunity in Morocco at the Conference of Algeciras led to the first world coalition against the two Central Powers. Not only Italy, but the United States of America, took part in the diplomatic opposition to Germany's economic advance in northwest Africa; and at the same time the failure of the German Government's attempt to protect the industrial enterprises of German firms in Morocco led to domestic trouble and made the Mannesmann interests and their many associates in the German industrial area of the Rhine, Wupper, and Ruhr definitely hostile to the "feeble" policy of the Chancellor, Bethmann-Hollweg.

Pausing in this story of industrial imperialism at the threshold of the War we must take note of one difficulty faced by German commerce and industry which even the strongest impulse toward centralized effort in the service of imperialism could not get rid of. The geographical distribution of industrial centers did not seem to be of cardinal importance in peace-times. Irregularities mainly consisted in leaving the northern and northeastern provinces—the mainstay of Prussia—and the southeastern part of the Reich—Bavaria in the narrower sense of the term—comparatively untouched by industrialization. When war became imminent, however, the capital importance, to an industrial plant, of being situated near the frontier of an enemy country and, therefore, near a potential invader, presented itself to industrialists and politicians alike. In a country which depends on coal, iron ores, and potassium as its chief native elements of industry, the location of industrial centers is not a matter of planning or policy. Silesia, near the Russian frontier, the Saar area in the immediate vicinity of France, and the Ruhr and Westphalia, which could be reached from Belgium in a day, were places ordained for industries connected with the mines. According to pre-war conditions and possibilities the Government might as well have sought to transfer the harbors of Hamburg or Bremen to Munich or Frankfurt, as to have the main industrial works transferred to Thuringia or Franconia, where they might be safer from the enemy. If the question of abandoning a frontier province to the enemy, at least temporarily, had to be faced, the conflict between the western and the eastern centers of industry would at once have become acute, and a rivalry which had always existed without doing great harm would have torn and rent the great capitalistic forces of Prussia. As it was, the outlying territories which in 1914 had to be sacrificed to strategical considerations were preponderantly agrarian, and the choice between freeing either eastern Prussia or upper Alsace from the enemy was a political choice, not a question of preferring one group of industrial concerns to another. Still, the problem had presented itself, and those on whom rested the responsibility of deciding it realized that if industrial imperialism should survive the War, new means for overcoming the geographical disparities, especially in the matter of west and east, must be devised. Industrial plants would have to be mobilized if they were to be transferred from one site to another; and new industries, independent of local supplies of raw materials, must be created in the interior of the country, as far removed as possible from the scene of war.

In the meantime two other problems involved in the close connection between industrial imperialism and the War claimed the attention of the Government. During the War a propaganda for annexations in the case of military success, which itself became one of the most serviceable tools of enemy counter-propagandists, was voiced by the Pan-German Association, which was probably responsible for the lack of restraint with which it was advocated. It actually originated with the desire of German industry for a dependable supply of certain raw materials and a market which could be held open to their products by political force. Again, it was the dream of the *geschlossene Handelsstaat*, of possessing an area of well-balanced production and consumption governed by a central political authority in the interest of maintaining that balance. But this time, with it went the fatal error that territories containing people of other nationalities might possibly be included in this entity, or *Einheit*.

The opposition to the "civilian" Chancellor which led to his dismissal at a most critical time and to a series of dismal failures in chancellorship from 1916 to 1918 would not have been successful, and the second submarine campaign would not, therefore, have been started, if the political opponents of a cautious policy and of the supremacy of civil power had not had the support of the most powerful group in German industry, the same that had urged a policy of the "strong hand" in the Moroccan affairs.

Again, during the War, centralizing tendencies of an industrial and financial origin combined, as a matter of course, under the obvious necessity for a united national effort and driven by the need for a uniform and consistent direction of military and political affairs. If Germany had had a Chancellor like Mr. Lloyd George he would probably have obtained their unstinted support even against the military commanders. As things were, those in supreme command, especially General Ludendorff, seemed so manifestly superior to the civil authorities that it was to Ludendorff that the economic forces had to turn if they wished to support the strongest central authority. War pressure had not automatically brought to an end the traditional antagonism of the southern German states, led by Bavaria, to Prussian predominance in the Councils of the Reich. There were many cases, at least after the first enthusiasm had subsided, in which differences of opinion between Berlin and Munich (and Dresden, Karlsruhe, or Stuttgart) became very marked. The same industrial and commercial interests were always found supporting the larger order, in this case that of Berlin, instead of the smaller (and perhaps in some cases safer) order from Munich or one of the smaller states. The central provinces of Bavaria had, up to the end of the War, only an insignificant share in national industry and banking, their strength being in agriculture and the arts and crafts. A bureaucracy which had a greater affinity with its Austrian cousins than with Prussian administration had in more peaceful times quietly but efficiently opposed the growth of industrial rule in this part of Germany. It was now the turn of industry to point out that great industrial achievements presupposed not only the largest possible area of administration but also a considerable measure of self-government for industry over and above the powers delegated by the State to other local authorities or organizations. Moreover, the War Emergency Bureaus, the *Kriegsämter*, were many of them (like the War Claims Bureau, or the different Raw Materials Bureaus) in close and daily contact with the centers of industrial activity. Almost all had their central offices in the capital of the Reich, and were trying to standardize the rulings for all cases dealt with throughout Germany, in order to allay suspicions of and complaints of favoritism. That followed almost of itself. But concentration and standardization had to come, in the wake of the War, irrespective of any actual need or justification for it. But before we enter upon that, we must first note a few minor changes which the War introduced into German industry.

The most important of these changes is an effect of modern warfare as such, and results from the new conception of war that has prevailed since 1914. War had ceased to be a military enterprise carried out according to scientific rules of strategy and tactics. Far less was it a mere raid or expedition into an enemy country. It was a life-and-death struggle between the belligerent nations. It involved all their human and material strength and resources. From the beginning of such a war, industry, or all the different activities in the life of the nation, ceased to be anything other than a *"potentiel de guerre."* It was an asset in the total amount of national power to be hurled at the enemy. It disappeared as a real and living thing, entered the mobilization plans, and was there transformed, transplanted, destroyed, or enlarged. A chemical works for the distillation of perfumes became a laboratory for poisonous gas or artificial food. A grain depot became a hangar for aeroplanes. An establishment for the mass production of cheap toys became an ironworks for the building of tanks. The demand of the hour was "Everything must yield to the needs of war!"

That would have been bad enough in any case, because it implies a break in the natural, healthy psychic relation, in industrial works, of both employer and employees to the material they worked with and the quality of their production. Or, to put it in still plainer words, it was a blow at what ought to have been their pride in their work. In the case of Germany in 1914 it was probably worse than, under any circumstances, it could have been anywhere else. Invidious as are such comparisons between the characters of different nations and the attitude of their workers to their work, it is probably true that the personal relation between a man and his work and his pride in his workmanship was, as a rule, unusually strong in the German worker, and that the people as a whole, beginning with the family and extending to the public opinion of almost every quarter of national life, expected not only a craftsman or an artist, but every workingman to take this attitude. A German might hate his school and the teacher and might say so with the utmost vehemence[8] with-

8. Leonhard Frank's novel *Die Ursache,* which traces the real origin of a cold-blooded murder a man commits back to the injustice with which his victim, a high-school teacher, treated his pupils, is one of the most instructive books in modern German fiction. But quite apart from such extreme cases, it comes almost as a surprise to hear a German speak well of the school he attended.

out losing the respect of his audience; but most people would look askance at him for speaking ill or even slightingly of the work he was occupied with. Hero worship, at least in its true form of spontaneous acknowledgment of great virtue in a leader, was conspicuously absent from German life. But in its stead Germans showed a marked inclination to admire accomplishments as such, and to give unstinted praise to good work done, apart from its creator; and this amounted sometimes to an almost absurd overestimate of individual accomplishments in workmanship. There was nothing of the Englishman's sane confidence in the all-round ability of Britishers, in their staying power, and in their sound common sense which helped them to master a situation which their best experts declared to be hopeless. Germans distrust the parliamentary system because it presupposes a belief in the ability of a politician to grasp and to master problems of which he has no expert knowledge; and it is just that reverence for the expert, the *"Fachmann,"* that dominates every phase of public life in Germany, from the Reich Cabinet down to the smallest district registrar's or business office.

If a German statesman or a great judge, lawyer, or poet found international recognition he was sure to be described by the press of his own country as a man past his prime or as *"undeutsch"*; and there would always be many people who could honestly say—and did say—that they did not know such a man existed until the newspapers announced that a Nobel prize or some other outstanding trophy of international fame had fallen to him. But public opinion in Germany unanimously exults in the number of prizes that come to German chemists for their laboratory work, to builders and engineers, to champion riders, or swimmers, or tennis players or boxers, to the conductors or soloists who represent Germany in foreign capitals. The *"Dichter und Denker"* complex had long become a thing of the past. Not what a man was but what he was able to do had come to count with the Germans. The achievement was the thing, not the person.

Industry, before the War, was not so much one big branch of the economic service of the nation, a column of national statistics along with those of agriculture, commerce, the liberal professions, and science. It was the process by which there was created or perfected goods of a certain kind—and no other—by the common effort of employer and employed in the interest of the factory. And this, even in the period of fiercest conflict between trade-union and employers' association, could successfully be appealed to. It might be a case either of matches or of monster engines, of tin soldiers or Zeppelins, beer or the printing of an edition of the Bible in a difficult African or Asiatic language, the making of grand pianos or of children's rattles—provided it *was* matches and not engines, tin soldiers and not grand pianos, tropical outfits and not sledges for expeditions to the Arctic that were being produced. Skill was highly specialized. Competition was quite as much a matter of ambitious pride in the honor bestowed by the international exhibition as it was a striving for the greatest possible profits to be attained by the greatest possible sales.

The change brought about by the War was tremendous. Unemployment, due only in part and indirectly to the War, enforced and made general a condition of things under which a workingman was of necessity potentially a casual laborer, and in any case could not count on finding work of the type to which he was accustomed or in which he was an expert. He became an exchangeable item in the industrial processes of the nation. Before the War, stability in employment was so much an understood thing in Germany that tenure of office in industrial and commercial employment was modeled as far as possible on that in the civil service, with old age pensions; not insurance, but pensions given by the individual firm as a reward for long service, with perhaps this added, an opportunity to live in some little house near the old factory when old age had come. The War reversed all this. Instability of industrial and commercial employment so largely prevailed that it extended itself to the public services. One battle cry for the demagogue in Germany was a demand for the reduction in, or the cancellation of, earned pensions. And, to the former German conception of public order and private morals, both reduction and cancellation would have seemed equally inadmissible. An official in the civil service owed no stronger allegiance or more loyalty of body and mind to the State itself than did the workingman or commercial employee to *his* firm or factory. That is gone, and if unemployment has played a part in this change, the greater part has certainly been due directly to the War. It began with the first weeks of the War. The fact that it came as a surprise to everybody, including the ministerial department in charge of industry and commerce, only aggravated the shock of the change, once it had begun to manifest itself.

The belief was firmly held in Germany that the War would be fought by the military forces alone. It would leave civilians to continue their peaceful trades or professions even during such a battle as that of Leipzig or Waterloo, and even when the battle was fought only a few miles away. It would, of course, call for the entire capacity of the munition factories and other special war-supplies concerns. They were equipped for such a contingency and well manned with skilled, trustworthy men. And if the War was unexpectedly long such factories would be enlarged and their staffs and working forces would be increased. But that would be all. It would have been an almost criminal skepticism in the face of the greatest military organization in the world and the machinery it had at its disposal to assume that any outside help would be needed, or that the offer of such voluntary and necessarily amateurish help would be regarded as anything but a nuisance, to be summarily rejected and perhaps punished as an unwarranted intervention in the affairs of Government and military command. But, after a few weeks of warfare under modern conditions, and with Great Britain as the determining factor in everything that concerned the conduct of war, it was seen that all the resources of the nation were involved. All machinery, and every kind of industrial plant, the equipment for driving the machinery, and the men working at the machines were all alike subject to requisition, and to change beyond any recognition. The men of military age gave place, as the War went on, to the old and infirm, to the invalided, to the women and children. The children in their turn were similarly transformed from objects of education into labor volunteers with a terrific sense of their own importance. And then most of them were simply to learn, after a year or two, that they must change a second time. The women had to return to their household duties or to the inactivity of the unmarried state, which in a country with a growing surplus of women was the fate of many tens of thousands. The young people had to go back to the school-room or to undergraduate life after the factory with its freedom and war wages, or to the barracks and the auxiliary services in the war zone.

The dissolution of what in pre-war time seemed an indispensable moral bond between two sides of the labor process, human effort and the production of goods, had a permanent effect on employers and employed alike. A lessening of the grip, which the idea of production, perfect in quality and growing in quantity, had on the mind and soul of the worker, had of necessity to lead to his giving more and more—and finally exclusive—attention to another side of the business—to wages.[9] It must be either heads or tails, heads being the satisfaction that comes from accomplishment, and tails the satisfaction of earning one's livelihood. During the War the industrial coin was turned upside down forever so far as we can judge, after sixteen years of post-war development; and there is no doubt that it was not the loss of the War or the depreciation of the currency or the crisis of 1930 that we must blame for the change, but the War itself.

Günther, speaking of the general tendency of wages, irrespective of the kind of work, to rise during the War, says:

Important changes of income have thus been introduced. The inflation of money-wages and money-prices later on found a soil well prepared during the World War. Tendencies became visible to measure wages by the cost of living, without any too much consideration for

---

9. Cf. Zimmermann, *Die Veränderungen der Einkommens—und Lebensverhältnisse der deutschen Arbeiter durch den Krieg,* pp. 364 ff. On the side of the employer we find the same phenomenon. They—even those who were the opposite of the profiteer or the *nouveau riche*—had to give their minds to the financial aspect of their businesses instead of to successful production and sale, or the maintenance of an old and honorable good will. In many cases they had to suspend operations, and accept some fair compensation. It would not have profited them to argue that an honest business efficiently conducted is an asset of national wealth which cannot be expressed in terms of money, and the loss of which is, in the literal sense of the word, inestimable. Most of them wrongly held that the money paid them in compensation was one of fortune's windfalls. The work of a peace industry, they were told, was useless in war; money was the thing which counted. Furthermore, there were two ways of using the profits that the manufacturer derived, whether he derived them from the making of war supplies or as a result of closing down altogether and accepting compensation. He could either invest such profits in his own business—enlarging it in proportion to his gains, acquiring adjacent land, constructing new plants, etc.—or he could try to build up a huge private fortune in stocks and shares. The latter course, in most cases, led to complete loss, not through taxation on war profits, which never took any very large percentage, but through inflation or, after 1924, through the severe crisis following stabilization. The former course, however, proved to be the more dangerous thing for the economic reconstruction needed after the War, for it was the beginning of that *"Fehlleitung"* of capital, which even the stoutest defenders of capitalism recognize as having contributed very materially to the crisis of 1930 and 1931.

the production. To be fair, it should be said that when measured by the poor nourishment, the efforts put into work were, on the whole, very great. It became more and more difficult, moreover, to maintain, as a basis for the calculations, the balance between production (work performed) and wages of work. A very large, continually growing part of the national production was done for purposes the ultimate value of which—as mentioned above—depended upon the outcome of the World War, but it could not be calculated by itself. The State made its payments in paper money, to the rapid increase of which one became accustomed. The laborer also was given paper money, and the employer was willing to increase this paper wage whenever he was sure of drawing a higher income for himself, through the higher prices of war supplies. (This income, however, was not only on paper, but for the time being could be invested legitimately in commercial paper and in commodities.) The middle class, with certain exceptions, did not take part in this race between the producer and the laborer for higher paper incomes. What large parts of them had to offer: intellectual and cultural values, were —again with certain exceptions—least in demand during the War. The causes of the decline of the middle class go back to the World War, whereas the upper classes not only maintained but bettered their position.[10]

This was a result of industrial development during and because of the War, a result that showed most conspicuously in the working classes, and in the owners of small- and middle-sized industrial establishments. Another effect of the War on German industry may be seen in the sphere of the bigger concerns, and in the case of both light and heavy industry. Here, as in general politics, war led to centralization, "efficiency planning," and overorganization.[11] Before the War there were syndicates, trusts, and combinations; and they had the same common goal—that of forming trade monopolies in their particular branches of business, with a consequent lowering of all costs of production coupled with the certainty of high domestic

10. Günther, *Kriegswirkungen in Deutschland*, pp. 137 ff. speaks of a process of immobilization of German industry which began early in the War, due to a miscalculation as to the chance of prosperity being restored after the War. "Ein erheblicher Teil der heute durch die Unbeweglichkeit des Kapitals und den Mangel an flüssigen Betriebsmitteln gegebenen Schwierigkeiten in Produktion und Einkommensbildung ist damals schon begründet worden."

11. For the best summary description of this hypertrophy of organization again compare Günther, *op. cit.*, pp. 150 ff.

prices[12] and an organized sale in foreign markets. In regard to wages in Germany the system of regulation by agreement between employers' associations and trade-unions had been generally adopted, and had made for centralization throughout the Reich, in spite of the obvious impossibility of making the same nominal wages and salaries buy the same commodities and cover the same general household expenses in the differing parts of such a country, one in which there could be found, and all alike typical, northern, western, and southern ways of life, habits, and standards of social entertainment. Except for the general rule in the case of wages, indeed, and except for the prices of a very small number of commodities manufactured under conditions of practical monopoly, these varying habits and tastes in Germany had maintained themselves against the many attempts to make the German public accept standardization. Competition between members of the same branch of industry within the same district was a stronger factor in the economic life than all endeavors to regulate and normalize the needs and demands of the consumer. Germany was in that respect a distinctly "old" country, one in which, save for areas that have known a rapid increase in prosperity, the preëxistent demand of the consumer creates the supply. Or at least it sees that it is given what it wants by the producing industries and their salesmen.

During the War and in the first period of reconstruction after the War the producers were able to turn the tables on the consumer. His individual wants seemed unreasonable, even criminal, at a time when the watchword of the nation was coöperation and common sacrifice. He might try to satisfy them by violating law and decree. But if he wished to remain within the law he had to be content with the things which his individual purchasing card allowed him to buy in the open market. He had to recognize, further, that in the opinion of competent, independent advisers the lack of an efficient and highly

12. For a special study of the most important pre-war case in Germany, the *Kali-Syndikat* of 1910, see J. Schönemann, *Die deutsche Kaliindustrie und das Kaligesetz* (Hannover, 1911); Flechtheim, *Deutsches Kartellrecht* (Leipzig, 1912), Vol. I; Görres, *Gesammelte Aufsätze und Abhandlungen zum Kaligesetz* (Essen, 1916); and W. Musold, *Die Organisation der Kaliwirtschaft* (Berlin, 1926). As to the transformation of the pre-war syndicate into its new form see R. Kahn, *Rechtsbegriffe der Kriegswirtschaft* (Leipzig, 1918), and the official reports by Wissel and Von Moellendorff in *Deutsche Gemeinwirtschaft* (Jena, 1919), fasc. 9; Schlegelberger in *Deutsches Uebergangsrecht* (Berlin, 1920), II, 508 ff.; and *Verhandlungen der Sozialisierungskommission über die Kaliwirtschaft* (Berlin, 1921).

industrial life of the provinces owned by them. The chemical industry, textiles and paper, lighting and power, and public utilities generally had a corresponding interest both for the liberals and radicals and for the left wing of the Catholic party—with the latter mainly through the municipal governments in the Catholic provinces. Last, but not least, the trade-unions and, through them, the Social Democrats, though officially opposed to the Imperial régime and the "ruling classes," were in more than one way bound up with the prosperity of the big industrial concerns and, therefore, with the policy of subordinating the general interest of the nation to plans for making the hold of German industries on the world stronger and stronger.

The cessation of party strife, which is one of the most striking effects of war under modern conditions, did not, for these reasons, affect the representation of industrial interests through the usual means of parliamentary and municipal parties. On the contrary, industry—seen as a political unit with naturally expanding tendencies—seemed to be such a faithful ally of the armed forces that even the more egotistical manifestations of its will and energy appeared to represent the united interest of the nation, while, at the same time, there was no doubt as to the distinctly and sometimes openly oppositionist attitude of the leaders and spokesmen of German industry toward the Government in the matter of the War, and of the peace which was to follow it.

A similar conclusion can be arrived at when we take a different point of view. During the later stages of the War the possibilities of informing the Emperor and his chief advisers upon the political and economic situation and the prospects of a negotiated peace became more and more important. It was an open secret, however, that at military headquarters the Emperor, Valentini, the head of his Civil Cabinet, and the first war Chancellor, Von Bethmann-Hollweg, were held to be subject to attacks of undue pessimism and to morbid qualms of conscience which made it imperative to keep unfavorable news, especially any connected with pacifist tendencies or with the Roman Catholic Church, from the Emperor's ear. Those qualified to express opinions on international affairs were constantly being asked not to do so, as the Emperor might be led to take some irrevocable step toward what the military leaders and the patriotic front regarded as a premature peace. The Emperor had had a large circle of personal friends apart from the court and the members of his

Civil Cabinet—that secretariat which, independently of the Government also advised him, within the domain of his private prerogative. Scientists and university professors, travelers, sportsmen, architects and engineers, a few bankers, and many amateur politicians had from time to time been admitted to a circle of intimate talk which, if it had continued during the War, would have afforded him ample opportunities for independent information. But not only because of the obvious difficulties of such informal meetings during the War, but also because of the general feeling that the monarch ought to be spared all news and opinions calculated to add to his own doubts and misgivings, a real conspiracy of silence reigned about the Emperor's person, and those who tried to break it were easily detected and frightened away. Again with one exception. The spokesmen of industry and of the shipping trade—the closest ally of Rhenish and Westphalian industry—had every facility to put their views before the head of the State. They were probably in a better position, in that respect, than the German princes or the Emperor's male relatives. So far as political responsibility rests with those who influenced or might have influenced the titular heads of the Government, the representatives of the great industrial and shipping concerns share the responsibility for most of the important decisions taken during the War on questions of non-military character. Nor have they disclaimed such responsibility. One of them, the head of a steamship line, felt it so much that he took his own life at the end of the War. Others were destined to fall victims to the strain of politics in the years that followed the War. Some who reappeared after it were under a cloud when the occupation of the Ruhr, inflation, and the reëquipment of industrial plants from 1925 to 1929 had initiated a new era of industrial prosperity in northwestern Germany.

Two men may be said to represent these two groups which in German industry are usually spoken of as if they had no connection, those "light" and "heavy" industries. These two men offer a striking contrast in almost everything, from their origin and social backgrounds, their early successes and failures, their share in pre-war public life in Germany, to, finally, the conflict between their policies when the War was over. One was the heir of a man who had built up one of the greatest industrial businesses in the country. The other was a self-made man. One belonged to the capital. The other always did his best work in the provinces. One was a German Jew, gifted with that intense but entirely unhappy love for the German mentality which causes a rift in so many lives of men of foreign descent who live in Germany. The other was a genuine, unsophisticated German. He represented both the mental attitude and the physical qualities of the pure-bred German of good average bourgeois stock. One was *au fond* an amateur and a romanticist, with a deep aversion to the ugly truth; and, as is often the case with such men, he was almost entirely concentrated on himself, not a flame, but the view of a flame reflected in a mirror. The other was a healthy cynic, and impressed his own personality on others without taking the pains to consider what that meant. There is as much ego in Hugenberg's articles and outgivings as in Rathenau's. But Rathenau's case is that of an ego puzzled by itself and trying to understand itself for its own sake. As for Hugenberg's it is an ego fully armed and satisfied with itself, and it is out to conquer, to annihilate, or to dominate others. Above all, Walther Rathenau, the democrat or even Socialist, as many saw him, was a man alone, one out of touch with the crowd though always sensible of its presence outside the politician's door, an "aristo" in the argot of the French Revolution. Hugenberg, a conservative or even reactionary, the defender of the old order against the revolt of the masses, became a force only when he got in touch with tens of thousands of men. He organized the means of dealing with them, ministered to their mass mind, and directed their fears and hatreds toward an end where they would serve his purposes.

In this picture of personal contrasts the most marked feature, however, is one which alike puzzled Rathenau's friends, his critics, and his enemies. In his writings he professed a loathing of materialism and mechanization and a sense of the spiritual values in human life that won him many sincere admirers in his country and, in his later years, throughout the world. All the best evidence afforded by his life, and not least by the way in which he met death for his country, points to the sincerity of his convictions. How was it, then, that his part in the War—and not a part taken on command, but one chosen on his own initiative, and one he was proud of to the end —consisted almost entirely in creating and perfecting the means by which a power alien to him, if not inimical, sought to attain an end of which he, Rathenau, was either ignorant or disapproved?

The early survey of war supplies and the organized effort both to secure all available supplies and to find substitutes for those that in time would become scarce or wholly disappear, which was Rathenau's contribution to industrialized warfare, meant a prolongation of the War through mechanical devices without any regard to the consequences that the transient success of the plan might have for the morale of the nation. It was the contest between the blockaded country and the blockaders as such that appealed to Rathenau's imagination; he spoke in glowing terms, at the time, of German resourcefulness in the struggle against the combined forces of the world, and, indeed, against nature itself; for nature had placed Germany where she could be surrounded and cut off from the open sea. To prolong, by an almost miraculous feat of industrial efficiency, a war that should have been decided on the battlefields of land and sea was to serve not peace but war. Rathenau, whom the annexationists hated and who, in the end, was killed by the bullet moulded by their newspapers was, more than anybody else, instrumental in creating the belief that the contest was one between the economic strength of Great Britain and that of Germany, with all the other nations mere seconds in the duel; and from that belief it was only a brief step to the conclusion that the spoils of the War should fall to the industrialists who had been the protagonists in the contest. Whether the spoils should consist in the elimination of a foreign competitor, a *"Sicherung,"* or in the annexation of territories that would be dominated by the victors was secondary. The main question was that of the peace itself; it might be a peace concluded by statesmen and soldiers after the decisive ending brought about by military strength, or it might be a peace of exhaustion, and one arranged by a conference of experts. In 1915 it could have been a peace concluded then and there, with military honors equal, or a prolongation of the War, as economic war, into a distant future that went far beyond the formal armistice. Rathenau failed to see this. In his war work he served the policy of Hugenberg and his group, unwillingly but nonetheless efficiently.

An explanation of these contradictions may be found in the fact that, with all his literary accomplishments and with all his enthusiasm for a purer state of society, Rathenau, when it came to politics, was an industrialist first and last. To him politics, nation-wide organization, literary propaganda, and in the last resort even war, were means, or stages of transition, toward the goal of a purified, scientifically organized, and perfected national industry, with a greatly increased capacity for production. To Hugenberg organization, propaganda, the War, and the effects of the War on industry were means to attain definite political ends, both for Germany in the domain of foreign affairs, and for the increase of the power of his own party in domestic policy. How these two men and the groups represented by them acted under the stress of the War, and how the War reacted on them merits the attention of the historian though he may be aware of the dangers that beset the writing of biographical history.

Walther Rathenau[1] came of German Jewish stock. His grandparents and great-grandparents had been people of importance in the commercial communities and of some social standing. They were townspeople, most of them in Berlin and Frankfurt am Main, bankers, industrialists, and merchants. One of them, Liebermann by name, was the man who, during the Napoleonic Wars and at the time of the first great continental blockade, introduced the process of calico printing into Prussia, a process which until then had been an English monopoly, a curious coincidence in view of his great-grandson's activities during the World War. Walther Rathenau's father, Emil, began his career as the joint owner of a small engineering works in the northern part of Berlin. He employed from forty to fifty workmen, and the chief output consisted of turbines and machinery, not for use in factories, but for the State theater in Berlin where grand opera, in the era of Meyerbeer and Spontini, required a great deal of mechanical equipment. The business had to go into liquidation shortly after Walther's birth. But the parents' fortune remained intact; and Emil Rathenau, after some rather desultory years spent brooding at home or visiting international fairs and exhibitions, found his opportunity. At the Paris Exhibition of 1881 he met Edison who was exhibiting his new electric bulbs. Rathenau bought the patents and, in 1883, founded the German Edison Company, with a capital of five million marks. It grew to be the Allgemeine Elektrizitäts-Gesellschaft. Few men, even in that time of industrialization, have had such outstanding success as he had in this second period of his life. He was a marvelous combination

1. Cf. in addition to his own writings the biographies by Count Harry Kessler (Berlin, 1928), H. F. Simon (Dresden, 1927), and E. Federn-Kohlhaas (Berlin, 1927).

of technician and businessman, very sound in his judgment, very strong-willed and highhanded in his financial dealings, and above all, one of the first men on the continent to realize that a new invention, if it were only made an article for mass consumption, could create a market of itself, sell by the million to the consumer, and thus support thousands of workmen as well as their employer.

Walther Rathenau was a schoolboy when the A.E.G. began to conquer the world. He showed all the traditional crown prince's spirit of opposition and wrote essays on the curse of money and the mechanization of life. But finally he went to a small place in the country, Bitterfeld, halfway between Berlin and Leipzig, and in seven years of hard work and no pleasures made a prosperous enterprise of the Electro-Chemical Works which had been established there. Also, having shown what he could do for himself, he went back to Berlin and became the head of the A.E.G.'s department of power-station construction. He supervised the building of stations in Amsterdam, Manchester, Buenos Aires, Baku, and other places. In 1902 he joined the Berliner Handelsgesellschaft, a solid but rather inactive banking concern, and reorganized their industrial undertakings. Between then and 1914 he made himself one of the best-known financier industrialists of a period when success seemed to come almost too easily. He was spoken of as one of those men who sit on more than a hundred boards of directors;[2] and in one of his own articles, wherein he exposed the shortcomings of the financial system,[3] he used a sentence which, afterward, was often turned against him. He spoke of the "three hundred men, every one of them knowing all the others, who among them controlled the economic life of the continent." One of his biographers mentions a group of thirteen, himself included; and from 1911 to 1914 he was in constant intercourse with the other twelve. By name they were Prince Henckel-Donnersmarck, C. Fürstenberg, Franz von Mendelssohn, P. von Schwabach, F. von Guilleaume, Krupp von Bohlen, Salomonsohn, E. von Bodenhausen, Albert Ballin, Klöckner, Louis Levy-Hagen, August Stinnes; and they were representatives of the mining, banking, and shipping in-

---

2. A detailed list given by Count Kessler cites twenty-four electrical works, seven chemical and ten metallurgical plants, eight mining companies, fourteen railway syndicates and telegraph companies, but can mention only five banks.

3. See the Christmas Number of the Viennese *Neue Freie Presse* (1909).

terests as well as of that electrical industry of which, after his father's death, he had become the head.

Two essays and a memorandum on Germany's African colonies in 1908, 1912, and 1913 express Rathenau's views on foreign policy before the War. Like the director of the Deutsche Bank, Helfferich, who was his bitterest enemy, and to whom Count Kessler openly attributes Rathenau's assassination,[4] what he aimed at was a planned and pacific penetration; and, in common with all those who were engaged in opening new markets to an increasing German production, it was in England that he saw Germany's chief rival. With France, he says in the memorandum on the colonies, fear of our growing population is the principal motivating factor. With England it is the irritation caused by ever more and more efficient competition. In the essay, "*England und wir*" (1912), he finds that the first of four reasons why England regards Germany as dangerous is that England realized she was being outdistanced by German technology and industrial production.[5] In the "Eumeniden-Opfer" (1913), he goes on to say that by her new military-service law France had set her seal of certainty on the coming war "and that as a tool of an England that will not unchain it [the war] accidentally, but when she chooses."

It was the industrialist, not the politician or the pacifist, who wrote these sentences, and as an industrialist Walther Rathenau looked at the War and acted in the War when it had come.

He saw it "not as the battle of both armies, but as the contest of the two economic rivals who had, except for very small enclaves based on profit-economy, divided the globe between themselves into two gigantic state-socialistic organizations." And the final issue of the War was "not the defeat of the German army but the defeat of the German economy—*Bedarfsorganisation*—by the blockade and the convoy-system which frustrated the German counter-attack, the unrestricted submarine warfare. . . ."[6] A phrase which recurs very often in Rathenau's thought is that of war fulfilling a predestined

---

4. *Op. cit.*, pp. 335, 336.
5. His prediction, in the same essay, that in the case of a war the United States would always derive the biggest profit, has been strangely falsified by the events. He could not foresee participation in the War by the United States, nor the non-payment of war debts.
6. Count Kessler, *op. cit.*, p. 194.

function in the life of the nation—"war as fate."[7] And, *in concreto*, he expected the war of 1914 to put the constitution of German industry—a faulty constitution as Rathenau had often pointed out—to the test, and lead to its correction: "Our economy today rests on the free play of energies, upon egotism, will-power, hatred, possibly even upon quickness, a slyness, ability to talk. That is no basis upon which to build God's heritage; and I am thoroughly convinced that the transformation will be accelerated by this war, which is the long-expected world-revolution, though not in the Marxian form, but in the great noble form of heroic battles and sacrifices."[8]

The story of his initiative in the first days of the War, which resulted in the huge organization of the Prussian War Ministry for the production of war supplies has often been told, most graphically by Rathenau himself in his lecture (December 20, 1915) on "Deutschlands Rohstoffversorgung" (Berlin, 1917). On August 8 and 9 Rathenau had successive interviews with the Director of Department in the Ministry of War, Colonel Scheuch, and the Minister of War, General von Falkenhayn, and in these interviews he stressed the need for an immediate survey of all available war supplies in Germany and of an organized effort to secure a sufficient supply of the necessary materials in the event of a war of unexpected length. The Minister gave Rathenau practically full powers. With two friends and collaborators, Von Moellendorff and Klingenberg of the A.E.G., he set himself to work. A fortnight later they were able to tell the Minister that the available supplies would last, approximately, one year, and that measures of uncommon rigor were, in their opinion, called for to inventory it, to seize it if necessary, to take every possible step to supplement it, either by purchase from neutral countries, by sequestration in the occupied territories, or by finding substitutes which could be produced in Germany.

Rathenau tells a vivid story of their first days in the Ministry of War, when they worked in four small rooms, and had no technical appliances to help them.

It was the middle of August. Outside my window a mighty maple tree spread its branches and overshadowed the roof. Down below, in the well-

7. Cf., e.g., a letter to Frederick van Eeden, dated September 28, 1914.
8. Address to a group of his collaborators on his fiftieth birthday, published in *Vossische Zeitung*, August 8, 1924, by Dr. H. Spiero, one of his deputies in the K.R.A., Ministry of War, 1914.

kept gardens of the War Ministry a sentinel paced slowly to and fro. Two old field pieces stood on the green, peacefully and quietly basking in the sun. Behind all this rose a tall factory chimney. It seemed a symbol of the gigantic area of German economic life that stretched from beyond this garden to the frontier, in flames about Germany. This area, full of thundering trains, of smoking chimneys, of blazing furnaces, of whizzing looms, an immeasurable domain of industrial life, spread itself before my thought. To us had been given the task of taking in our hands the whole of this agitated world, of making it serviceable for the purposes of war, of forcing upon it our uniform rule, and of awakening its titanic strength to the needs of our defense.

Of the more idyllic part of the description some things might have been a poet's dream. But the chimney must have been there, truly enough, looming over the offices of state and their sheltered gardens. And it characterizes the man that, in the midst of his practical office work, he thinks of industry as part of the corporative State, as a public function, not as the combined activity of human beings. The chimney is the symbol, not a workingman or a soldier. The factory is the real thing, not labor. And, above all, the power of a single intellect, directing the enterprise so that it may serve the War in the most efficient way.

Four points presented themselves to Rathenau and his collaborators as the most important in a program of rationalized industrial warfare. First, all raw materials, including the half-finished products made from them, should become *"zwangsläufig,"* "emergency materials," in the sense that they could, at any moment, be seized by the military authorities to serve the needs of the army. Second, raw materials to supplement the German stocks would have to be procured from foreign countries, by force if need be. Third, every indispensable article of war which could not be so obtained would have to be manufactured in Germany. Fourth, materials which could only be obtained with difficulty must, wherever possible, be replaced by other materials more readily obtainable. There is nothing out of the ordinary in all this, except perhaps the second point: It the military censor deleted from the first printed edition of Rathenau's speech. But on the whole it was nothing but a formula for things that, as a matter of course, the director of a war under modern conditions must be well aware of. That Rathenau's plan, at the time, seemed a striking innovation, almost the creation of a genius, is solely due to the fact that here was a civilian, an outsider from the point of view of the *"Beamtenstaat"*—the civil service State—who told the authorities—in fact, the supreme command itself—that they were not at the beginning of an ordinary war in the traditional style, an expedition or campaign, that would end in victory or defeat on a battlefield. They were entering upon a conflict which had been shaking the world since August, 1914, and which was still raging twenty years later. The need for certain raw materials is obvious even for a short campaign. What Rathenau saw and pointed out was the need for stocks of raw materials that could be maintained indefinitely.

The authorities fell in with Rathenau's suggestions almost at once and supported him unstintedly. Opposition came from his fellow industrialists, who were reluctant to furnish the necessary information about stocks and supplies to what seemed to them to be a combination of a department of state and a rival industrial enterprise on a gigantic scale. After some time, however, they, too, coöperated. In one of the most remarkable passages of his famous address, Rathenau told how quickly the collaborators who had been independent businessmen and industrialists changed their methods and even their ways of thinking to those of civil servants. Their fiscal outlook became a standing reproach among those who a short time before had stood on the same platform with them and sought to defend business, banking, and the manufacturing industries from State intervention and control. Rathenau himself tried to further this process of change by placing the men he chose as his collaborators at the head of subdepartments that dealt with things which had been outside their province in their former activities. They were expected to forget that they had been experts in business. An electrician was in charge of the leather department, a coal and iron man had to deal with chemicals, a professor of economics with textiles. And, still more significant, every one of those men had to create, to organize, and to direct the affairs of his department, not by building them up from below, but by giving orders from above. "Unter jedem Dezernat wuchs nach abwärts eine hierarchische Pyramide"—the sentence gives a vivid impression of the inverted state of things, for it implies nothing less than the building (or "growth") of a pyramid beginning at the top of it. Just as Rathenau himself felt that the War Raw Materials Department, the Kriegs-Rohstoff Abteilung, or

"K.R.A.," had emanated from his brain, the special departments concerned with the different raw materials, with metals, chemicals, jute, wool, rubber, cotton, leather, hides, flax, linen, horsehair, or timber had to emanate from the men who were at the head of them.

Too much, I think, has been made of the new form of sequestration Rathenau claims to have introduced. To a lawyer the distinction between confiscation and the different grades of sequestration seems clear enough. The latter abstains from depriving the owner of his title to his property. But they are alike in taking from the owner the essence of the right of property—the right to dispose of it. Owners of sequestrated raw materials or half-finished products were allowed to keep them and deal with them in any way which made them more ready for final confiscation by the military authorities, but not otherwise. Metal works possessing a stock of raw material could not continue manufacturing plate or cutlery or fancy articles, nor could they hope to sell their supplies at a good price to the Government and close down. They had to change over to the manufacture of arms, ammunition, or other articles needed by the army or let their stocks lie waste until the Government required them. Ownership of raw materials on the list of the K.R.A. became a burdensome responsibility, and if the matter had rested there, war profits might have been very small.

In the end, however, in spite of the public spirit shown by the members and staff of the K.R.A., the thing could not be put through along the lines of a department of state with its strict code of integrity and unselfishness. The spirit of commercial enterprise, with its zeal for success if not for private gain, had to be called in to help. The K.R.A. had to allocate a growing number of *Kriegswirtschaftsgesellschaften*—war-work companies—to itself, trading companies formed on the lines of ordinary business firms; these companies which afterward became the target for most violent attacks from both Nationalists and Independent Socialists, had to form the connecting links between private business and the authorities; and they had the threefold task, first, of taking stock of the available raw materials,[9] second, of distributing them at fixed prices to firms working to meet

9. The German expression for this (*"erfassen"*) is misleading and has in some cases given rise to misunderstandings. It sounds much like actual seizure or confiscation of the object which is *"erfasst,"* while in practice it only meant that the object had been registered with a view to being eventu-

the needs of the armed forces, and, third, of being intermediaries between the manufacturers and the exchequer, where the latter had not directly contracted with the former. The companies were forbidden to make any profit or to distribute dividends on their capital; they were placed under government supervision and control by special commissaries. But the actual power in the hands of their most important divisions, the smaller committees for the valuation and distribution of the supplies of raw materials, was such that suspicion of occasional unfairness toward an eventual competitor or of favoritism could hardly be avoided. Rathenau himself cannot be held responsible for any abuses which resulted from ulterior developments in these various "war companies." They did not originate, for one thing, in the War Ministry with which the K.R.A. was associated; moreover Rathenau left his official work with the K.R.A. on April 1, 1915, under circumstances which have not been fully explained.

His interest in the conduct of the War never flagged whether he was in office or not. Twice he seems to have come near to a decisive influence on the course of events. In 1916 he opposed the policy of the Government[10] in the matter of the occupied parts of Belgium, and especially the deportation of Belgian workingmen, but gave in —or at least did not record a protest—at the decisive meeting of industrialists in the Ministry of War on September 16, 1916, when Dr. Duisburg led the group which demanded the strongest coercive measures for German war industry. Again, in 1917, Rathenau tried to convince General Quartermaster Ludendorff of the dangers of the unrestricted use of submarines, but failed to do so, and henceforth ceased to offer advice to the General. Neither Rathenau's let-

---

ally seized, and could not be disposed of in any way to make it inaccessible or diminish its value for war purposes if required.

10. The differences of opinion between the Supreme Command, the Foreign Office, and the Governor-General of Belgium on the question of the deportation of Belgian workingmen to meet the shortage of labor in northwestern Germany are described in some detail in Dr. von Köhler's volume, *Die Staatsverwaltung der besetzten Gebiete,* pp. 145 ff. Rhenish-Westphalian industry had been asking for such a measure from the beginning of 1915 and, on the refusal of the Governor-General, had tried to draw Belgian labor to Germany through the "Deutsche Industriebüro" in Brussels. The bureau had branch offices throughout Belgium. The Rhenish-Westphalian group in this as in other questions acted in close connection with the Supreme Command.

ters nor the comments of his biographers give sufficient indication of what was in his mind when he first opposed the measures advocated by the strongest organization of German industrialists, and then at least outwardly condoned them. The best explanation I can find is this, that Rathenau always tried to take the longest view—that was where, as a business leader of great experience, he deliberately differed from both military leaders and politicians—and that he regarded the actions in question as mere interludes, mere temporary spurts in the race for victory which could not lead to final success and therefore did not offer occasion for an objection on principle.[11]

His opportunity came at the end of the War, too late, as it proved, for his voice to be heard. He was the only man in a responsible position who, when Turkish and Bulgarian resistance had collapsed and the German command had insisted on the necessity of negotiations with the enemy, called for a Gambettian *levée en masse*.[12] He was out of touch with the mass of the people, partly because he had seen things coming which they had been prevented from seeing, and did not feel he had been betrayed and deceived as millions of Germans did at that time—and partly because he had always been out of touch with the feelings of the multitude. From it the greatest things he did for his country brought him and his political associates only the bitterest hatred. One of those things was the creation of the K.R.A.: through the *Kriegsgesellschaften*, which in the mind of the uninitiated became one and the same thing with it, anti-Semitism grew to be one of the strongest subterranean forces in German life, and Rathenau became its principal target. The Wiesbaden agreement of October 6, 1921, following the Spa Conference of July, 1921, between Rathenau and Loucheur was another of those things in which today we see Rathenau to have been unquestionably right,

11. Although Rathenau was free from the more sentimental notions of pacifism, and the conflict between the industrial power of Germany and Great Britain seems to have appealed to an instinct for war in him, he suffered acutely from what went on around him, and his judgment occasionally was blurred by the violence of his emotions. On one occasion he said (and had it printed afterward) that the blockade of Germany would in the end work against England because Germany, through the blockade, had become an autarchy with a currency circulation limited to her own territory, while England was able to buy everything she desired and would therefore automatically endanger her currency.

12. See article in *Vossische Zeitung,* October 7, 1918.

both from the German point of view and from that of the European powers in general. But it was the Wiesbaden agreement which for the first time gave rise to the suspicion that a combination of international financiers was trying to "suck the last drops of blood out of the German people." Rumors, the origin of which was said to have been found in the circles that surrounded Hugo Stinnes, attributed to Loucheur and Rathenau a plan for establishing a gigantic electrical trust throughout Europe with the help of the agreements concluded between Germany and France. This was a first instalment of that efficient propaganda against international agreements which has been instrumental in molding German politics since 1924. Rathenau's last important act, the conclusion of the Russo-German treaty at Rapallo, preceded his death at the hands of a group of young Germans by only a few weeks; and that death opened an era of political assassination such as is not to be found in German history.

The impression made upon us when a man stands alone, does his duty to his country, and thereby evokes such terrific hatred is a feeling that can only become stronger and more sinister in its significance for the history of mankind when we come to realize the conformity of his intimate connections with the programmatic utterances of those who fought him and to whom his assassination was one of the earliest promises of victory to come. Of the revolution of 1918 Rathenau said:

A revolution in outward form has taken precedence of the inward revolution the German people needs. That is why even today, hardly a year after it broke out, it shows all the degrading signs of a mere clash of interests and egoisms. . . . Only a second revolution can save us, but it ought to be a revolution of our whole being, a new mental attitude, not a revolt of disbanded soldiers. . . . The German revolution which has still to come is one which will spring from a sense of individual responsibility to the nation. . . . It will owe much to the War because war has extricated humanity from the meshes of mechanization. It will be based on a new understanding of the relations between a leader and his followers. The leader will be one of them, known by them even as he knows them. . . .[13]

National life, in a future era of peace, is to be organized in order

13. The sentences are taken from Rathenau's pamphlets, *Die neue Wirtschaft* (1918), *Kritik der dreifachen Revolution* (1919), and *Zur Kritik der Zeit* (1920).

to be ready for war. "Never again can, nor should it happen that we enter a new war insufficiently prepared economically. All future years of peace must contribute to the utmost to this preparation. . . . A general plan for economic mobilization must be created, and constantly renewed. Economic mobilization orders should be drawn up, and distributed by the thousand. . . ." The man who imbued himself in such a thorough manner with the spirit of war, and who was killed by the discords of peace, may teach us at least one unmistakable lesson. Both his successes and his failures are bound up with his being more a brain than body and limbs, the human type of a centralized organism. We find not a trace of the provincial in him; the capital was his natural home. In almost every branch of human industry, except two, a modern European capital is practically self-contained. It unites, as in one big office, manufacturing, industries, and banking—a most unusual combination in the provinces—administration and science; every kind of influence that can be brought to bear on public opinion; centers of learning and education; parliamentary institutions so far as they survive; the chief national sports arenas and parade grounds; the central transport offices, in fact everything except raw materials and food. The intellectual development of modern science tends to make great cities more and more independent of raw materials, and to find substitutes and develop new sources of energy. Food, however, remains indispensable; it has to be brought in, to be commandeered if it cannot be bought. In an industrial leader who represents the spirit of the capital, as Rathenau represented Berlin, all these features are reflected. He is able to combine a genius for financial operations on a great scale with the technique of building up and directing industrial enterprises; but he lacks the instinctive familiarity with agricultural life, and is easily misled by an overconfidence in his own ability to organize supply, just as he can organize demand. And there is another drawback in the constitution of a capital and in that of a man who by nature belongs to it: they cannot do teamwork. Provinces may compete on a footing of equality and finally coalesce, states may form a league or even a union; a capital has to stand alone, and by itself. Its claim to superiority, the superiority of intellect over matter, one of the most obviously dangerous fallacies in politics, is an inevitable ingredient in its composition; and the man who lives by his self-trained intellect rather than by his physical qualities and his natural disposition, is exposed to the same dangers as the great town that has bred him.

The figure of Walther Rathenau, detached from group, association, or party, as it remained to the last, even during his membership in the Cabinet, has often been paired off as the opponent of another outstanding member of the commercial or industrial world. Hugo Stinnes, the coal baron of Mülheim-Essen and the strongest representative of the "horizontal trust" school in the post-war period, seemed to be a kind of anti-Rathenau at the time of Rathenau's negotiations with Loucheur. But the two men hardly had any contact, whether unfriendly or friendly, during the War or in pre-war times; and after Rathenau's death Stinnes indicated that they had just reached some understanding about their general attitude on reparations and the reëquipment of the German industrial plant. Karl Helfferich, the director of the Anatolian Railway and the Deutsche Bank, and an influential member of the war cabinets from 1915 to 1917, was an avowed enemy of Rathenau's; and, as I have intimated above, one of the latter's biographers has publicly arraigned him as being responsible for the assassination of his antagonist. But the conflict between the two, both of whom, within the same short space of time, met with violent death amidst the ruin of most of their efforts, was much more a conflict of personal ambitions and a clash of temperaments than a positive and essential antagonism in questions of public policy or national economy. It might be too much to say that Rathenau, in Helfferich's place, with his physique and upbringing, would have acted exactly like Helfferich, and Helfferich, in the same contingency, like Rathenau. Rathenau certainly was more genuine than Helfferich, who born of Bavarian parents in the Palatinate, by choice adopted the northern German capital as his domicile. But their politics during the War had more in common than they would have liked to own. The "Berlin-Bagdad road" and the contest in strength, initiative, and resources between Germany and the British Empire which it implied, could not but appeal to Rathenau's imagination, while Rathenau's conception of the War as a national task, far surpassing mere military operations, must have been more or less willingly accepted by the man who was mainly responsible for the financing of the War in its critical stage.

The man who ought to be set up as Rathenau's real foil in every walk of life and in every move of the political game was a man whose name was as often mentioned in connection with a group or business as Rathenau's was allowed to stand alone, Dr. Alfred Hugenberg.

The origins and early successes of the Hugenberg group have been portrayed by one of the members of the group, Professor Ludwig Bernhard of the University of Berlin, with so vivid an art that it stands out from all other industrial and banking groups of the same period like an orator on a platform before a background of statistical wall charts. To speak of Dr. Hugenberg only as the man who led the Conservative party into the wilderness of uncompromising opposition to the reigning system after the 1927 elections, and who returned triumphant with almost a majority of Reichstag members behind him in the Hugenberg-Hitler coalition, after two years of virulent denunciation of the Young Plan and international Jewish capital which, he claimed, was behind this plan, was a mistake even at the time. The things he said of the Governments that followed the stabilization of the mark, whether Socialist, Catholic Center, National Liberal, or Conservative, were, in substance, the same as those said by him against the various Imperial Governments he had known ever since he had entered politics at the beginning of the century.

The circle of friends out of which the Hugenberg group grew up and gained its special character as an "interest," maintained by industry but directed toward a policy of aims that were preponderantly agrarian, had its nucleus in a common passion of its members for what was called the *Ostmarkenfrage*, the question of maintaining the eastern frontier regions of Prussia as the great farming belt of Germany, with a highly organized and even socialized system of coöperation between the great estates of the East Prussian and Baltic type and smaller farming settlements of the Posnanian kind, worked in part by cheap Polish labor, chiefly seasonal, from Russian Poland. The group was formed in the first years of this century, almost simultaneously with the British Round Table groups in South Africa; that is to say, at a time when the Anglo-French Entente on Mediterranean policy was not even in its infancy and European policy had not yet taken its turn toward the system of alliances and counteralliances which ended in the War; at a time, however, when Pan-German agitation had been fanned to the scorching point— with great gusts of smoke—by the Boer War. Great Britain, through her African policy, seemed to offer herself as a target for the Pan-German politicians who were insisting on the need of new areas for

German settlement. A war between Germany and France or between Germany and Russia seemed farther off, at that time, than at any other since 1871.

Ludwig Bernhard describes[14] how in 1904 when he was appointed professor of economics at the Prussian Academy in Posen, he felt himself drawn toward a group of seven men, six of them civil servants, and one an economist like Bernhard himself, who were trying to evolve an economic policy of their own and carry it through in the Eastern Marches of Prussia, sometimes against, and more often independently of, the official policy of the Prussian administration of Posnania. Leo Wegener, the economist, was a pupil of Max Weber. Like Bernhard, he had suffered disappointments in his academic career, and felt that he had a contribution to make to the greatness of the German nation; and, to do so, had to overcome bureaucratic routine by a passionate effort of personal will power and creative energy.[15] Of the other six, Von Schwerin, Wahnschaffe, Gonse, Katte, Meydenbauer, and Hugenberg, the first had worked as an assessor with the Prussian Settlement Commission, and later on as district commissioner at Thorn on the Vistula and as lieutenant governor of Frankfurt on the Oder. He felt convinced that a systematic settling of peasants on large areas, these to be farmed by a great number of small landholders individually, but at the same time in close coöperation, and all accompanied by a far-reaching system of standardization of produce and coöperative selling, seemed to be the ideal way of building up a strong reserve force of peasant population in a country which was, by the irresistible trend of events, in danger of being completely commercialized and industrialized. The second in age, Arnold Wahnschaffe, was also decisively influenced by experience gained in his official functions. Between 1897 and 1905, he had been an assistant member of the Silesian Board of Agriculture, and he had been in the District Office at Landsberg on the Warthe— in the *"Neumark,"* adjoining the present Corridor, once a part of the former province of Posnania. And, later, he had been a director

---

14. Ludwig Bernhard, *Der Hugenberg-Konzern*, pp. 1 ff.
15. Bernhard, *op. cit.*, p. 5; Wegener, *Der wirtschaftliche Kampf der Deutschen mit den Polen um die Provinz Posen* (1903), *passim*. It is to be noted that even where members of the group speak of a "personal" effort, it is always in the plural that they mention such efforts.

in the Prussian Ministry of Agriculture and a member of the Settlement Commission.

Alfred Hugenberg, born in 1865, was of the same age as Wahnschaffe. He was the only member of the group without the regional contacts which, with the others, made the question of peasant settlements in the eastern provinces of Prussia one of vital importance. Hugenberg came from western Germany. The mobility of the Prussian civil service was the only constant and effective mobility of population in a country which otherwise followed the old rule of staying at home and finding a useful occupation there. And one stayed at home in surroundings made familiar by the traditions of five, ten, or even more generations of landowners, holders of the same offices, occupiers of the same shops or workshops, inns or mills, post offices or dispensaries. It was the routine peregrination of a civil servant through the different parts of the Prussian area of administration, from the Baltic provinces and Posnania to Alsace-Lorraine and from the western Rhineland to Upper Silesia, that brought Hugenberg into touch with the question of land settlement in the east. He was appointed an assessor to the Settlement Commission in 1894 and stayed till 1899. Even before he went east, however, he was ready to take up an attitude of marked independence and even opposition to departmental rule and the official mentality. His master at the university, Georg Friedrich Knapp, had been one of the great individualists of that period, an avowed enemy of conventional teaching and officialism of any kind, an economist whose pupils distinguished themselves by their open-mindedness and their keen powers of critical appreciation, when the actions of Government and the routine of public administration were concerned. A brief period in office in western Germany did not make any great impression on Hugenberg's mind. But as soon as the *Raiffeisen* plan of developing German agriculture by coöperative credit and methods of marketing had caught his attention, it became the central moving force of all his activities. With him it was always organization on the biggest possible scale, but with a political motive, that mattered. Local influences were not as strong with him as with the other members of the group. The scene of his activities might change from Posnania, where he acted as director of a newly founded Bank of the Agricultural Coöperatives in close connection with the Central organization of German Agricultural Coöperatives, to the Prussian Ministry of Finance at Berlin. Then, after a rather sudden resignation and retirement from the civil service almost at the beginning of his career, he might go to Frankfurt am Main, and to Essen. There, in 1909, he became in turn president of the board of directors of the *Friedrich Krupp A.G.* and after the revolution, the leader of the German Nationalist party and a cabinet minister in the first cabinet formed after the National Socialist revolution. But under the most differing circumstances and with almost ceaseless changes of fortune, Hugenberg never wavered in his two characteristic attitudes toward public life, a stubborn sense of independence in the face of officialism and bureaucratic complacency, and a keen appreciation of the possibilities of mass propaganda.

To move faster, or even to override the civil service in its slow, painstaking attempts to "colonize" Posnania was the mainspring of the Hugenberg-Wegener group. With the exception of the latter, all its members were civil servants at the beginning of their career, men in their thirties or perhaps early forties. Risking their future, they formed what English parliamentary jargon in the Victorian era called a "cave." Their historian, Bernhard, speaks of a shadow government, a "*Nebenregierung*," which they had maintained in the eastern provinces. Through the administrative work of the Settlement Commission they had first come to hate and despise, and later on to annul or to circumvent, the petty jealousy, the counterplay of the different State departments with which the settlement work in Posnania had to deal. They did not challenge it to pitched battles; they worked its destruction from the inside of the bureaucratic system. While the heads of departments in Berlin were quarreling over a question of competence, the men on the spot had completed their own plan and carried it through by presenting it to a departmental chief who had just seen his own scheme defeated by the veto of a neighboring department, and who was glad to prefer it to the proposals of his next-door rival in the ministry. The forces which offered a real contest to Hugenberg and his friends were not those of the civil services; their antagonists were men of their own class and political creed. The landowners in the provinces east of the Elbe were by no means friendly to a plan the success of which would necessarily have meant the triumph of the peasant farm over the big estate and would, moreover, have blocked the supply of farm labor from Russian Poland. The agrarian laws of Prussia had, during the nineteenth century, favored the growth of a strong peasant class in Posnania.[16] The Wegener-Hugenberg group tried to make use of this old Prussian tradition of agrarian reform and to make the settlement of German peasants in the Polish districts, which was their national and political aim, a social program that was to be supported by the full administrative power of the State as against the interests of the landlord group. The members of the Hugenberg group were more consciously nationalist than the administration of Prussia as a whole, and more than any single department of state could afford to be[17] they were stronger partisans of the agrarian interest of Prussia than the big landowners themselves; and they had a firmer hold on the agrarian credit system in the eastern provinces than the agrarian banks and the industry connected with these banks, for they had the hold possessed by the "man on the spot."

When Hugenberg transferred his energies from the east to the west and from agrarian to industrial policy he and his little group of fellow workers had evolved a method which since then, and throughout the War and its aftermath, has been applied on a tremendous scale to German industry. The men who have adopted it have regarded their property and its administration not merely as a means for accumulating wealth and improving industry—both in quality and in quantity of output—but also as an instrument of political power in domestic affairs and as an element of the nation's strength

16. The Land Act of 1823 had been applied here in a greater number of cases than in the other Prussian provinces; and Posnania had, at the beginning of the present century, a few farms of the smallest size, that is, a size too small to support the owner. Some of them contained less than 2½ hectares, or 6.75 acres. Many were between 15 and 30 acres, that is, sufficient for the owner and his family and servants. And still more were between 30 and 150.

17. Their organization's independence of the central political authority had become so absolute that the change from German to Polish government in 1919 could occur without the organization as such being fundamentally affected. "Our organization's complete independence of the central government," said Leo Wegener in October, 1918, at a meeting of agrarian functionaries of the province, "has, as you know, been fought for during a struggle of many years, and eventually obtained by me long ago. We stand on our own strength. We need not alter our constitution. We shall be able to keep ourselves going whether under a German or a Polish Government." Wegener himself remained in the province after the War.

and prosperity. In the case of the Polish provinces, it was likewise a means of exercising authority over foreign elements that were poorer and lacked technical education. It was precisely this neglect of the more human side of industrial ambition, that is, of the love of an owner for his special field of activity, of his traditional family pride in an estate or a great establishment that has descended to him from men who founded or conquered it many centuries ago—it is the replacement of these older forms of industrial activity and ambition by a new conception of the "powers" of industry that made the Hugenberg method a formidable weapon during and after the War. It fell in with the conditions of war much better than with those prevailing before 1914. War forces industries to change their production and to alter their whole status to serve the national purpose, that of winning the War. This new attitude fitted even better with the task which the end of the War and the first period thereafter laid upon German industry. It had to remodel itself on new lines, entirely contrary to its old predilection for specialized "*Qualitätsarbeit*"—"high-class production"—it had to try to reconstruct its foundation by forming extensive horizontal trusts in the management of which the single plant or business—whether shipyard, ironworks, newspaper-press, estate agency, or cinema—counted little compared with the capacity for production and the selling power of the concern as a whole.

It seemed an irony of fate that, at the prime of life, the pioneer of these new ideas got hold of the management of the industrial family property which represented the most conservative and correct type of German industrial enterprise, that of Friedrich Krupp, and was able to use it as a lever for carrying his policy to victory. But fate, in permitting the ardent organizer of German colonization in the eastern provinces to become a director of Krupp's and, for a period of years, the guiding force behind the huge, unwieldy bloc of the Rhenish Westphalian coal and iron companies, was certainly doing more than playing a game of change of residence from Posnania to Essen on the Ruhr. Fate submitted to its own inexorable law of necessity. The old order of things in industry was bound to break down under the stress of the War. A man, or a group of men, had developed a new policy for handling industry—and, incidentally, everything else, from the meanest by-products of metropolitan life to agricultural settlements at the other end of the social heirarchy.

The man or group of men used such things as instruments of political power instead of serving them as something worthy of disinterested service because of their own merits. And he and his associates had to step in where the old aristocracy of the land and the great merchant houses and industrial plants had had to retire into the background of the national emporium.

It was not only the purpose of their policy, however, which the Hugenberg group had decided on when dealing with land settlement in Posnania, and which had made them, long before 1914 and almost immemorially long before 1932, the leaders of the "national opposition," one that opposed every kind of painstaking, scrupulously conscientious, bureaucratic civil government (whether bourgeois, clerical, or socialist) which has ruled Germany during the last thirty years. The methods, too, that were to be applied in the struggle for power had likewise been chosen and tried under pre-war conditions. Both aim and methods were exactly fitted to the War and the post-war period in so far as the latter took its character and development from the War. The aims coincided with the aims of those who fought for decisive victory in the War—a victory implying annexations, privileges, and indemnities—and the methods were the same as those used for propaganda in a modern mass war.

One of the Hugenberg group's chief means of attaining success was the timely, rigorous use it made of an innovation of the early present century, the so-called matrix news agencies ("*Matern Korrespondenzen*"), for disseminating news from a central agency to the organs of the provincial press, independently of the big newspapers and the political parties. In the land-settlement work the group had made the settlers feel that the Government did not care, or lacked the power to help them; they had to rely on their own local resources and on the support of men like the members of the group, who though they were themselves high officials or directors of banks and industrial concerns, felt with the common, hard-working man in the street or farmer on the land, and were ready to act even against instructions from Berlin, if need be. In the same way the local newspaper which had been dependent on some bigger daily in the next state capital or in Berlin for its news—news which was prepared for the next day's issue by the sub-editor's scissors and paste—was given to understand that it had only to apply to the Hugenberg office for its matrix newssheets, if it wished to emancipate itself from the Government and from the party secretariat in the capital and become a force of its own in its own district.

The most striking incident in this line of development was the acquisition by Dr. Hugenberg of the Scherl newspaper concern—and that did not occur when he took the lead against the policy of paying reparations or when he directed the referendum against the Young Plan or formed the alliance with the National Socialist party with a view to depriving the Socialists and the Catholic Center of their influence on the Prussian Government. It took place between 1912 and 1914, at a time when Prussia was the uncontested domain of the Conservative party, and the Chancellor of the Reich himself was a more reliable member of the Protestant Church and the Conservative party than any of his predecessors in the office.

Hugenberg had been chairman of the board of directors of the Friedrich Krupp Company since 1909; and in 1912 he had become president of the *Bergbauliche Verein*. This was made up of the mining companies and associated industries of the Ruhr area; and even before Dr. Hugenberg's time it had been well known for its efficient organization and the loyal coöperation of all its members in the question of prices, tariffs, industrial competition, restriction of output, and the like. The articles of the association, however, were in the main concerned with the relationship between its members. What concerned the outer world, especially the consumer, was only a by-product of the transactions among the industrialists themselves. In that respect the advent of Dr. Hugenberg worked a rapid and a radical change. The heavy industries, under his guidance, became more and more united in their attitude toward the Government, toward the banks, the other industrial groups, and the political parties. The means used to cement the union were as simple as they were, in the Germany of 1912, surprisingly new. Dr. Hugenberg opened the eyes of the wealthier members of the mining area to the fact that, as individuals or through their firms, they had been continually approached by people soliciting contributions for all kinds of public institutions and undertakings and even, sometimes, by the Government itself, and had in a number of cases given more than was necessary simply because they did not know that their fellow industrialists contributed to the same cause, or had given to unworthy persons—and what seemed worse, had given without exercising efficient control over the use of the money, and seeing that its use conformed with the interests of the donors. To stop this evident waste a secretariat under the personal control of the president of the association was created. To it the members agreed to send all such applications as they received. It would compare them with similar applications, it would prevent double payments for the same cause, and advise the rejection of demands if they came from persons or organizations that were unreliable or otherwise suspect; and, finally, it would supervise all the various social and political activities toward which money had been contributed. The effect was almost magical, in both directions. The members of the association saved money and trouble. They knew that the secretariat would not advise them to support an institution or person that was not known to it, and had not given proof of loyalty to the régime and of usefulness to the interests or the prestige of the association; and if they had to refuse a request they felt they were free from any blame which otherwise might fall on an ungenerous Croesus, for they had acted on advice which almost amounted to instructions. In this way they drew more closely together, and at the same time came more and more under the control of Dr. Hugenberg's central office. More than they were aware of at the time, too, they disclosed their private relationships with political groups, with their banks, their customers, and with public bodies. In another direction the accession of power to the Hugenberg secretariat was still greater. Everybody in the Reich came to know that an application to any member of the mining industry of the Ruhr and the neighboring areas for sympathetic interest or support could only succeed with the good will of the secretariat; and the secretariat, moreover, came to possess an almost unlimited knowledge of the financial needs of institutions, associations, or private individuals, as also their activities and their weak points, where, if they become obnoxious, they could be attacked. A list of persons in the habit of presenting themselves as secretaries or agents of the applicant bodies or as the authors of plans that required support forms itself almost of necessity in such a secretariat, and those in charge of its files are, at any given moment, enabled to engage such people, many of them ready to undertake any conceivable kind of activity and to work for any master who pays them well and protects them efficiently from eventual pressure from their former employers.

The common knowledge that all applications went to the secretariat reinforced its hold on public opinion, more than the money actually paid out on its advice. The entire wealth of great members of western Germany's steel, iron, and coal industry, such as the Reusch, Klöckner, Thyssen, Stinnes, Kirdorf, Stumm, Springorum, and Phoenix companies, the Bochumer Verein, and many others, seemed to center in Dr. Hugenberg's cabinet. Adverse comment on its activities spoke of corruption and of wholesale buying up of public opinion. That was, to say the least, an overstatement of the facts. One of the merits of the system, we must remember, consisted precisely in the fact that it prevented any lavish spending of money and allowed, as a rule, only the kind of expenditures that would bring direct returns.[18]

It was under conditions such as these that the event took place which made the influence of the Hugenberg group one of the decisive factors in German politics after 1913, the financial breakdown of the newspaper proprietor August Scherl and the halfhearted and finally unsuccessful attempts on the part of the Government to reconstruct the Scherl concern as a semiofficial news agency. Hugenberg used the opportunity to the full. For obvious reasons, all the results of his control over an unrivaled apparatus for political publicity[19] did not become noticeable until the end of fifteen years of

18. A letter from Dr. Hugenberg himself to one of the industrialists, published by Professor Bernhard, offers a good instance of the way in which applications were handled, and explains a good deal of the confidence put in the secretariat. "The enterprise which has been recommended to you," it says, "is the precise opposite of what is required, for here we have a case of collecting money for no other purpose than that of maintaining the considerable number of superfluous associations which undertake these collections. I fear that only a small portion of the money would reach X; the cost of organization, especially with such an association as this, would absorb the greater part of it. I therefore advise you to refuse. I will mention the affair at the meeting of . . . and will, moreover, inform Mr. Y, and so enable him to warn all our friends by telephone to have nothing to do with this matter."

19. Control over the most important cinema interest in Germany, the Ufa, with a special eye to the contents of weekly news reels, was added to the newspapers and news agencies after the War, and finally became the most influential part of the system. Somewhat inexplicably, broadcasting was left out. Even the Republican governments regarded broadcasting as more or less their own domain. But it is through it that the National Socialist State acts directly on the masses; and it controls even the minutest details of personnel, program, and listening-in.

warfare and domestic conflict. But the propaganda against the "policy of debt paying" and the Young Plan carried the coalition of Nationalists and National Socialists to victory at the polls. The War certainly helped to consolidate the strength of the Hugenberg line, if it is permissible, in such a chain of thought, to borrow an expression from the language of military tactics; but it gave scant opportunity for using it except to secure preparedness for the reorganization of industrial life after the War. The trade-unions had to be conciliated. Wages did not count during the War. The activities of Parliament were sometimes difficult to bear with patience. But on the whole the energies of Parliament spent themselves in keeping the Chancellor and his civil colleagues occupied with the abstract questions of a negotiated peace while the industrial interests and their publicity, hand in glove with the military authorities, worked for a decisive victory. During the War, moreover, the vexed question of the rival claims of agrarian and industrial interests to paramount influence in the framing of domestic policy did not arise. It was to be expected that sooner or later Dr. Hugenberg himself would turn his attention to agriculture and land settlement; a greater Germany, to a man like him, could not mean merely an extension of markets for industrial products nor even colonial expansion. His ulterior aim was the one to which the labors of his first period had been devoted, that of firmly rooting a German peasant and landowner race in the vast, fertile area of agricultural land between the Baltic and the Adriatic Sea. It is too early to sum up a life of unbounded vitality, but Hugenberg's biographers will probably agree that he was happiest, though least successful, during his tenure of the Reich Ministry of Agriculture in 1932 and 1933. During the War, however, agriculture had a policy of its own. Germany was a blockaded country, both on land and sea, so far as agricultural products were in question; for, even apart from the control exercised by the Allied Powers, neither Switzerland nor Holland could have supplied Germany with products of their soil, and Germany's allies needed more themselves than they could give or let pass. The production and distribution of food had been placed under government control. Landowners had lost their independent power of trading more completely even than the armament industry. The Hugenberg group, therefore, had no occasion to form contacts with the economic or political associations representing landowners or peasants, or to place its organization at their service. Individual contacts were formed or maintained through a common allegiance to a program of war aims that went beyond the declarations of the Government. But, apart from that, the industrial groups of which Hugenberg became the exponent had as little direct understanding with the landed interests as the groups from which Rathenau had emerged.

If such a vast field of human energy, ambition, strength of purpose, and error of judgment as the German industrial community during the War could be justly described in an antithesis, one might be tempted to say that the contrast between the two schools consisted in their differing attitude to the War itself. In the view of Hugenberg and those around him, the War must be made to serve German industry, for on its strength and power the fate of a Germany of the future, one stronger and more powerful than the Germany of Stein and Bismarck, would depend. In the view of Rathenau, German industry, by exerting itself to the utmost in the service of the War, would be able to win it, and thus thwart the attempt of the enemies to overthrow Germany. Rathenau saw the chief asset of German industry in centralized leadership exercising its intellectual skill; to Hugenberg it was mass organization and propaganda, the massive foundation of Rhenish Westphalian and Silesian mines and factories, and of eastern Prussian agriculture, and above all an instinctive belief in the primitive forces of racial physique on which he relied. Rathenau, whom his enemies called a pacifist, served the War to the utmost of his ability and it was in the nature of things that the War should kill him, while those who had made the War serve them emerged from it clad in armor, which though blackened, had been made only the harder to pierce.

CHAPTER XIV

SOME POST-WAR EFFECTS

IN the field of national industry and wealth two separate and distinct movements must be noted in the general trend of the post-war period —through inflation to retrenchment and reconstruction, and finally to deflation. One of those movements was characterized by a rapid local growth and decline. It alternately shot up and dwindled down again in the same place like a *jet d'eau* in a French garden. This movement was entirely devoid of economic utility; in a certain sense it even defied economic laws.

The other movement was more lasting in its effects; it was horizontal and implied a transfer of property from one district or province to another. So far as frontier provinces with a lively trade across the frontier were concerned, it meant a corresponding loss or increase in national prosperity as a whole. In any case, it was a disturbing influence for the stability of national wealth and the tax-paying power of the community. For the province which lost in wealth and earning capacity to a neighboring district would immediately make its losses felt in the annual national balance sheet, while the gains of the newcomer in prosperity might remain invisible for the next two or three years.

The upward-downward movement was a direct outcome of the War, and of the suspension of sound economic relations between effort and success, or between work and wages—for which the War was responsible. The horizontal movement had not the same direct relation to profiteering and such other phenomena of war industry. But, in the case of Germany, war had at least had a determining influence on its origin and growth. The duration and the geographical peculiarity of the War, the temporary occupation of the western part of Germany by Allied troops after the War, and the permanent change in the former hinterland of the eastern section of Prussia, all gave this movement a strong impetus. At the very beginning of the War, industrial plants had to be transferred from the danger zone on the western frontier to the center and the east of Germany. After the War part of southwestern and western Germany and the whole of East Prussia found themselves cut off from old trade connections. But, while East Prussia was definitely outrivaled by Poland and Czechoslovakia, and economically starved by the conditions which followed the creation of new economic units with strong tendencies to high tariffs and a policy of autarchy, the west was quickly drawn into a current of—partly illegitimate—trade far stronger than there had been in the normal times of peace.

The movement excited more curiosity, between 1919 and 1923, than it merited. Fortunes which, during the War, had been won or had been vastly increased by means of army contracts and by business done with the occupied areas were in some cases lost, in other cases further increased by speculations in foreign currency during the inflation period. In the great majority of cases deflation destroyed the last vestiges of that sham prosperity which had surrounded the dwellingplace of the war or inflation profiteer. Excessive profits from army contracts, from financial credits to the Government or some incorporated branch of a belligerent state had been normal effects, one might even say necessary elements, in the wars that were waged during the past two or three centuries between countries which had exchanged the barbaric conditions of primitive economy for civilized capitalism, and had not yet become ripe for the communist type of war, one that must be carried on as an effort freely given by all alike. It is one of the *contradictiones in adjecto* by which the history of mankind moves along and develops new conceptions and modes of life that war, though it relies on the ability of a people to endure physical hardship and on the soldier's knightly virtues, at the same time favors the ugliest kind of easy profits through speculation and usury, and evenly distributes both honors and spoils among the best and the worst. It has been said that, on the whole, it was war, at least in the old world, which had created all the big fortunes, in the shape of great landed estates. For the land was given in fee in return for military service, or for grants of men and goods to help the sovereign in his wars. It had also been true of great capitalist fortunes, for they began with the commissions and brokerage fees which the "court" Jews of the European princes earned by financing royal military enterprises in the seventeenth and eighteenth centuries. In more recent times—the Rothschilds furnish the best-known example—the special news service maintained by their commercial agents in foreign countries was the money-making power. For such a news service could inform the home office of an imminent war before the governments concerned could themselves become aware of it. And huge gains resulted from the buying or selling of the stock of a belligerent country in the neutral exchanges. Finally, it is still true of the great fortunes in the world of industry and commerce. For, under modern conditions, the supplies needed for mobilization and for the first months of warfare may be accumulated by a few enterprising firms with some inside knowledge—and not too much patriotic sentiment—and be almost monopolized before war actually breaks out. No government could, in the haste of mobilization or under the pressure of the first war clashes, afford to haggle about prices or try to buy in the open market such small quantities of war materials as remained in outside hands. The price demanded must be paid, whatever it may be. And the seller may even tell the buyer that he can get the goods much cheaper through him than by introducing a system of forced economy, with its expensive bureaucratic machine, its waste of time, and the almost inevitable petty corruption it leads to. These three ways of accumulating great fortunes, by feudal land grants in return for military service, by commissions on war loans and credits, and profits from army contracts and "*Aufkauf*,"[1] "forestalling," are as old as war itself. As to the last two methods, in the times of the religious wars, the Thirty Years' War, the "succession" wars of the seventeenth and eighteenth centuries, and those of Napoleon, the methods used gave rise to accusing broadsheets and pamphlets without number. The generation of Germans that had to bear the brunt of the World War had, in so far as it had been brought up on books, learned all about it from two of the greatest war books in world literature, Goethe's *Kampagne in Frankreich* and Tolstoy's *War and Peace*.

A fourth possible source of war gains has now been added to the three older devices of the profiteering tribe. Speculation in currency is made easy whenever a belligerent country is led to lower the value of its money, abandon the metal standard, declare a moratorium, and

1. In the German language of the late fifteenth and early sixteenth century the expression "*Aufkäufer*," meaning one who forestalled, who bought up foodstuffs and other necessaries of life and sold them at exorbitant prices during the war he was able to foresee, was a very common one. Many of Hans Sachs' poems on the events of his time deal in forceful language with these parasites of the many sieges and military enterprises of that period.

finance its war through domestic loans which, on account of their unbearable burden of interest, will have to be liquidated at the end of the war either by bankruptcy or by subsequent inflation. Speculation of that kind forms perhaps the best example of the *jet d'eau*-like changes within the boundaries of national wealth of which we have just spoken. But in this case it is an enormous, volcanic explosion, a veritable geyser of wealth spouting up from a small, contemptible piece of ground which nobody had thought worthy of consideration till it disclosed its resources. The geyser spends itself in gushing energy and effort to reach incredible heights, dwindles, and in the end leaves the old black hole from which it sprang an exhausted, desolate—perhaps a cursed—place. The wealth which is nominally won under such conditions represents no value at all, it springs from nothing, and in the first stages of the process there are no losers who contribute in proportion to the gain of the *nouveau riche*. It is only when the new fortune, by growing out of all rational relation to the value of property and income in the neighborhood and perhaps even in the whole national community, automatically accelerates the depreciation of money and so diminishes its buying power that others begin to lose. The general loss, in that case, follows; it does not precede or accompany the rise of the new individual fortune.

The last and most depressing peculiarity of this phenomenon consists in the fact that the dwindling away and disappearance of the great fortune does not as a rule mean that it is being divided into small public gains or is passing on to some other rising power in commerce or industry. It is a dead loss, and for the onlooker it is like being a belated visitor to a public garden when the fountain is turned off, the jet grows smaller and smaller, and ends by disappearing with the faintest of little gurgles.

While such phenomena as these show themselves in almost every case of war and, apart from their moral consequences, do not mean permanent changes in economic conditions, those war profits which, during the war itself and the first post-war period, arise from the transferring of money from the pockets of one part of the people to the pockets of another, or, to use a current term, come about in a "horizontal" way, are of a more serious character. Transactions of this kind deal with real things. The transactions may consist chiefly in exaggerating the value of these things out of all proportion to their real usefulness. But the commonwealth cannot but recognize the importance of an "*Umschichtung*," to use one of the terms which became familiar through the War, or of the transfer of valuable property from one group or class of the nation, or from one part of the country to another.

Such a transfer seems to have occurred on a much greater scale during the World War and the years following than in any other war within the living memory of mankind. In Germany one of its most striking examples was the change in the economic structure of such a place as Cologne. Cologne had an old tradition of rather quiet, solid banking and commercial business, based on the patrician feelings of an important, self-governing city of the old German Empire, on conservative if rather tolerant Catholicism, and on its geographical and ethnical nearness to the Dutch Netherlands and the Flemish part of Belgium. Cologne's most representative banking house, bearing the name of its founders and owners, the Freiherrn von Oppenheim, had, through its association with the Phoenix Mining company, an influence on the metal industry of the Rhineland and the Ruhr which far exceeded the usual part that a moneylender and financier plays in the industrial enterprises of his client. During the War, however, the Oppenheims were ousted from this position. They maintained their social standing and their personal fortune. But they were ousted by newcomers who represented an economic process the reverse of the traditional one of capital nursing industry. Two self-made men, Otto Wolff and Ottmar Strauss, dealers in ironware before the War, laid the foundation of one of the greatest post-war financial and industrial companies in Germany, one constituting a decided power in politics, by a lucrative deal in tin plate at the beginning of the War. Coöperating with a successful banker, Louis Levy-Hagen,[2] they obtained interests in some of the industrial concerns of the "heavy" type. After a brief resistance on the part of the Oppenheim interests, they wrested the Phoenix concern from the hands of its former rulers, mobilized its huge powers, fused industrial production with trade in metals—the refining and sale of metals having a closer affiliation than other branches of industry and com-

2. The 1922 *Who's Who* speaks of him as Hagen, Louis, commercial councilor, owner of the banking firm A. Levy, president of the Chamber of Commerce, member of the boards of directors of forty-four companies, Cologne.

merce—and finally, at the time of the inflation, crowned their success by supporting, and in the end taking over, Cologne banking. For the latter had exhausted its reserves while the commercialized industrial concerns of the Rhineland and the Ruhr district were at the height of their power.[3] The losses of the losing bank, which before the War had held the dominant position in the province, were more than made up by the profits of the successful competitor acting in concert with the metal trade. But the general loss of influence which the banking interests of Cologne suffered through the change is undeniable. Even the strongest of them now depends on its industrial connections in spite of the natural tendency of industry to look for credits from some old and famous local bank. The Wolff-Strauss group is an entirely new economic factor.

In addition to these social and economic changes within the limits of single districts, we are faced by the fact that increased prosperity in one German state or province often meant a corresponding loss in a neighboring or even in a more distant part of Germany; and the Rhineland is, again, a conspicuous example of this kind of change. Between 1919 and 1928, Cologne, in spite of the almost revolutionary alteration in her own economic structure, was able to strengthen her position as the chief city in the province and the center of the Rhine trade. But, at the same time and to almost the same degree, Frankfurt am Main was losing ground. Throughout the duration of the old Holy Roman Empire these two cities had been more or less friendly rivals, with a slight preëminence for Frankfurt; for it was associated with the ceremonial crowning of the German kings. In the first half of the nineteenth century Cologne had won the regard of the Romantic movement, and the fervent religious feelings of King Frederick William the Fourth of Prussia had led him to regard Cologne and her Cathedral, finished during his reign, with a favor as warm as that of those young Germans with whom Cologne was sentimentally bound up with the lyrics of Heinrich Heine. Frankfurt, however, regained its hold on the nation; in the Forties

---

3. Cf. Fried, *Das Ende des Kapitalismus*, pp. 68 ff., Levinsohn, *op. cit.*, p. 73. Fried contrasts what he calls the *"wendige Händlertyp, der Konjunktur und Spekulationsgewinne in der Industrie anlegt"* with the hereditary wealth and stable power of the Krupps or the Thyssens, Hoesch or Stumm, and with the conservative ways of the older private banks like those of the Oppenheims, Schröders, or Rothschilds.

its Paulskirche saw the meeting of the first German Parliament; and, under the new Empire, the preëminence of the Protestant free city on the Main over the cathedral town on the Rhine seemed firmly established. Frankfurt attracted the best administrators as mayors, among them Miquel and Adickes, foremost of the representatives of progressive communal enterprise in the Wilhelminian era. It was the first among the great centers of commerce and industry to create a new university adapted to its special needs, and, a sign of a strong renaissance of civic pride, the first university in Germany not entirely dependent on one of the states. For, in the case of its university, the city of Frankfurt and a local foundation shared the administrative power with the Prussian Ministry of Education.

The War ruined the position of Frankfurt. The importance of its exchange dwindled. A famous old house like Neufville's Bank closed. Others lost all influence on the German market as a whole; and there are hardly any firms of more recent growth with enough new initiative to take the place of the old ones. Frankfurt would seem to offer many opportunities for financial coöperation with the metal trade, the dye industry, and the manufacturing of automobiles, all of which interests are represented by leading representatives in Frankfurt itself or in the neighborhood; for example, the Mertons for metals, the Weinbergs, of Casella and Company, and Meister, Lucius, and Brüning for chemical dyes, the Opels for automobiles, Merck of Darmstadt for pharmaceutical products, and so on. The university attracted more students than its founders might have expected, and some of the leading scientists of the day. But in spite of such isolated indications of means of recovery, the depression soon became general. It showed clearly in the precarious position of the *Frankfurter Zeitung*. The incomparable prestige of its tradition as the only German newspaper of international standing and the uncontested merits of its financial supplement were barely sufficient to save it from passing out of existence. It showed, too, in the slow but unmistakable decline of the theater and concert life of the town. And all this was taking place at a time when Cologne was rising by leaps and bounds, founding its own university, doing pioneer work in opera and playhouse, and, above all, heading the new German development in town planning.

The decline of Frankfurt and the corresponding rise of Cologne was also a fact of some international importance. The War with

France had placed the three trade centers on the Rhine—Mannheim-Ludwigshafen, Frankfurt-Mainz and Düsseldorf-Cologne—in the same plight. Almost over night they found they were no longer industrial and commercial communities of the most active type: they had been turned into mere strategical points, bridgeheads, and railway stations. Their natural lines of communication had been cut off, and all they could do during the first period of the conflict was to forget that they had had an existence and functions of their own, stand aside, and let the troops from the west and the fugitives from the east pass through. They were almost equally affected by the complete cessation of commercial intercourse with France; and the particular hardships visited upon the zones nearest the fighting line, with air raids as a special reminder, were felt alike by all of them. After the War the occupation struck Mannheim hardest because its twin town and main industrial quarter, Ludwigshafen on the left bank of the Rhine, was occupied by French troops, and the bridge was practically closed for private use. Cologne was the headquarters of the British army of occupation, while Frankfurt experienced only a brief occupation by French troops at the time of the Ruhr conflict. The three centers suffered—in so far as an artificially and economically unsound stimulation of illicit or at least abnormal trade can be called an infliction rather than a benefit—almost equally from the enormous amount of "contraband" coming in and going out through the so-called "hole in the West" at a time when Germany was trying to limit imports, but could not exercise full control over either imports or exports on her western frontier. Given similar conditions in the three Rhenish centers, industry and commerce would have had equal opportunity to maintain their northern and southern connections. Holland and Switzerland were both neutrals, and the restrictions imposed by Allied control upon their export trade were of the same kind. The increase in the importance of Cologne and the diminishing influence of Frankfurt and the other southern trading centers after the War corresponded to a marked *rapprochement* between Germany and Holland, while German-Swiss trade was slow to regain its old importance.[4] The decline of Frankfurt signified that for the time being Amsterdam and Rotterdam had won a success at the expense of Basle and Zürich.

4. It should here be said that strong currents of commercial and family relationship existing between Frankfurt and Antwerp were first deflected

How far does this fall in with some general law of economic evolution through war? Is it possible to conclude from such and similar facts that war favors the commercial position of a coastal state and imperils that of a landlocked country? Was neutrality more difficult to maintain—and therefore commercial intercourse with one of the belligerent countries subject to stricter supervision—in the case of Switzerland, with its obvious French sympathies in the western cantons, than in that of Holland with the close contact it had with some of the Belgian provinces suffering the most terrible hardships of the War? Was it easier for Holland to invest capital in the industrial works of the Rhineland and the Ruhr than it was for Switzerland to support the German financial market through the old channels of credit which existed between the northern Swiss and southwestern German exchanges—for in Basle and Frankfurt there were many families among the patrician bourgeoisie which, through their several branches, belonged alike to both towns. None of these questions can be answered by a clear affirmative. The conditions that made for a continuity of relationship with both countries were equally good. Both were financially sound and could dispose of sufficient capital for foreign investment at high interest. Both felt equally safe from any danger of sharing the fate of Belgium. From both countries Germany tried to obtain as much food and as many other necessaries of life as possible wherewith to mitigate the effects of the blockade upon the civilians in the industrial regions of western and southern Germany. They, of course, suffered more directly from the scarcity of food than did people in the agrarian provinces of eastern or southern Germany. To both countries Germany had something to offer in exchange for food, and that was, mainly, coal. It is certainly curious, then, to see the difference in post-war conditions between the upper and lower German Rhineland. In part the explanation may be found in the material benefits which the occupation by British troops bestowed on Cologne and the surrounding districts. But, in part, it

from their traditional course by the inevitable militarization of life in the occupied area of Belgium. This halted the intercourse between individual Germans and Belgians even where it would have survived the shock of the War; and later on the obstacle was the understandable suspicion with which Belgians regarded the German connections of a Belgian subject. This was an additional reason for the handicapped position in which Frankfurt found itself after the War.

also lies in the fact that before the War the ties between Switzerland and Frankfurt or the towns of Baden had been much stronger than those between the German towns on the lower Rhine and their Dutch neighbors. The mingling of trade and even of the private lives of many prominent citizens of Basle, Freiburg, Strassburg, Karlsruhe, Mannheim, Mainz, and Frankfurt made them feel the rupture occasioned by the War, the moratorium, and the censorship on private letters as a terrible rent in the texture of their common descent and race, and one which could not be restored as soon as the War ended. Switzerland, saved from participating in the fate of Belgium by the rigid exercise of military precautions and self-reliance, held back during the later stages of the War. Holland, with no such strong pre-war interdependence, had nothing to withhold her from coöperation, when consistent with neutrality, during the War, and much less after it, when Belgium had been restored to her former position as a friendly rival in trade.[5]

Broadly speaking, however, the changes in German industry must be traced back to the War itself, not to its political consequences or the attitude of foreign countries. The first years of the era of attempted reconstruction completed the work of the War. To quote once more from Professor Günther's volume:

War and *Kriegswirtschaft* had made familiar the organizing of everything. Surprising results had in fact been reached by the armed forces in union with industry, when concentrated upon the War. The technical side of organization had no secrets. There were many people who had earned their living during the War by activities that were connected with organization as such; and they tried, after those opportunities had vanished, to find new bases for similar work and the profits accruing from it. With many of them, indeed, a highly individual policy of increasing their incomes became the motive and the foundation of a social policy of higher incomes for the masses! Resultant upon this organizing zeal came cartels and trusts, combines, partly industrial, partly commercial, of the well-known "vertical" type; coöperative societies, syndicates, export trade bureaus and coördinated secretariats for the

5. Similarly, on the eastern frontiers, it made a considerable difference whether the neighboring countries were Lithuania and Poland, on the borders of Prussia, Czechoslovakia alongside Saxony and northern Bavaria, or Austria and Switzerland, adjoining southern Bavaria. Württemberg was in a specially favorable position in having only a friendly neutral (German Switzerland) and no belligerent country as a neighbor.

regulation of prices as between industrialists and middlemen; trade-unions, coöperative stores, and central offices of workmen's and shop stewards' councils in the camp of labor. Employers and workingmen organized in associations, and unions negotiated their agreements through central committees; they coöperated as *au pair* members of several public boards and met in the provisory *Reichswirtschaftsrat*, the new Imperial Economic Council; they fought one another before the special labor courts, conciliation boards and wages' committees; they concluded general wage agreements, and together formed committees to fix index numbers, and so on.

The administration supported these organizations in many ways; it even created them in some cases, and, at any rate, tolerated them. In a certain measure the State itself had the benefit of all this exuberance of organizing zeal, the various attempts at planned economy and *Sozialisierung* owed much to it, and it brought forth the "fundamental principles"—if such an expression be permissible in such a connection— of economic and social policy during the inflation. The personnel of the civil service in the Reich, the states, and the civic administrations, whose members had been further increased after the end of the War, found themselves fully occupied when participating in or dealing with such organizations. As members of the suffering middle class tried more and more to obtain public jobs they made the existing hypertrophy of organization, rules, and ordinances, with all its evil consequences, still worse.[6]

The end of the inflation brought a setback to modern industrial methods; but even the impressive spectacle of the sudden collapse of the Stinnes companies and a few minor events of the same character were soon forgotten. The years of sham prosperity which followed were the worst imaginable for returning to the pre-war tradition of work for work's sake. The specific dangers which beset Germany in connection with the world crisis of 1930 were certainly due to the general effects of war on the attitude of an industrialized nation toward its work.[7] The series of failures, some of them aggravated by

6. *Op. cit.*, p. 150.
7. For details of industrial reorganization see James W. Angell, *The Recovery of Germany* (1929), Chapters IV and V, and the tables in Wl. Woytinsky, *Zehn Jahre neues Deutschland,* pp. 53–92. At the annual meeting of one of the leading iron and coal companies, the Klöckner-Werke A.-G., December 12, 1931, the board of directors was reconstituted by the resignation of three experts, the reëlection of three bankers and directors of companies in Cologne, Bremen, and Berlin—the seat of the company is Duisburg in the Ruhr district—and the addition of another Berlin banker, one of the

corrupt practices and laxity in the matter of prospectuses, balance sheets, and accounts—from those of Favag and Nordwolle to the Darmstädter and Dresdner Bank and that of Schultheiss-Patzenhofer—can easily be traced to the general lessening of actual and effective connection between the owner and his property, the industrialist and his output, and that which should unite the banker, his creditors, his debtors, and the use made of money lent.

Among the "captains of industry" in Germany none is better qualified to give his opinion on the general lines of development during the last thirty years than the former president of the *Reichsverband der Deutschen Industrie,* the Imperial Union of German Industry, Dr. Duisberg, one of the leaders of the German dye trust during the period of its rise to the rank of an industrial world power. Dr. Duisberg was a self-made man, owing his position entirely to his personal qualities, his unbounded energy, his driving power, and his courage. A simple chemist in a large dye factory, the *Bayer'sche Farbenfabriken,* in the Eighties, he rose to be the director of the business. He made it one of the largest establishments in Germany, in Europe, in the world, the nucleus of the "I. G. Farben," and one of the key industries of the war and post-war period. In another sense he is one of the representative figures of the second German Empire, closely connected with public affairs, the bearer of every academic honor Germany had to confer, conspicuous as the benefactor of students' welfare work, research fellowships, and the international exchange of young scholars, the man, perhaps, who took the most important part in supporting the policy of both Emperor and Imperial Government, that of industrializing and technicizing Germany that began to function about 1900. Actual accomplishment in, and official protection for, industry are almost equally represented by his forceful personality. It is a noteworthy fact in the history of the War and the post-war period that his activities, far from being broken, doubled and trebled after 1918, and that he was

directors of the "Commerz- und Privat-bank." The chairman of the board said in his report that the most hopeful signs in the present distress were the recent arrangement for international coöperative selling in the wire trade, that is, through the International Wire Export Company of Brussels; an international sales office for *Formeisen,* and later on for other products of the steel mills. And it might be expected that these arrangements would succeed in raising retail prices.

one of the first Germans with whom, in spite of his uncompromising hostility toward the treaties of 1919, the leaders of French and British industry once more dealt on a footing of equality, and even with respect for the power he wielded.

In an article on the economic crisis of 1930,[8] Dr. Duisberg pointed out that it had at last become clear to all honest-minded men that the roots of this crisis lay in the economic consequences of the War. It was

the economic ebb after the great floodtide of the War. War destroyed capital to such an enormous extent that it could not be built up again after the War; the liquidation of the War continued to absorb capital and had withdrawn it from its normal function, quite apart from German indemnities; it was all a consequence of the War having been financed by bills payable after it, with the result that war debts everywhere prevented a reasonable use of capital.

It may be too early, here amidst the débris of the organic structure of the pre-war world, to pronounce a definite judgment on the relative importance of the indemnity payments, payments on Inter-Allied War Debts, the destruction of capital during the War, and the necessarily faulty and sometimes unscrupulous use of capital during the reconstruction period. From the point of view of capitalism, all are unlawful if not destructive elements in the economic setting of the western world. One of them is peculiarly offensive to the vanquished country; another is especially obnoxious to some of the victorious powers. Another kind of peace, with a more realistic view of the possibilities of reparation might have saved both sides much of the trouble. But of the last two we can say that they are felt equally in every country that took part in the War. Destruction not only of specific capital in a specific country, but of the value of capital itself, and, consequently, a falsification of the future use of capital are necessary complements of a modern war.

8. Released by *Nordische Gesellschaft* (Lübeck, November 29, 1931).

PART IV

CONCLUSIONS

CHAPTER XV

MATERIAL EFFECTS

An attempt to account for the effects of war on one of the belligerent countries such as I have made in these pages would of necessity be doomed to failure were complete records of the material consequences of mobilization, battle, blockade, and treaties of peace the aim of the Economic and Social History of the World War. At the end of the War, Germany had the terms of peace imposed on her. Through circumstances which, partly at least, had no direct connection with the War, reparation and recovery were forced to take forms that violently agitated and disturbed international relations; to such a degree, indeed, that the post-war period is now commonly described as a continuation of the War by different means. And this period led, in Germany, to a revolution much more radical in its program and in some ways much more closely connected with the War than the revolution which coincided with its last stage.

For all these and other reasons it would in any case be beyond the scope of this volume to cover the whole field of national industry, and determine at every point whether the change since 1914 is due to the War, to the loss of the War, to the revolution, or to the developments in foreign and diplomatic policy from 1919 to 1934. But a few points may perhaps be made without too great a risk of error. I propose to deal here with questions that lie mainly in the field of economics, and to postpone the moral considerations to the last chapter.

1. *Planned economy.* As a theoretical conception, planning on a national scale is as old as conscious statecraft. Modern warfare, from 1916 to 1918, has demonstrated its practical possibilities, especially in the case of Germany. Russia followed suit. The essential differences, however, between war planning and peace planning remain in full force. Walther Rathenau, the initiator of war-planned economy in Germany, has been quoted as saying that the lesson to be drawn from the experiment is to undertake intense preparations, during the next period of peace, for planned economy during the next period of war. That is a different thing from planning such as

is implied by the N.E.P. in Soviet Russia, or the N.R.A. in the United States. Planning during a war and for a war originates with the necessity of making every industry in the country and the whole organization of exports and imports subservient to the production and accumulation of war material; and it ends with the rationing of food, clothing, housing, and even of medicinal drugs for the population of the "nationalized" area. It has the character of an emergency measure, and any argument drawn from the ulterior consequences it may have must be rejected as irrelevant because war planning cannot take future conditions into account. Planning in peace-time, on the contrary, starts with an attempt to coördinate the various industries. It aims at a general strengthening of the capacity for production, at an increase in the exchange of goods, both by domestic and by foreign trade, and finally at a rise in prosperity which will obviate the need of a mechanized distribution of goods. But in spite of these differences in the character of planning for a war, present or future, and planning for a period of peace, all the plans our age has witnessed have one common and essential feature. Such planning is not the result of voluntary coöperative activity, of deliberation and resolution on the part of those to whom the plans are to be applied and whose needs they are expected to satisfy. Planning is decreed from above; a force which is professedly independent of the individuals, groups, or corporations involved in the scheme of the plan, conceives it, proclaims it indispensable in the interest of the commonwealth, stigmatizes opposition to it as unpatriotic and destructive, makes non-participation punishable as an act of sabotage, and, so far as the plan succeeds, disposes of the material profits. Peace planning, obviously, would not proceed—and, in the past, did not proceed—in that way, if left to itself. Federations of industry, agricultural coöperative societies, institutions for scientific research, guilds and trade-unions are, as a rule, jealous of their independence and prepared to work out their own salvation, without interference from non-members. They claim the privilege of the expert who knows his own business best; and their impatience of any foreign opinion, be it even that of a judge in court, has often been remarked upon. When planning on a national scale began, in the first stages of the War, it seemed to imply a reassertion of the value of the expert, the industrialist, the engineer, and financial administrator, as opposed to the combined forces of civil and military governmental power. But after a few months the movement was reversed. Expert planning began to take the form of partly military, partly bureaucratic regulation. At the end of the War, planning has assumed the character which it has kept since the War and of which it seems unable or unwilling to rid itself. Planned economy means economic relations governed by rules devised and decreed to be in force by, say, some politician, evangelist, military commander, demagogue, lawyer, or newspaper editor, by anybody—that is, except those whose work, whether in theory or in practice, has made them familiar with such economic relations. Another legacy bequeathed to planning by the War is that it has come under the sway of the propagandist who looks to the possibility of being able to make it seem a glorious innovation: It will "change defeat into victory." It will "set the pace for the recalcitrant and hostile world," and so on. The planner thinks less of the lasting effects it will have *"après moi."*

It is not too much to say that planned economy in its present methods is an outcome of the War, and not of the loss of the War or the kind of peace treaties in which it ended.

2. *Planned money.* This question, perhaps, needs special consideration. Among the host of theories that have grown up from the hotbed of alternative inflation and deflation, Sir Basil Blackett's indictment of the War as the chief instigator of trouble in the monetary system is particularly worth quoting for his calm and well-poised method of stating the case.[1]

Various circumstances have of late years focussed attention on the financial mechanism of modern civilization with special reference to questions of currency. During the Great War all the belligerent nations frankly subordinated every other consideration to the major purpose of organizing victory. Most of the recognized rules of what was called a sound currency were thrown to the winds. So long as the War lasted money was treated as nothing more than one instrument among others for mobilizing[2] the national resources for the winning of the

1. Sir B. Blackett, *Planned Money* (1932). Also his "The Era of Planning," in *Great Events in History* (1934). The quotations in the text are taken from the latter work. The attack upon planned economy in this chapter is in line with the author's philosophy of liberalism. It was not intended, however, as a complete analysis of this very complicated problem. *Ed.*

2. The term "mobilization" is strangely misleading. Actually, mobilization means that life has to stand still and all its resources become immobile in

war.[3] . . . The Great War thus provided an object lesson of the truth, still imperfectly assimilated, that money is nothing more than a means for facilitating the production and exchange of goods and services. . . . The new discovery, known theoretically as long ago as the days of Plato, but only now emerging as a practical possibility, is nothing more and nothing less than a realization that so long as men and women are willing to make use of a piece of paper or a credit instrument in suitable form as money and to accept it for all ordinary purposes as representing a given value expressed in money, confident that they in turn can pass it on to others on the same terms, there is no need for money to have intrinsic value of its own. There is no need for it to be made of some precious substance and no reason why the authority issuing currency should keep in reserve some precious substance, gold or silver or anything else, equivalent in value to the face value of the currency which has been put into circulation, or even as "backing" or "cover" for part of that value. All that is needed is that the currency authority shall so manage and control its issue as to secure that anyone into whose possession it comes at any time is satisfied that he can at will exercise in any way in which he wishes the power of purchase which that currency professes to convey.[4]

All this may be said and has recently been said about the managing of its currency by a government which lives in certainty of peace; the benefit accruing to the export trade of a manufacturing country from a cautiously depreciated currency can be a sufficient motive for governmental action in that direction. But the main point, even in such a case, is not precisely the action of the currency authority. The main point is the willingness of the public to accept the "piece of paper" as money, "confident that they in turn can pass it on to others on the same terms." The confidence does not follow from the willingness; the willingness is the outcome of the confidence. Within the limits of domestic trading and intercourse the confidence can be created by a decree which makes the acceptance of paper money obligatory.[5] That is what the War has done to such an extent

order that a certain prearranged artificial movement may be carried out according to a plan which is also immobile. Sir Basil Blackett might have said with more reason that the national resources were immobilized for the winning of the War.

3. *Op. cit.*, p. 897.   4. *Op. cit.*, pp. 898–900.

5. The painful consequences of such a decree if applied to foreign territories occupied during the War show the inherent weakness of this kind of "planned money."

that "to-day in all but a few backward spots—even among the unsophisticated natives of remote villages in countries such as Northern Rhodesia or Nigeria or the Congo which are under European rule—gold coins have disappeared altogether for the purpose of circulation and silver coins pass simply as tokens for values far above the intrinsic value of the metal they contain."[6] It must not be forgotten, moreover, that the War taught governments and other directors of currency policy another, and a more dangerous lesson. The management and control of the currency which, as Sir Basil Blackett points out, should satisfy the public need for stable purchasing power was, during the War, for reasons of national policy, practically without limit. It has remained so. Even at a time when parliamentary institutions and democratic control were supposed to function, both inflation and deflation were beyond that control, and newspaper criticism was commonly held to amount to a criminal lack of national discipline. Here again, the War itself, and not the peculiar consequences of the War for a country which had to accept the conditions of the enemy, must be held responsible for post-war developments.

3. *"Forged Money."* Taking a position deliberately the opposite of that held by Sir Basil Blackett, and best indicated by Sir Basil's term, "planned money," Mr. J. B. A. Kessler wrote two articles for the London *Times*[7] which he entitled "Forged Money," on the problem of the monetary crisis and the remedies to be applied. The principal points of the writer of these articles were: First, the system of credit and monetary exchange which has been developed with the growth of international trade is in itself indispensable for the intercourse between producers and consumers, but that credit and the money system generally have been misused; and the writer emphasized the fact that the misuse began with the outbreak of the War. Second, even among those who were mainly responsible for managing the world's affairs, lack of understanding as to the mishandling of the monetary system still continued to be fairly general. It should be recognized that a right to consume exists only in so far as the would-be consumer has produced, or, to a certain extent, can be relied on to produce in due course, a corresponding amount of goods.

6. *Op. cit.*, p. 899.   7. September 6 and 7, 1934.

The money with which to buy things comes to him as the result of the sale of the goods he or his predecessors have produced, or of the credit given to him in expectation of future production by people who in their turn have produced and sold their products. During the War, consumption was bound to exceed production. The production of useful goods was neglected in a way to benefit the production of war material. And the capacity for future production was considerably diminished if not entirely destroyed. None of the criteria of sound money, therefore, remained valid. If the war is a regional affair, the fact that both consumption in the belligerent countries and credits given to them by neutrals and allies are economically improper may be disregarded, and the disturbance may pass away without lasting consequences; especially if the war is conducted as continental European wars were conducted before 1914, that is, as a contest of military strength between the armed forces only. But in a world war and with the increasing readiness of the wealthier allies and all neutrals to lend money to the governments of belligerent countries, credit giving must in the end have a destructive effect on the monetary system. The credits were, in fact, based not on the prospect of future production[8] but on the pressing need for consumption, a consumption, moreover, which by its peculiar nature extinguished the value of the consumed goods without any compensating economic effect. The final result in such a case is that while creditors continue to consume on the assumption that war loans will be redeemed and war indemnities will be paid, in spite of the fact that the ability of the debtors to produce salable goods or acceptable service has diminished almost to a vanishing point, the money used for international transactions becomes virtually forged money. The public refuses to accept bank notes at their face value and tries to acquire goods of, presumably, a more stable value than that of the official token. Hoarding of gold and the equivalents of gold is not the cause but the effect of the public realization that the monetary system of the world is using the methods of the forger. The same is true of import duties, import restrictions, foreign-exchange restrictions, and similar measures. They aggravate a crisis of which

8. In most cases the lenders of the money were, on the contrary, bound to hope for a complete annihilation of the competitive economic forces of the country which they encouraged to continue the war by extending credit to its industry, its banking, its municipalities, etc.

they are not the cause but the unavoidable consequences, just as anti-enemy propaganda, spy hunting, and in general the "moratorium of the Sermon on the Mount," however much they did to envenom the War and however much their own effects outlasted those of the War itself, were not causes but corollaries of the War.

The remedy, then, can only be found in systematic, reasoned opposition to the spirit and, consequently, to the practice of war, not in applying principles and methods of war or following the habits of war in peace. Public opinion must realize—and get the governments and the public to act on it—

that honest consuming power is only created by useful production; not by increasing the cost price and reducing production. . . . Those who think that the time has come when we can do without gold and silver for our monetary and credit system do not understand that, in order to allow the production process of the world to continue, we want an honest token to prove our economic right to consume or to give credits; that those tokens have been tampered with on an unprecedented scale; and, thirdly, that that has caused the crisis. This is the worst time to contemplate removing from our monetary and credit system the only tokens that cannot possibly be forged. Confidence in our money must be restored—not further undermined.[9]

Sir Basil Blackett and Mr. Kessler agree upon the main point. They attribute the deterioration in the monetary system to the War. It should be recognized, then, that two sets of circumstances peculiar to a long period of war have to be removed before the world can hope to return to peaceful economic relations. The habit of wrongful consumption which is made possible by credits given at a usurer's risk and on a usurer's terms must be abandoned, and the right of the public to decide for itself on the honesty of the "token"—a right which is taken away as soon as war is proclaimed—must be restored to the full, with all its implications as to public control over public finance and parliamentary discussion of the budget; and it might even be restored with additional safeguards in the matter of the international value of money. The defender of sound capitalism and the adherent of national socialism should find no difficulties in agreeing as to the direct relationship between the economic and the monetary troubles of the war and the post-war period in Germany, though

9. J. B. A. Kessler in the London *Times,* as above.

they would differ as to the desirability of restoring pre-war conditions.

4. *Taxation.* Compared with the effects on the monetary system, and the constitution of national economics generally, the permanent effects of the War on taxation have been remarkably small. During the War itself the resources of the treasury in a blockaded country are practically dried up; taxation has to be readjusted as the taxpayers called up for military service become entitled to remission or respite. Foreign investments become more and more sterile; and public income through taxation which normally represents almost four-fifths of the total income is reduced to an insignificant part of the annual expenditure, the rest being raised through loans and confiscation. At one time the partisans of a highly progressive tax on large incomes and capital, and of higher death duties, believed they had found new justification for their proposals; for popular indignation at the easy war gains of the profiteer and a general feeling that in war lives must not be understood to have been sacrificed for the protection of domestic wealth and money power would have ensured strong support for drastic measures of taxation on the part of the Government. But the conservative forces in the Government were strong enough to withstand the pressure, the success of which might have been accompanied by the collapse of the Prussian electoral system and which, in any case, had a revolutionary flavor. The army did not take sides, and the sentiment of those who later on formulated the program of the National Socialist movement was still inarticulate.

A comparison between the revenue of the German Reich, states, and municipalities in 1913–1914 and in 1926–1927 shows an increase in the income tax,[10] 2,635.9 million marks as against 1,390.2 millions; in the tax on capital, 359.5 millions as against 78.8; in the tax on land and buildings, 1,009.6 millions as against 435.5; in the license tax, 644.6 as against 179.3; and in several other special taxes amounting to 2,879.1 millions as against 1,270.2. In the receipts from death duties there was a decrease from 61 millions in 1913 to 34.7 in 1926. A radical change in the substance of taxation was in-

10. The change in the buying power of the mark between 1913 and 1926 accounts for a part of the rise in the totals; but the actual rise after due deduction on that account is still abnormal.

troduced by the imposition of a sales tax and a tax on unoccupied buildings, provided that, as mortgaged property, they had been relieved of part of their indebtedness by the inflation. In 1926–1927 the latter brought 1,524.8 million marks, the former 882.6 millions, an entirely new source of income, and one that represented about one-fourth of the total income for the budgetary year.

If the government of a belligerent state must be regarded as entitled to stake its financial policy on a victorious ending of the war and to throw the onus of the consequences of defeat upon the financial clauses of the peace treaty dictated by the enemy powers, inflation and the special taxes which come in its wake can be listed as among the individual and independent policies of the post-war period. If, on the other hand, we are correct in assuming that the financial policy of the Reich during the War was misdirected, and that it should have tried to provide for the expenses of the War through taxation instead of war loans, the new taxes may be said to have made good what had been lacking in the war years, and that the inflation from which they seemed more directly to proceed was only an intermediary stage from war to post-war finance. In any case, the War indirectly affected the German system of taxation in more than one way. Its centralizing influence was strong enough to transfer the taxes on income and capital from states and municipalities to the treasury of the Reich. If the War had not undermined the position of the civil service, which had been the mainstay of State sovereignty under the constitution of 1871, the so-called Erzberger reforms in 1919–1920 could not have been formulated, much less carried through. They weakened the hold of the States on their subjects. They burdened the Government of the Reich with a load of political patronage for the use of which the unbalanced party system of the Republic was not equipped. In a still more surreptitious way the War habit of trying to circumvent obnoxious regulations of the D.O.R.A. type gave the habitual tax evaders a new feeling of security. Their favorite excuse for defaulting—"If I paid my taxes I would be the only man in the neighborhood who did, so why should I?"—was an excuse that had taken on a semblance of justice during the period of the *Brotkarte* and the daily struggle for fuel. Even one of the best things that occurred during the War, the generous response which the people as a whole made again and again to appeals for voluntary contributions, was rather detrimental to the collecting of taxes when the demand for them followed the free gift of a last remnant of savings.

5. *Traffic and communications.* Of all the public services and the industries connected with them railroads and shipping suffered most acutely. If the effect of the peace treaty be added to that of the War, it amounted to the out-and-out destruction of practically the whole matériel of transport services and, consequently, service interruptions of the most serious character. For nowhere is continuity of training and practice needed more than in the personnel of the railways and the commercial fleet. Nowhere else does recovery through repair seem to be fraught with greater difficulties than in the case of damage done to the complicated mechanism we see in the organization of a modern transport service. In Germany, moreover, State railways labored under the special burden of foreign control which, even with the greatest tact and good will on the part of those in charge must always create friction and lessen energy. Against every reasonable expectation, however, both railways and shipping made a quicker recovery than most other branches of industry. Ten years after the War, in spite of the supervening embarrassment of inflation, traffic had, on the whole, made good, and in part even showed a decided improvement over 1913. In the matter of matériel hardly a trace of the wear and tear of the War or of the havoc made by the delivery clauses of the peace treaty could be seen in 1926 or 1927. Tonnage of goods on the railways had risen from 467 millions in 1913[11] to 481 millions in 1928, and from 57,282 million ton-kilometers in 1913 to 73,180 millions in 1928. The number of persons traveling on German railways rose from 1,577 millions (and 36,599 million kilometers) in 1913 to 2,009 millions (and 47,649 million kilometers) in 1928. Statistics of communication by inland navigation tell a similar tale. Though Germany in 1919 lost 12 per cent of her navigable waterways, the tonnage of goods shipped on German rivers and canals rose from 97.2 million tons in 1913 to 107.7 millions in 1928.[12] The German merchant fleet which in 1914

11. Based upon the present territory of the Reich, that is, without Alsace-Lorraine, the province of Posnania, northern Schleswig and the Memel Territory.

12. The War and the treaty of peace altered the importance of sea traffic for the different parts of Germany; and in spite of the efforts of the North

MATERIAL EFFECTS 275

numbered 4,935 ships, with a total gross tonnage of 5.2 million had, by 1919, been reduced to a tonnage of less than 50,000. In 1928 it had again risen, to 4.1 millions. There, a lasting effect of the War was made evident by the position to which the German merchant fleet had fallen in international shipping. From its second place, in 1914, it had dropped to one of the lowest among seafaring nations. In 1928 it occupied the fourth place, and its share in world tonnage had fallen from 11 to 6 per cent. But this, again, was a result of the loss of the War, not of the War itself.

On personnel and efficiency of service the War left no impression at all. The problem which today occupies the attention of the State departments and the boards of directors that deal with traffic is one which has no connection at all wth the War, viz., the growing competition between railroad and traffic by motor car and truck, between inland navigation and roads, and between aerial transport and former methods of communication. It is probably safe to say that without the War the development of the automobile, road building, and traffic regulation would not have been much different from what they had been since 1919, given the monopoly of State railways and public postal service. The development of flying was hampered by the restrictions of the Treaty of Versailles, not by the War.

The German system of communications during and after the War offers an instance of most speedy recovery from the severest shock[13] —a real recovery, too, in the sense of a return to, and a continued development of, the standards of 1914, not a new departure after salutary and wholesale destruction, as in Russia.

6. *News services.* The mechanization of the news service through national broadcasting is a post-war phenomenon. It has developed

German Lloyd and the Hamburg American Line to regain their full share of trans-Atlantic business, and of the support given by the Government, in 1928 foreign shipping took 71 per cent of the traffic offered by German ports as against 62 per cent in 1913. This, as well as the decline of the German ports on the Baltic and the rise in importance of places like Duisburg-Ruhrort or Mannheim-Ludwigshafen is almost entirely due to the political changes effected in eastern Europe by the Treaty of Versailles, and not to the War as such.

13. The recovery in this field of industrial activity was independent of general planning and centralizing tendencies. Both German and foreign observers have criticized the measures taken, and in particular the govern-

in neutral and belligerent countries alike; and the differences between France, Italy, Germany, Great Britain, and Russia, or the difference between the United States and the European systems cannot be traced back to the distinction between victors and vanquished, or between an "associated power," and the Allies. It was a movement which had got under way before the War and which, without the War, would have begun to expand three or four years earlier than it actually did, and just as much. But it was, nevertheless, influenced by the War, in Germany at least, in so far as the War allowed a test to be made of the usefulness of broadcasting to influence public opinion at home and abroad, and the possibility of government control of the contents and the dissemination of news. Full credit was not given to the lessons of the War in that respect until 1933. By its semiofficial connection with the news and lecture service of the broadcasting stations, the Socialist-Centrist government of Prussia had tried to defend its position in the face of growing dissatisfaction. But it had to reckon with the twofold fact that first the administration of the broadcasting service was in the hands of the Postal Department, controlled by the Reich government, which meant a conscientious neutralization of the news and, second, public opinion in the provinces was still governed, to the exclusion of practically every other influence except that of the clergy in the Catholic parts of Germany, by the local newspapers, most of them of the *Lokal-Anzeiger* group. During the War, they had been willing organs of the publicity bureau established by General Ludendorff's staff. After the War they became professedly non-political, while they showed their lack of sympathy with the Governments of the Republic whenever those Governments were in need of sympathy. With the strengthening of Nationalist opposition that followed the election of President Hindenburg, the Treaty of Locarno, and Dr. Stresemann's death, they also went into more or less open opposition to the

ment subsidies paid to some of the shipping lines, as economically unsound and creating a deceptive appearance of returning prosperity. But with the devastating effects of the War on these single industries staring him in the eyes even a farsighted statesman could hardly, at the time, have refrained from acknowledging special governmental responsibilities calling for special measures of support and subsidy. If the war strikes with peculiar hardship at some spot in the nation's area or some branch of national industry, the government which bears the responsibility for the war—whether instrumental in causing it or not—is entitled to apply special measures of relief.

Government, which had so far withstood the attack of the Nationalist and National Socialist forces, notably in Prussia, the Hanseatic towns, Bavaria, Baden, and Hesse.[14] The renaissance and final victory of the war spirit in 1932 and 1933 led to the nationalization of the news service throughout Germany, and, incidentally, to an almost complete superseding of the local newspapers by the news and lectures section of the *Reichsfunk*, or imperial broadcasting system.

The element of danger in such a situation is obvious. Individual opinion, if effectively silenced in public, revenges itself in private conversation. A small group of educated people who remain in touch with foreign public opinion, with foreign newspapers and foreign broadcasting, become estranged from the mass of their countrymen. A centralized broadcasting service from an office in the capital is, moreover, as recent events have shown, liable to be the first object of a revolutionary attack, and a handful of determined lawbreakers may spread civil war over a country if they succeed in such an attack. The fruits of war cannot be enjoyed without an ingredient of danger.

7. *Industrial development: individual cases.* Shipping has been cited as among those industries which were hardest hit by the War. The textile industries are another instance; emergency legislation and the blockade deprived them of their raw materials. On the other hand, cases of single industries remaining comparatively unhurt by the direct effects of the War are by no means rare; and an outstanding example of one that was helped by the War is to be found in the German chemical industry. The rise of the I. G. Farben to its present position among the most efficient industrial combinations in the world was directly due to the War. One of its centers, the plant at Mannheim-Ludwigshafen, along with the Darmstadt factories, was dangerously near the western frontier. During the War, therefore, when supplies for the army and for agriculture depended on an increased output of chemicals and on the production of substitutes for foreign raw materials, the works near Bitterfeld and Halle, situated in a very favorable position because they were far from the theaters

---

14. The Thuringian states, Brunswick, Oldenburg, and Mecklenburg had gone Nationalist, while Saxony and Württemberg, with a stalemate between Right and Left in their Diets and the Communists refusing coöperation, had non-party governments that were sympathetic to moderate Nationalism.

of war, were enlarged and the Leuna factories added. After the War, Ludwigshafen took the lead again, partly for personal reasons. The demand for efficiency suggested a combination of the Saxon, the Palatinate, and the Hesse-Rhineland groups. The plan for this, a union of the largest chemical works, was realized and acted upon with a precision and singleness of purpose worthy of the greatest strategical movements of the War.[15] Two special features of the I. G. Farben which contribute to its success also date from the War, a close coöperation between industry and science, with able administrators as middlemen,[16] and the adoption of the mechanism of the "vertical trust." In this case the "vertical trust" included the mining of coal and potash, smelting and other metal industries, and manufactures of chemical salts, dyes, perfumes, paraffin, and, finally, textiles and artificial silk.

A modest branch of industry which has, apparently, not been in any way connected with the War, the making of watches and clocks, shows a development surprisingly akin to that of chemicals. The total value of watch and clock production rose from about 50 million marks in 1913 to 110 millions in 1929, or, in detail, from 10 million clocks to 13.5 millions, and from 1.5 million watches to 4 millions. The German share in world production of clocks rose from 60 to 70 per cent, and the value of exports came to exceed that of imports by almost 200 per cent. Trusts and cartels, favored by the centralizing forces of war, have played their part here as elsewhere. According to the report of the *Enquete-Ausschuss* (1931), four concerns controlled among them more than 60 per cent of the production of clocks and more than 90 per cent of that of watches, although the latter had, until recently, been a typical peasant home industry.

On the whole, the material effects of the War, reflected in these isolated planes of German life, seem to correspond to the essential char-

15. In 1930 the total value of the production of German chemical industries was estimated at 3.6 billion marks, with an excess of exports over imports of about one billion.

16. Dr. Bosch, the I.G.F.'s director, is in himself a combination of scientist, administrator, and industrialist. For the rest, the names of scientists like Professor Haber and Bergius, industrialists like Dr. Duisberg and Herr Schmitz, and administrators like Dr. Bücher and Dr. von Simson might be mentioned.

acter of war as opposed to peace. Peace must always try to prolong its reign; indeed, it must try to become eternal peace, and it can do so only by making human life and its relationships more perfect and harmonious. War, on the contrary, even from its own narrow point of view, must intend itself to be of short duration, exhausting its span of life by a superhuman effort. Its goal is victory, to be won as quickly as possible; its hope of fulfilment is based on the weakness or the faintness of heart of one of the opponents who thereby is made to acknowledge defeat.

War, therefore, goes with the energies concentrated on a present achievement—or pleasure, whichever it is—without regard to the future. It goes against efforts to secure permanency of tenure, security of power and stores of wealth. History, in itself one of the companions of peace, has recorded the industries of the human mind through which it plans to outstay time. Writing, designing, building, perfecting useful tools for the handicrafts, for forestry and agriculture, all these things are neglected, despised, or falsified by war. But it will help an industry that discovers deceptive substitutes, and it will teach people to speak into a vacuum and to listen to sounds without meaning which thunder from the hollow of an amplifier.

CHAPTER XVI

MORAL EFFECTS

The conclusions we have so far been able to reach are far from satisfactory. War, if we look at it from the point of view of its lasting effects, presents an aspect unexpectedly different from that of a revolution. Neither the political, cultural, nor economic life of the nation seems to have been changed in its substance or, to use a musical term, to have been transposed to another key—as is likely to be the result of a revolution. By war some things have been taken out of that life, and others added to it; some things demolished, or split off, and others hastily put in their places. One might almost say it has been like a picture puzzle, broken up and put together in the wrong way, with certain pieces lost, and others mutilated to make them fit together.

But if that is true of the material consequences of the war in question, what, then, of its moral influence upon the nation? Have men and women been pitched to a new key? Can the sacrifice they had to make be called an expiation? Has the death of the innocent made the guilty repent and taught them to mend their ways? At the time of the War it seemed so natural to use the word superhuman in speaking of the deeds of the soldiers, or the sufferings of the people at home. Has the nation been lifted out of the drudgery of the daily struggle for life that makes poets and philosophers speak with scathing contempt of police-protected peace; and has it become a kind of superhuman being which, in its turn, may teach the millions of its human members to live in a higher atmosphere, nearer to transcendence?

Historians of the future will be tempted to draw comparisons between the changes wrought by the great national wars of the last three hundred years in the national character of the two peoples which had to bear the heaviest part in them, Germans and Frenchmen. The Thirty Years' War, the Wars of the Spanish Succession, the Seven Years' War, Napoleonic wars, the wars of the Sixties and Seventies, and the World War—each of them must have given the warring people something, as well as taken something away.[1] What was it?

1. Of the 300 years from 1618 to 1918, roughly 125 have seen Germany

If we compare the effects of the Napoleonic Wars on the German people with those of the War of 1914, the conclusion seems almost inevitable that the change which follows war is a change for change's sake, or, in other words, that war teaches the next generation to react vehemently against the opinions, manners, and institutions of the pre-war period, whatever they may have been.

The Napoleonic Wars left Germany torn and rent, her constitution torn to pieces, and the western and southern parts of the country half annexed by, and half allied to, the Emperor of the French in his war against northeastern Germany, Russia, and Great Britain. French armies had been sent to give battle, first to the Austrians, then to Prussia and the Russians, through the length and breadth of German territory. Thousands of Germans had been recruited to fight Napoleon's battles in the Tyrol, in Russia, and in Spain; dismissed or deserting at the end of the war, they remained as dangerous crowds of adventurers. The continental blockade against England had dislocated international trade; currencies had collapsed. The material change was tremendous.

The period in which the mind of the generation of 1799 to 1814 had been formed was a period of skepticism. The "age of enlightenment," the *"Zeitalter der Aufklärung"* had—or believed it had— dispelled superstition, and in so doing had done away with much of the religious zeal Catholics and Protestants alike had retained ever since the wars of religion in the sixteenth and seventeenth centuries. A striking example of the change that had come over the mentality of Germans in the second half of the eighteenth century is made evident by the fact that Johann Sebastian Bach's Passion music had been forgotten and discarded for a full hundred years, following the date of its first performance in St. Thomas' Church at Leipzig, in 1729. The *Passion according to St. Matthew* un-

(including Austria), or parts of Germany, involved in warfare, mostly on German and Austrian territory. The longer periods were 1618 to 1648; 1672 to 1679, Louis XIV's Dutch War, and the Swedes against Prussia; 1681 to 1699, Turkish wars in Austria and Hungary; Louis XIV's "Orleans War," and the burning of Heidelberg; 1700 to 1718, the War of the Spanish Succession, and the Swedes under Charles XII against Saxony, Prussia, and Holstein; 1740 to 1748, the War of the Austrian Succession, with Dettingen, Kesselsdorf, and Fontenoy; 1756 to 1763, the Seven Years' War; 1792 to 1796 and 1804 to 1815, the Revolutionary and Napoleonic Wars; 1864 to 1866 and 1870 to 1871, German Wars; and 1914 to 1918.

doubtedly was the purest expression of the spiritual life of Germany since Luther translated the Bible; one which today seems inseparable from the very being of the nation. Yet in spite of that it was completely discarded for what, even in the life of nations, may be counted a very long time, a time, moreover, which was taking its watchwords from men like Frederick the Great, Immanuel Kant, Gotthold Ephraim Lessing, and Goethe. Religious feeling had not disappeared, nor had it ceased to find expression in sacred music. The oratorios of Handel and Haydn found admiring audiences everywhere. But, with Bach, religion and art had been of the inner life; he prayed, or mused about himself, or, at most, talked to his wife and children and a few good neighbors. With Handel and Haydn even sacred music was of outward things, a hymn in praise of creation or a *te deum* for a victory won by the King. Pride in the prosperous and healthy state of the country, and enjoyment of the pleasures of natural life had replaced the severer meditations on sinfulness and salvation to which previous generations had been addicted. Optimism led to activity in reform. Liberal opinions were in the ascendant, and justified themselves by an almost flawless rational-logical explanation of deity, man, and creation. Such was the spirit in Germany of the age into which the men and women of the Napoleonic era were born.

In and after 1815, the result of Napoleon's wars was a renaissance of the belief in the value of faith above everything else, and especially above mere intellectual reasoning. In some people it was tempestuous and romantic, the brain found itself in a time of storm. In others there was faith expressed by quiet strength and clear purpose. Even agnostics, when speaking of the conclusions they had reached, spoke in terms of religious revelation. Friedrich Rückert, the poet of the War of Liberation gave expression to a nationwide feeling when he asked the Savior to descend to the earth again and establish his reign of peace, breaking the power of kings and military leaders. It was a peace that was not of this world, and not in any way connected with the nationalist arguments that nationalist worshipers of an idolized state are likely to use when they make protest to the world of their peaceful intentions.[2]

The change which the World War brought about in Germany was hardly less drastic, nor could it be expected to be otherwise. The

2. The words of the German patriot of 1814 contrast so strangely with

period of warfare was considerably shorter than that of Napoleon's time, and the war was not allowed to carry into German territory the pillage, devastation, and recruiting by force which it had seen between 1804 and 1815. But the infliction of war, taken as a whole, was certainly more terrible, and the War was much more inhuman than the wars of a hundred years ago had been. The individual had to go without that comfort which even in times of great national distress may be drawn from the sense of sacrifice, freely and bravely made. Men could do no more than serve the machine which was pouring forth death and destruction; they could not even know where the shell they had thrown would burst. It might hit some enemy force preparing deadly attack. It might hit an ambulance where wounded prisoners, the gunner's compatriots, lay side by side with their former enemies. It might hit a munition depot or a church filled with womenfolk and cripples praying that able-bodied men might be spared. Modern war makes a fetish of invisibility, and the price it has to pay for that is that it must strike blindly.

The Napoleonic Wars transformed a people that prided itself on its intellectual development, its freedom of conscience, its outspoken opinions, and its industrious pursuit of the civic professions, arts, and sciences, into a nation of fervent idealists, converts to a sincere if romantic faith, and to a cult of nature full of non-rationalistic sentiment. The sons and daughters of 1814 had grown up to be warriors of heaven, instead of a paid soldiery in the service of some foreign power, or crafty traders, merchants, and bankers. The wars had taught them to work out their own salvation in the affairs of this world as in those of the other. That is one of the missions that war has to fulfil in the history of mankind. But to the youth of 1820

the sentiments by which the patriots of our own time are moved that it may be worth while to recall them to memory:

> *O mächt'ger Herrscher ohne Heere*
> *Gewalt'ger Kämpfer ohne Speere,*
> *O Friedensfürst von grosser Macht!*
> *Es wollen Dir der Erde Herren*
> *Den Weg zu Deinem Throne sperren,*
> *Doch Du gewinnst ihn ohne Schlacht.*
> *O Herr von grosser Huld und Treue,*
> *O komme Du auch jetzt aufs neue*
> *Zu uns, die wir sind schwer verstört.*
> *Not ist es, dass Du selbst hienieden*
> *Kommst, zu erneuern Deinen Frieden,*
> *Dagegen sich die Welt empört.*

and 1830, working out their own salvation did not mean to act in a body; it meant freedom, for every man's and every woman's body and soul, freedom to find out what their lives were meant for, and freedom to act on what they believed they had discovered; freedom, above all, from the conventions of manners and morals and from the bond of the *Contrat Social* to which their pre-war progenitors had devotedly offered service, long before Jean Jacques Rousseau had coined the phrase.

There is a difference. The German people in the second half of the nineteenth century, young men at the time of the Franco-German war of 1870 and '71 and the foundation of the Second Reich, or those who were sons of the men who had fought for German unity, grew up in an atmosphere of self-reliance and consciousness of national strength which did not permit of even a shadow of doubt so far as the position of Germany and German citizens in international affairs was concerned. In domestic affairs, however, German national character appeared as diversified and as inclined to centrifugal movements as it seemed united and concentric in face of the outer world. Class consciousness was more marked than ever before, in both employer and employed. It was favored by a system of education which practically reserved all access to the universities, and therefore to the higher grades of the civil service, the church, and the liberal professions, to boys who, from their tenth year, had attended a certain kind of high school. The conflict between the Christian churches, which had almost subsided during the past hundred years, broke out afresh, and at the same time a militant anti-Semitism began a campaign in which Stöcker, a court preacher in Berlin, the historian Treitschke, and a dismissed educationalist, Ahlwardt, became the precursors of the "Aryan" creed of today. Elections were fought on strictly party lines, and the violence of the verbal injuries which used to accompany them, especially when a party or coalition of parties was open to the accusation of "ultramontane" or internationalist, that is, "unpatriotic" conduct, was only surpassed by the degree of animosity which, during the period preceding the War, had grown up between agrarian and metropolitan interests. In the time of William II, and even in the Federal Council, majority decisions arrived at only after a prolonged struggle were not uncommon. Indeed, such struggles had been envisaged by the framers of the constitution, who had made careful provision both against Prussian predominance and against an out-numbering of the larger states by the smaller ones. The strongest elements of cohesion were the Protestant pastors and college professors, the civil service in its lower grades, especially in the railways and postal services, and the commercial middle classes. The social system into which these differing elements had been fitted stood firm during the War and for a short time after the War. Then the shock of the monetary difficulties broke the resistance of those who had stood for a united national and liberal German State in its old form; and the passion for strife seemed to have found unlimited scope. It even threatened social disruption. But the real change effected by the War did not show until, from 1929 onward, the National Socialist movement began to sweep the country. No compromise with any of the former unitarian forces was sought. Of the four great parties of pre-war times, Conservatives, Catholic Center, National Liberals, and Social Democrats, the two last named, both of them strongly unitarian, are two that have completely disappeared. The new spirit which entered into the youth of Germany, first into a few soldiers who were disappointed in their immediate prospects and hopes, and later on into thousands, hundreds of thousands and millions of their fellows in suffering, has been variously called a spirit of comradeship, of solidarity, and of unity. But its most significant—and favorite—designation lies in the adjective of the new German State: "totalitarian." Uniformity of action, for instance, a vote that was "Yes" by almost 95 per cent, desirable as it may be, has been recognized as being of only passing merit. Uniformity of mental attitude, attained through uniform education and a prescribed common stock of knowledge in a community of one single racial denomination, is the gift of the War to the German nation.[3] The change, from 1913 to 1933, was at least as great as it was from 1803 to the eighteen-twenties; but it has been changed in the reverse direction. The lesson to be drawn, so far, is that each post-war generation feels itself compelled to adopt an attitude divergent from and, perhaps, contrary to the *Haltung*—"the stand"—of the last generation before the War.[4]

3. Other religions or creeds have sponsored dualism, or believed in the superior merit of the Three or the Seven. The new national faith has adopted the number One. Even in journalistic slang one remarks a strong predilection for expressions containing this number, like *"einmalig"* or *"eindeutig."*
4. If it were true that the *"Generationenproblem"* is common to all people

Within this general change, however, two or three distinct displacements in the moral character of the nation may be detected, of minor importance, but directly connected with the War. The caution against generalization which has been given in the preliminary remarks must be repeated—we have to deal with the peculiar effects of war on a country which for the best part of four years saw its life at home practically cut off from the life of the armed forces. Or, in other words, the life of its women, children, of its boys up to eighteen, and its men over forty-five—or roughly that—cut off from the life lived by all the able-bodied men who during those four years chanced to be between eighteen and forty. By "cut off" in this connection we do not mean the physical separation; we mean the difference, or division, or even estrangement in morals between the two groups, which was caused by the clash between the actual and material life facts as severally presented to them. The difference was not in loyalty to the cause of the country; the women and boys and girls served it as faithfully and, on the whole, as uncomplainingly as the men in the fighting forces; and most of the older men were as eager for victory as any of the officers in the field. The difference was in this: The men in the trenches saw the War as it really was, and the people at home saw it as the newspapers pictured it. Underground rumors and tales told by prisoners and the wounded were hardly calculated to give a better insight into the essentials of the conflict than official bulletins. The difference was here: The men in the trenches had comradeship to comfort them, while the people at home, as soon as the blockade made itself felt, had to face competition and the struggle for life in its ugliest form, and likewise had before them, day after day, the spectacle of the prosperous and influential profiteer.[5]

and all times, whether of peace or war, the change mentioned in the text would, of course, lose its connection with the War. The experience of Germany during the last two hundred years seems to show, however, that longer periods of peace or war do make a difference.

5. The situation was made worse by the distorted view which both the men at the front and the people at home used to take of the *Etappe* that, as soon as the struggle had settled down to trench warfare on more or less rigid lines, had established itself in northwestern France, in Belgium, and in Poland. The *"Etappe"* was partly commissariat, partly a semicivil administration of occupied enemy and neutral territory, and partly the headquarters for many kinds of hybrid activities which were neither a part of the fighting

Pre-war Germany was praised by some observers, and blamed by others, for the general respect paid to old people, especially to those who had risen to a high rank in their professions, by dint of lifelong effort. The comic papers might poke fun at the Excellencies, and a few radicals might attack them, but they had no need to take much notice of that. They were masters in the house, and the young men of forty or forty-five hardly dared raise their voices when they were present. A deep-set trait, and one that was common to people of all classes and professions, this attitude of younger people toward their elders resisted the shock of the War for a considerable time; the

force nor of the ordinary civil government. It contained hospitals, bureaus for the identification of unknown soldiers and for enquiries after the missing, rest cantonments for shock troops, newspaper correspondents' quarters, offices for the dissemination of war literature and many other similar things.

The vocabulary which the soldiers used when discussing the doings of the *"Etappenschwein"* was appalling, even under war conditions. Undeniably in the *"Etappe"* there were many abuses of a position of comparative safety, and one of greater ease than either the soldiers or their people at home experienced during the War. But on the whole the reputation of the *"Etappe"* was due to the falsehoods and misunderstandings which must necessarily arise under that system of strict censorship which drives all information underground and makes people thrive on the loose talk of soldiers on leave, correspondents, nurses, chauffeurs, propaganda lecturers, and other occasional travelers between the fighting line and the country at home. Two members of my faculty, men well over the fighting age, were in charge of villages in northern France for several years (as *Ortskommandanten*), and I can vouch for their wholly admirable handling of one of the most difficult of situations. One of them, Robert Piloty, was, among all the men I have known, nearest to the ideal of the perfect gentleman. With a poet's gift of grace he combined the wisdom of a warmhearted old teacher and the knightly disposition of a born champion of wronged rights. The villagers in the invaded zone could not have wished for a better man to take care of them. The other man, though entirely without imagination, was at least a man with a scrupulous sense of justice and an uncompromising enemy of corruption of any kind. Both had their staffs well in hand, and tolerated no interference with their duty toward the districts they had to administer. In the country, the *"Etappe"* was certainly far better than in towns like Brussels or Lille, and the black sheep formed probably a very small percentage of the service. But just as before the War every Prussian was deemed to be a rank militarist, and after the War the people at home were said to have stabbed the army in the back and behaved like traitors, so during the War the *"Etappe"* was imagined to be peopled by bullies and sneaks, place hunters and profiteers, and people even worse than that.

change did not make itself known in its full significance till 1930. That it was directly due to the War, and not to the economic difficulties of the post-war period, cannot well be doubted.

The change was one in substance, not merely in form or manners. The thing was not so much in the behavior or utterances of youth, as in a general preference for youth and a youthful attitude even among the older people. The natural attributes of age, consideration in deed and wisdom in thought, had been discredited long before the outward respect paid to the old had ceased to be a rule of gentle conduct. Swift action became the one desired result of training, instead of slow and exact thought. The terms in which those preëminent in the newer educational arrangements were publicly praised indicated the origin of the movement; the terms used were almost invariably from the language of warfare, and, within the sphere of war, terms not of endurance or defense, but of attack and striking the first blow, and inflicting defeat on others.

An outstanding attribute of the average German attitude toward life before the War, well known to foreign observers, was a pride in, and an enjoyment of, one's household possessions, one that went far beyond the necessaries of life. The housewife's store of linen, or the man's store of books or the tools of his trade were the best examples of a habit of mind which, in weaker moments, led to accumulating trinkets, souvenirs, and half-broken bric-à-brac, and covering the walls with vastly enlarged photographs of several generations of the family. To their owners all these things were much more in the nature of living pets than objects of marketable value to be bought or sold. The Japanese legend of the doll that grew a soul and became a human being after having been the play friend of a dozen generations in the same nursery is, perhaps, a truer expression of how a German family of the older stamp feels toward the things of the house than all the cartoons of "Simplicissimus."

However that may be, the old attitude has been thrown to the winds. There is no time now for the leisurely pleasure of going to the wardrobe and taking out grandfather's old uniform or his student insignia—or, for that matter, his Bible—or great-grandmother's pattern book. There is no time to spin yarns about such things, before putting them back to sleep again. The play of youth is of another kind. It builds its castles of sand with a keen eye to destroying them again. It buys things to throw away. It forgets them. That is the sign under which the post-war people are fighting their battles. The Japanese doll has given way to the cheap Ford car. Construction itself, more perfect in technique than ever before, pays heed to the general intention to use things up as quickly as possible.

The change in recreation habits, between 1900 and 1930, of average middle-class people in Germany is striking. It is a complete break rather than a change; and one or two of the fissures that began to forecast and threaten it showed themselves long before the War, and independently of the various trends that led to the War. The movement for ways of enjoying life that were healthier and more active than could be afforded by the *Stammtisch*, the student's *Kneipe*, the formal picnic, *Landpartie*, or even tennis or skating had begun long before the War broke out. The *"Freideutsche Jugend"* had held its great constitutional assembly on the *"Hohe Meissner"* in 1913; and the *Wandervogel* had by then begun to look upon the generation of its founders as among the aged who were beginning to stale. But the youth movement, with its nature worship, its keen sense of physical fitness and its self-centered pride in responsibility, was by no means alone in dividing a decidedly before-the-war period from the immediately pre-war, the war, and post-war times which we think of as the present; and its influence was outweighed by that of a technical innovation of incalculable importance, the cinema.

One of the few public institutions that followed an unbroken course of development from the beginning to the end of the War and emerged from it stronger than ever while its rivals seemed, most of them, to have been utterly broken,[6] the cinema meant much more to Germany than to other countries because provincial theaters, concerts, and university lectures had meant much more to the Germany of the nineteenth century. Opera affords perhaps the most striking example. To take the German theaters, there was a court theater in every residence city of the German princes, one or more municipal theaters in every big city and in most of the smaller university towns, and all were repertory theaters. These theaters staged the operas of

---

6. Compare education in the public schools and at home, universities, theaters, concerts, literature, the fine arts, libraries, or, on a lower plane, society, clubs, racing, hunting, and similar entertainments and recreations in the first post-war period. The cinema was practically alone in having thriven throughout, even during a regional civil war, *putsches* of communists or reactionaries, during inflation and during deflation.

the whole world. They had outlived the Wagnerian attack.[7] They were reveling in the works of the neo-French and neo-Italian schools, in the newly discovered Russians, and light opera from Vienna and London. And then the silent film appeared and, during the War, seized that advantage over human effort which is apt to be given by war to the invulnerable machine. The twenty years that followed, including the years from 1914 to 1918, saw dramatic art such as Lessing, Goethe, and Schiller had given us fade out of German life. The public concerts for which Germany had been famous for the last hundred years will in their time become a closed chapter.[8] A renaissance of genuine old folksong and of German sacred music before the time of Bach is prophesied. If it comes, it will have had no connection with the War. The influence of the War, so far as it went, was entirely in favor of the cinema. The German newsreels owe their effectiveness in political propaganda to the lessons of the War. Their services vie with those of the radio.

The craze for public dancing which marked the first few years after the War in many countries where a cold climate and an uncouthness of bodily construction make hopping a welcome exercise, and no one is offended by the absurdity of the spectacle, formed a horrible anticlimax to the events of 1918. In Germany the fashion

7. Richard Wagner employed his extraordinary gifts to destroy the traditional friendly relations of the German people with musical art, sacred and profane, with Bach's "Passions" and his *Wohltemperiertes Klavier*, with Mozart's operas and sonatas, Haydn's oratorios and quartets, Schubert's and Schumann's *lieder*, and to replace them by a cult of grand opera of an absurd kind, one draped in the clothes of Teuton nationalism. Nobody doubts that he was a political genius; almost singlehanded, using the hysterical devotion of a madman, a few adoring women, an unscrupulous schemer, and a mixed lot of Jews and anti-Semites, he was able, by laying the foundations of Bayreuth, to anticipate the events of 1933. The War and what followed the War was needed to put the seal upon his work. Germany today rightly acclaims him as the precursor of her faith.

8. The understanding of music as a quiet friend of the soul of man has gone, not the capacity for performance. Statistics of the sale of gramophone records in Germany would show that well over 90 per cent are devoted to music of the other type: dance music, comic songs, military marches, adaptations of all kinds. Of the excellent records of great music only a few have been produced in Germany and by Germans. The best records of Bach's music come from France, England, and the United States, or from German conductors and soloists living in Switzerland and Austria.

has not passed. Dancing in a small circle of friends at home, very popular for a time, is rarer now. But dancing in public restaurants —a habit unknown to pre-war Germany except for a few fancy dress balls in carnival time—is still very common even in the smaller provincial towns.

Prowess in athletics is acclaimed more loudly than before, and delight in public sport is more general than it was at a time when military parades and the playing of the band drew the bigger crowds. That in itself is all to the good. But with a nation which deliberately prefers the attitude of youthfulness to that of riper age the physical effort does not count much compared with the mental change it has purposely to make. To abjure intellectualism is by no means enough. The cult of intellectuality never has got far with the masses; and, apart from isolated cases of civilian leadership won by the sheer power of some intellect that towers above others—such as that of Disraeli or Bismarck or Mussolini—the multitude can easily be persuaded to offer only antagonism to the superior gifts of mentality in a man who has neither wealth nor the privileges of noble birth nor the glory of success in war to cover his aloofness. The religion of national youthfulness is not content with denouncing the intellectuals; it has to spurn aestheticism, in the broadest sense of the term, as well. That is the element of danger it contains: it is the opposite not only of the scholar and the humanist but also of the monastic ideal. To a German who had imbued himself with the spirit of Dürer, Bach, and Goethe, *vita contemplativa* was the highest form of life. He learned to acknowledge wisdom, beauty, and perfect order in other human beings and in the works of creation, to enjoy things not his own without envy or covetousness, and with an enjoyment that became greater and richer the older he grew. Since the War, and because of it, the attitude of the German has, obviously, been the reverse of that. His task, he feels, is to act, and to become aware of his own existence through action is his purest pleasure. Things not his own are to be shunned, if not destroyed. In his leader he recognizes not a superior, but a man of the people like himself. He cannot learn wisdom from his elders nor wonder about the beauty of that which does not belong to him. He cannot bow in silence before an image holy to other nations. He cannot submit to eternal laws. His wisdom is drawn from the immemorial experience of the native soil. His senses are governed by the blood of his race, and he is a law unto himself, a youth born to war.

In a recent study of the British, French, and Spanish national characters one of the most acute observers of our time has tried to describe the influence which three things, the cult of honor in the case of his own Spanish countrymen, the respect for the law in the case of the French, and the Englishman's ideal, that of the gentleman, have had and still have in molding the men into whose hands has been given the fate of western Europe and, through western Europe, a great part of the destiny of the world. Modern war, with its robotlike disregard of individual effort, is bound to make the peculiar virtue of a nation an object of its attacks. Conduct that is honorable, just, and gentlemanlike must make way for a general belief in the dishonorable, false, and vindictive conduct of enemies and neutrals and, as soon as the war is over, for the belief that victory was directly due to the use of dishonorable, criminal, and barbarous methods on the part of the victor. The soldiers are comparatively immune to this deterioration of the national character; it is those at home who are subject to the worst attacks of war psychosis.[9]

9. A representative series of autobiographical memoirs and biographies of men prominent in German public life between 1900 and the present should be consulted by any student of the effects of the War in making or marring the lives of men. The great mass of those who emerged from the War resigned and discouraged, of course are silent. The bulk of such memoirs, therefore, favor the belief that war is one of the great forces of life. Men have to do battle, show themselves the master, in order to make plain their true measure of strength. Between the lines of these life stories, however, the tale of the scourge of war and its punishment of the good and great, and rewards for the coward and the braggart, is told in unmistakable signs. The following titles represent only a small selection from recent biographical literature:

Bernhard Huldermann, *Albert Ballin* (Oldenburg, 1921); Otto Baumgarten, *Meine Lebensgeschichte* (Tübingen, 1929); Rudolf Binding, *Erlebtes Leben* (Frankfurt, 1928); *Robert Bosch und sein Werk*, edited on behalf of the Verein deutscher Ingenieure by Conrad Matschoss (Berlin, 1931); Otto Braun, *Aus nachgelassenen Schriften eines Frühvollendeten*, edited by I. Vogelstein (Leipzig, 1920); Lujo Brentano, *Mein Leben* (Jena, 1931); Carl Fürstenberg, *Die Lebensgeschichte eines deutschen Bankiers*, edited by H. Fürstenberg (Berlin, 1931); Friedrich Gundolph, *Stefan George* (Berlin, 1920; 3d ed. 1930); Alfred Grotjahn, *Erlebtes und Erstrebtes* (Berlin, 1932); Julius Ferdinand Wolff, *Lingner und sein Vermächtnis* (Hellerau, 1930); Otto Lubarsch, *Ein bewegtes Gelehrtenleben. Erinnerungen und*

MORAL EFFECTS

It is not the English private in the trenches who ceases to behave like a gentleman; it is the politician in Parliament, the man in the street, the newspaper writer and the newspaper reader at home who, in dealing with the "enemy," loses the noble qualities of thought and behavior which made England one of the great countries in world history. It is not the French *poilu* who forgets that to be just and to be generous are twin virtues in the man who defends France. Again, it is the politician, the wealthy newspaper owner, or the director of a munition factory in whom the fair sense of justice is perverted into prejudice and partisanship, till sanctions seem to be the veritable mainstay of law instead of a mere *pis-aller* when justice has failed. It was not the German soldier who lost his sense of man's responsibility for the doing of his work, according to his abilities, or his loving gratitude to the land of his fathers and the mother earth on which he was born and grew up. His regional ties were never loosened: he had faith that his work would wait for him if he survived: he honestly believed himself to be defending his title to all he had left behind, to all he longed to return to. It was in the office, in the political club, in the editorial rooms, in the secretariats of trusts and combines, in the committee rooms of trade-unions that the national heritage of respect for individual probity of work was sold for a mess of pottage. There it was that annexationist nationalism, the reverse of everything the great builders of Germany had preached and practiced, was set up as an idol to be worshiped instead of quiet and devoted attachment to the native soil. It was then that the cult of massed and centralized power, culminating in the leveling down of education,[10] in a hollow mockery of socialism, and in a veritable

---

Erlebnisse, Kämpfe und Gedanken (Berlin, 1931); Harry Graf Kessler, *Walther Rathenau, sein Leben und sein Werk* (Berlin-Grunewald, 1928); Carl Ludwig Schleich, *Besonnte Vergangenheit* (Berlin, 1928; cheap edition 1931); Albert Schweitzer, *Aus meinem Leben und Denken* (Leipzig, 1931); Rudolf Olden, *Stresemann* (Berlin, 1929); Marianne Weber, *Max Weber. Ein Lebensbild* (Tübingen, 1926); U. von Wilamowitz-Moellendorff, *Erinnerungen 1848–1914* (Leipzig, 1929).

Among recent novels *Die Geächteten,* by Ernst v. Salomon (1930) might be consulted for an autobiographical sketch of the author, a member of the German *"Freikorps"* in the Baltic provinces and of the National Socialist movement; *Erfolg,* by Lion Feuchtwanger (1929), contains lively sketches of Bavarian ministers, industrialists, and intellectuals of the post-war period.

10. By a strange coincidence the strongest of all the influences on the

mania for misleading statistics, displaced the old virtues of personal honesty, of pride in sound workmanship, and that self-reliance which springs from local tradition and the ties with the past that it forms.

It is too early to seek to prophesy whether the reaction against the effects of the War which must set in sooner or later will come in time to be helped and directed by a few men and women who have kept the older German ways alive within them. If that is to be, public education in Germany will have to undergo a complete change. Instead of following in the wake of the War, as it has under the successive governments since 1918, it will have to set its face resolutely against it. Every word of what John Ruskin wrote of education in the England of 1884[11] applies to education in every country throughout the world today, but with special force to a country which has eaten the bitter fruit of war for more than fifteen years, and desires to change to other food before it is too late. Instead of centralization,

minds of young people and the one which was hardly touched by the War, that of moving pictures, conspired with the influence of war itself to achieve mental standardization. The cinema is not only an international institution, with the same successful plays attracting tens of thousands in New York, London, Berlin, Paris, and Stockholm; above all, it is a means of leveling education and making it stereotyped. Each country produces its own films, and it needs little discrimination to know a Russian production from an Italian or British, or a French play from an American. But the films are produced to be shown to every class of people, from the sophisticated professor of philosophy to the village dunce, to be shown in the biggest cities and in the remotest parts of the country, to old and young, rich and poor. The only difference among the millions of spectators is this, that a few educated people of independent mind know the historical, the ethnographic, and the domestic pictures of modern life to be fakes, every bit of them, while the great mass of those who get their ideas of other people's manners and morals by attending the local cinema, believe that the picture must be true because it is reproduced from life by mechanical means. Broadcasting also tends to standardize the minds of the listeners-in: with the proviso, however, that most of it does not leave any impression on the mind of the listener, and that, for the rest, his critical faculties are often as much alive during a radio lecture as they are lulled to sleep by the concerted sound and sight of the moving picture.

11. *Fors clavigera,* Letter XCV on *Fors infantiae.* Ruskin insisted upon having education varied according to the circumstances in which the child grows up, and protested against "the madness of the modern cram and examination system" maintained for the purpose of fitting the student to make his way in the competitive system of modern society.

metropolitanism, and uniformity, the dominant rule for the association of human beings must again become regionalism, a frank recognition of natural differences, and a mutual respect among honest men professing different opinions.

INDEX

Anti-Semitism, 104, 123, 162, 233; its modern beginnings in Germany, 284. *See also* Jews
Autarchy, 204, 210, 250

Bach, 281, 282
Baden, 156–158
Bavaria, 116, 156, 160, 166, 185
Berlin, authority centered in, 116, 118, 119, 123, 151
Bethmann-Hollweg, Theobald von, 209, 210, 221
Bismarck, 60, 61, 64 *n*, 106, 107, 117, 156, 205–207, 208
Bourgeoisie, 96, 97, 99, 105, 129. *See also* Upper Middle Classes
Brüning, Dr. Heinrich, 41, 128, 152
Bundesrat, 106
Bureaucracy, 33–37, 42, 197. *See also* Civil Service
Business and allied interests: post-war enemy of officialdom, 33, 34, 36; in politics as *Wirtschaftspartei,* 200–201; wrecks constitution, 202; deadlocks Parliament, and unites with National Socialist party, 202, 247. *See also* Industrialism

Catholic Center Party, 161 *n*. *See also* Political Parties
Censorship, 5, 6, 27. *See also* Etappe
Centralization: during War, power centered in Supreme Command, save for Reichstag, 117, 118. *See also* General in Command. After War, 120; proportional representation, 121, 122; Kleinstaaterei, 123; unity, 125; National Socialist party, 126; Erzberger financial measures, 150, 151; National Service Law, 125, 158–160
Civil Service, the *Beamtenstaat,* 230; Hugenberg and, 239, 240; Rathenau and, 230; undermined by War, 273; after war, 35; salaries attacked, 37; and pensions threatened, 214
Cologne, 253–256

"Dagger Thrust" legend, 80
Dawes Plan, 198, 199
Deflation, 86, 88, 249, 250, 253
Devaluation of money, 58, 285

Dictatorship, 88, 106. *See also* Leadership
Duisberg, Dr. Carl, 232; effects of War, 260, 261

Education, 37 *n*
Eisner, Kurt, and Bavarian revolution, 166
Erzberger, Mattias, 150, 151, 163
Etappe, hated barrier between soldiers and people at home, 26, 27, 28, 286 *n*, 287

Financial Mobilization and Financing War: early pre-war plans, *see* Miquel, 60–65, and Wermuth, 67, 68. 1914; disregard of economic laws, 44 ff.; emergency decrees, 45–48; long war not taken into account, 49, 56; overconfidence in resources, 47, 55–59; internal war loans, 50, 53–55; general summary, 69–74, 86–88
Frankfurt am Main, 62, 254–258
Free Cities (*Freie Reichsstädte*) and the Big Towns (*Grosstädte*): early character, 129, 130; loyalty to Empire, 130; in Parliament, 130, 131; in War, 132–135; examples of self-government, 136; freedom, responsibility, local pride, and individuality, 137, 138; effects of War, 138–142; post-war taxes and social welfare burden, 144–149; powers taken over by central Government, 150, 151
French influence, 101, 102
Frontier bonds and relationships changed by War, 102–105, 256–258

Ganzheit, 123
General in Command, The, exercises supreme war-time power, 108; civil servants displaced, 109; local censorships, 110; local and state boundaries disregarded, 111, 112; monarchs virtually dethroned and local government extinguished, 116
Geography, racial, 99, 100
German lack of sense of politics, 31, 32
Government, former attitude of people to, 96–98
Grimm, Hans, 92–94

Helfferich, Dr. Carl, 63, 76, 77, 82, 206, 226, 227, 236

Hindenburg Program, 59, 75, 76, 85 n, 86. *See also* National Service Law
Holland, 256–258
Hugenberg, Dr. Alfred, 161 n, 219, 222–225, 237, 240, 246–248; "colonizing" Posnania, 237–242; president of Krupp Company, 241, 242, 244; leader of "National" opposition to German Republic, 76, 243; hold on German press, 243, 244, 246; head of Ruhr heavy industries, 244–246

Industrial Imperialism, 204, 206, 208–210
Industrialism, political and war activities, 210, 211, 220–222; attitude to labor, 212–216; "efficiency planning," overorganization, and effect on old-time employer, 217; centralization, 211, 219; standardization, 211, 218, 219. *See also* Business
Industrial revival after War, 277, 278
Inflation, 58, 86–88, 198, 249, 250, 252, 259, 285

Jews, 94 n, 103, 104, 140–142, 219, 250. *See also* Anti-Semitism

Kleinstaaterei, 97, 204

Labor. *See* Trade Unions
Landowners, 100, 101, 104, 105
Lawyers and officialdom, discredited by War, 196
Leadership, 94, 94 n, 99, 106, 119, 120, 127

Middle classes, *see* Bourgeoisie
Military absolutism, 117, 118. *See also* General in Command
Military leadership, discredited by War, 197
Money, "forged," 269–271; "planned," 267, 268. *See also* Deflation *and* Inflation
Municipal extravagance after War, 37–43, 85 n, 86 n, 152

National Liberals, 12, 107, 130, 285
"National" parties, 161–164
National Service Law, known also as Hindenburg Plan, 75–86; necessity and origins, 75, 76, 81; an alliance of Government, industrialism, and organized labor, 80, 81; territorial army, works committees, and conciliation boards, 82; greatly increased power of trade-union labor, 80–84; Socialists strengthened, 86; forces of nation overstrained, and economic system impoverished, 85
National Socialism, prepared by War and centralization, 125, 152, 158, 160; absorption of Hugenberg's *Wirtschaftspartei*, 202, 237, 247; sources and beginnings, 285
New generation, character, 15, 288–292
News services after War, 275–277
Noske, 165–168, 170–172, 174, 175

Pacifism, 21, 221. *See also* Soldiers
Pan-Germanism, 206, 206 n, 210
Parliamentary system, distrusted by Germans, 213
Peasants, 101, 105, 106, 129
Pensions, 35, 214. *See also* Civil Service
Planned Economy, 266, 267
Political parties, 107, 115, 115 n, 116, 117, 120, 162, 220, 221, 285
Politicians, discredited by War, 195, 198
Profiteering in War, 251–253
Proportional representation, 121, 122, 123
Proust, Marcel, 9, 10
Prussia, new power given by War, war industries, and National Service Law, 158, 159, 164; Prussian electoral system, 84 n, 159, 160; Prussian intransigence and revolution, 160, 161

Race, German people highly composite, 95
Radio, 277
Rathenau, Walther, onslaught on military bureaucracy, 77; initiator of war-planned economy, 265; life, 225, 226, 234, 235, 248; character, 219, 222, 223, 225, 227, 234, 235; in War Ministry, 228, 230; attacked by both Nationalists and Socialists, 231, 232; principal target of anti-Semite hatred, 233; death, 224, 227, 234
Recreation habits, post-war changes, 289, 293 n, 294
Religion, effects of War, 14, 20–25
Revolution, general character, 154, 169, 173; Württenburg, 157, 160, 181–191; Prussian revolution, 158–175

Soldiers, disillusionment, 127, 128; post-war dream of peace, 173, 174; 292, 293
States, decline in power through War, 116, 117, 118; effect of Erzberger financial reforms, 150; "pattern states," 158
Stinnes, Hugo, 236
Stresemann, Gustav, 115, 116, 163

INDEX

Switzerland, 256–258

Taxation, in War, 50, 87; after War, 149–151, 272
Totalitarian state, the, 150, 152, 285
Trade-unions, alliance with War Government, 80, 81, 84; Manifesto, 82, 83

Unification, 121, 123, 125, 128
"Unitarian," 115, 116, 285
Upper Middle Classes, 11, 285

Wagner, Richard, 290
War, its absolute power, 7, 91, 279, 280; groups unaffected by, 7–11; moral destruction due to, 14, 15, 19, 20, 27–30, 92; effect of separation of soldier from home, 5–7, 26–27, 286, 286 n; exaltation and reaction, 26, 27; war industries, 79–80; theory and reality, 91, 115; changing traditional attitude of German subject to State and Government, 92; destroying age-old forms of Government, 113, 114; war and industrialism, 202, 203; comparative effects of former wars, 280–284
Weimar Constitution, 116, 123, 124, 153, 154
"Westerners" and "Easterners," 101–105
William II, 24, 50, 51, 60–62, 67, 68, 107, 117, 131, 156, 206–208, 221, 222
Woman Suffrage, 154
Württemberg, 155–158, 175–177. *See also* Revolution

Young Plan, 198–200, 247

ECONOMIC AND SOCIAL HISTORY OF THE WORLD WAR

German Series

DER EINFLUSS DES KRIEGES AUF DIE LANDWIRTSCHAFTLICHE PRODUKTION IN DEUTSCHLAND. *By* Professor Friedrich Aereboe.

GEISTIGE UND SITTLICHE WIRKUNGEN DES KRIEGES IN DEUTSCHLAND. *By* Professors Otto Baumgarten, Erich Foerster, Arnold Rademacher, *and* Dr. Wilhelm Flitner.

DEUTSCHLANDS GESUNDHEITSVERHÄLTNISSE UNTER DEM EINFLUSS DES WELTKRIEGES. *Twenty-one monographs edited by* Dr. F. Bumm. (Two volumes)

DEUTSCHE ROHSTOFFWIRTSCHAFT IM WELTKRIEG. *By* Professor Otto Goebel.

DIE STAATSVERWALTUNG DER BESETZTEN GEBIETE: BELGIEN. *By* Professor Ludwig von Köhler.

KRIEG UND KRIMINALITÄT IN DEUTSCHLAND. *By* Dr. Moritz Liepmann.

DIE DEUTSCHE STAATSFINANZWIRTSCHAFT IM KRIEGE. *By* Dr. Walther Lotz.

DIE EINWIRKUNG DES KRIEGES AUF BEVÖLKERUNGSBEWEGUNG, EINKOMMEN UND LEBENSHALTUNG IN DEUTSCHLAND. *By* Professors Rudolf Meerwarth, Adolf Günther, *and* Waldemar Zimmermann.

DIE DEUTSCHEN EISENBAHNEN IM KRIEGE. *By* Professor Adolph Sarter.

DIE DEUTSCHE KRIEGSERNÄHRUNGSWIRTSCHAFT. *By* Professor August Skalweit.

DER KRIEG UND DIE ARBEITSVERHÄLTNISSE. *By* Herr Paul Umbreit *and* Dr. Charlotte Lorenz.

THE WAR AND GERMAN SOCIETY. *By* Professor Albrecht Mendelssohn Bartholdy.